Published by Straight Talk Books
P.O. Box 301, Milwaukee, WI 53201
800.661.3311 · timeofgrace.org

Printed in the United States of America
ISBN: 978-1-949488-81-4

CLOSER
TO
GOD
EACH
DAY

365 daily devotions

JANUARY

Create in me a pure heart, O God, and renew
a steadfast spirit within me.

Psalm 51:10

When you're in the valley, think of the glory

Mike Novotny

Our lives, with rare exceptions, eventually pass through a valley—a difficult and wish-it-were-over season of life. Four big categories of such valleys come to my mind:

First, there are physical valleys. Something goes wrong with your body or brain. It could be intense anxiety or depression so bad you start to think some pretty dark thoughts. It could be the fear that it's cancer or the fear that the cancer is coming back. Second, there are financial valleys. When you already had enough debt and then inflation hit. Or the car breaks down or your kid needs braces you can't afford. Third, there are relational valleys. When your closest relationships are not going well. When your boyfriend won't commit or your wife is done with her commitment. Finally, there are spiritual valleys. When you've been trying so hard and praying so much yet nothing seems to be changing or growing.

I wish you never had to pass through things like that, but you either have or you are or you will. So what will you do in the valley? The apostle Paul suggests, **"So we fix our eyes not on what is seen, but on what is unseen, since what is seen is temporary, but what is unseen is eternal"** (2 Corinthians 4:18). Fix your eyes on the eternal blessings that are yours because of Jesus—forgiveness, love, heaven, hope—and you will make it through this valley.

Count your blessings. Not your physical blessings but instead every spiritual blessing that is guaranteed in Christ.

Acts of service
Liz Schroeder

I am a horrible person for whom to buy presents. "Gifts" is not my primary love language; "Acts of Service" is. My husband could have saved so much money when we were dating by forgoing flowers and jewelry. I feel loved when he vacuums out the car or makes me a salad. I teared up a little on Mother's Day—not because my kids gave me a gift but because someone had put a fresh roll of toilet paper on the holder. To commemorate the moment, I snapped a picture. (I also fought the urge to post the picture on social media lest I arouse the jealousy of moms everywhere.)

Have you ever wondered what God's love language is? Maybe it's "Words of Affirmation," because in the Bible he reminds us of his love for us. Or perhaps it's "Quality Time," because as we linger in prayer, meditate on his Word, and worship, our relationship with him is strengthened. What about "Physical Touch"? Is that one reason he gave us the bread and wine—his body and blood—in the Lord's Supper?

Let's read what the apostle Paul has to say: **"But God demonstrates his own love for us in this: While we were still sinners, Christ died for us"** (Romans 5:8).

Before I was baptized, before I made a public proclamation of my faith, while I was still God's enemy, Christ died for me. He gave his life for me. Is there a greater act of service than that?

How long, Lord?
Andrea Delwiche

Have you had a conversation with God when life's circumstances seem a dark contrast with what's written about God's goodness? In Psalm 89, the psalmist wrestles in this way with God.

He begins by noting and praising God's loving actions: **"I will sing of the Lord's great love forever; with my mouth I will make your faithfulness known through all generations. I will declare that your love stands firm forever"** (verses 1,2).

He acknowledges that living under God's justice and wisdom is humanity's best choice: **"Blessed are those who have learned to acclaim you, who walk in the light of your presence, Lord"** (verse 15).

But then he has hard questions: **"How long, Lord? Will you hide yourself forever? How long will your wrath burn like fire?"** (verse 46). He wrestles with God: **"Remember how fleeting is my life. For what futility you have created all humanity!"** (verse 47).

Perhaps surprisingly, he ends with blessing. He pleads for God to bring new blessing to his people. And he blesses the Lord: **"Praise be to the Lord forever! Amen and Amen"** (verse 52).

This conversation has a place in our lives. Sometimes it's passion filled and quick. Other times it's drawn out in thoughtfulness and anguish. Do you have hard questions for God? How could this be a model for your talk with the Lord? Find a quiet place for your conversation, and remember that authentic conversation requires good listening too. God be with you.

Always there
Clark Schultz

"Early in the morning, Jesus stood on the shore, but the disciples did not realize that it was Jesus" (John 21:4). If you're familiar with the accounts of Jesus showing himself to his disciples after his resurrection, then you know that this is the third time post-Easter that Jesus appeared to them. You might ask, "What? Why didn't the disciples realize it was Jesus?"

Maybe it's because it was early in the morning, they were 100 yards from shore, and they were not expecting Jesus to be there. Or maybe their minds were on something else that caused them to be distracted.

Does that sound a little familiar? What about you? What keeps you from recognizing Jesus in your life? I once came across this phrase: "Whatever you live for owns you." What consumes your thoughts 24/7? Is it your kids, sports, comparisons on social media, the political circus, or a person whom you think "isn't acting sorry enough"?

You and I might know the Sunday-morning Jesus. But have we put so many "important" life matters in the way that they cloud our vision of seeing our Savior in all the moments of our lives? Let's do some spiritual spring cleaning of our hearts and minds and toss out the idols that distract us from seeing our Savior.

Take the time to notice that Jesus is ALWAYS there.

January 5

Follow God's example
Jason Nelson

Reading the Bible upside down can be very discouraging. Focusing on the warnings, judgments, and bad acts of chosen people can diminish one's appreciation of Christianity. But these are not to be ignored, because that is how God builds accountability to him into our consciences. Reading the Bible right side up lights the flame of faith and moves us in the direction of godly living. The gospel is knowing who Jesus is right side up.

There was never a downside with Jesus. His love for sinners was on display in how he lived his life, in his willingness to suffer and die for them, and in his divine ability to overcome death. He promised to be with us always. Seeing Jesus right side up is what moves us to follow—to want to be Christians.

Jesus possessed every human trait we admire, and the fullness of God dwelt in him in bodily form. To be his chosen friends motivates us to live for him. People are inspired by watching others. Children are inspired to become great musicians or athletes because they watched great musicians or athletes in action as they were growing up. Children of God become humble servants by carefully watching the humblest of servants. We look to the pages of Scripture and at the lives of other Christians to see Jesus in action.

"Follow God's example, therefore, as dearly loved children and walk in the way of love, just as Christ loved us and gave himself up for us as a fragrant offering and sacrifice to God" (Ephesians 5:1,2).

Be you!* (Part 1)
Mike Novotny

What do the movies *Moana, Mulan, Brave, Beauty and the Beast, Coco,* and *Aladdin* have in common? The moral of those stories is almost exactly the same—Be you. Moana, your father wants you to be an island manager, but you are an ocean explorer—be you! Miguel, your family wants you to make the best shoes in Mexico, but your heart wants to make Mexican music—be you! Belle, Jasmine, and Mulan, you are not helpless princesses awaiting arranged marriages; you are book-reading, kingdom-running, sword-swinging warriors! Be you. Only then can we all live happily ever after.

"Be you" (a.k.a. "be genuinely you," a.k.a. "live your truth," a.k.a. "live authentically") might be the highest value of modern American culture, but what does God think? Does he want you to find the unique you that he created you to be and embrace it without apology? Or does he want you to repress those desires humbly and conform to what your family/culture wants you to be?

Don't answer too quickly, because God's answer is tricky. According to the Scriptures, God says, "Be you!"* God exclaims, "Be you!" and adds an asterisk that says, "Terms and conditions apply." In the days to come, I want to explore what it means to be biblically "you," but for now give some thought to Paul's words: **"Just as each of us has one body with many members, and these members do not all have the same function, so in Christ we, though many, form one body, and each member belongs to all the others"** (Romans 12:4,5).

Be you!* (Part 2)
Mike Novotny

It took me 35 years to figure out who I am. Now I know who God made me to be, what God made me to do, and how I am divinely gifted to help people. I have figured out that God made me to learn, study, write, teach, preach, mingle, and meet. Give me a series to preach, a book to write, or a group of strangers to meet, and I will be in my happy place. But give me a complex problem to solve, a situation that requires extra empathy, or a team to lead, and I will do more harm than good. That's me.

Who are you? Have you figured it out yet? Have you thought about your personality or experiences, the compliment clues to your gifts, and the complaint clues to your weaknesses? You being you, according to the Bible, is as important as ears being ears instead of trying to be eyes. We need you. Jesus' church needs you. This is why God emphatically says, "Be you!"

"For just as each of us has one body with many members, and these members do not all have the same function, so in Christ we, though many, form one body, and each member belongs to all the others. We have different gifts, according to the grace given to each of us" (Romans 12:4-6). You and I don't have the same gifts or same functions in life. Pray today that the Spirit would help you see whom God created you to be, uniquely and wonderfully made!

Be you!* (Part 3)
Mike Novotny

Do you know what David from the Bible did just before he ran off to fight Goliath? He decided to be himself. When King Saul, the trembling leader of Israel's army, looked down at the scrawny shepherd boy who volunteered to fight the Philistine giant, Saul offered David his royal armor. **"Saul dressed David in his own tunic. He put a coat of armor on him and a bronze helmet on his head. David fastened on his sword over the tunic"** (1 Samuel 17:38,39).

But as well-made as Saul's outfit was, it wasn't David. **"'I cannot go in these,' he said to Saul, 'because I am not used to them.' So he took them off"** (1 Samuel 17:39). When David fought to save his flock from a local predator, he didn't chase away lions and wolves with a sword and a shield. Rather, he used his sling and some stones. That was him.

The same principle is true for you. Going through life trying to be just like your father or sister or best friend or favorite celebrity isn't you. Just like David, God has given you unique gifts and experiences that you use to fight your battles and honor Jesus. The apostle Paul taught that **"we have different gifts, according to the grace given to each of us"** (Romans 12:6).

So use *your* gift. Few things make our gift-giving God happier than watching his children discover and use their gifts for his glory.

Be you!* (Part 4)
Mike Novotny

Modern culture has an infatuation with the phrase, "Be you!" In a way, these cultural voices are on to something, since God uniquely designed us and individually gifted us (read Romans 12:4-6). But to be thorough and biblical, it would be better to say, "Be you!"* Don't forget the asterisk. Don't forget the terms and conditions that God applies.

I sometimes ask my daughter, "Maya, do you think it's good to follow your heart?" She smirks and says, "What if my heart wants to punch you in the face?" Ha! She's pointing out that sometimes what's within us isn't good or selfless or right with Jesus. If you've ever been wrong, ever changed your mind about something, or ever felt afraid when there was nothing to be afraid of, you already know that being true to what you feel/want/desire/think isn't the best way to live life. Terms and conditions must apply.

The apostle Paul wrote, **"Do not conform to the pattern of this world, but be transformed by the renewing of your mind. Then you will be able to test and approve what God's will is—his good, pleasing and perfect will"** (Romans 12:2). That's a simple summary of the asterisk. Be you . . . as long as you are following the "good, pleasing, and perfect will" of God.

God cares about your passions, strengths, and desires. If you first filter them through Scripture, you will end up the very person whom God wants you to be, transformed by the Word instead of conformed to the world. That's what it means to "be you!"*

Be you!* (Part 5)
Mike Novotny

When I was back in grad school, I had an older professor who admitted, "I used to pray that God would protect me from my weaknesses. Now I pray that God would protect me from my strengths." The older I get, the more I understand what he meant. It's hard not to let good things go to extremes. Outgoing people can turn into conversation-dominating people. Compassionate people can become cowards who never have confrontational conversations. Organized people can be picky and pushy, and adaptable people can be unreliable and flaky. So how do you stay balanced, using your unique gifts while not letting those blessings become a curse?

This question might help—Am I selfless? Selfless people (1) use their strengths to serve others and (2) know they need the help of other people's strengths. For example, if you are a hardworking, box-checking, productive person, you will ask yourself, "How can I use this gift to help my family/my church/my community?" and, "Whose help do I need to make sure I am doing the most important things instead of just my own things?" Selflessness makes the body of Christ fit together as we all enjoy the selfless love of Jesus, our Head.

"So in Christ we, though many, form one body, and each member belongs to all the others" (Romans 12:5).

Be you!* (Part 6)
Mike Novotny

The Bible frequently tells us, "Be you!"* Be the unique you whom God made you to be. *And* make sure you remember the asterisk, the terms and conditions that God applies. No one does that quite like Jesus did.

Jesus was absolutely himself. When his family wanted him to calm down with his claims to be the Messiah, he didn't conform to their wants but rather was true to himself. When the Pharisees demanded he change his message, Jesus pushed back, insisting on being the only-begotten Son of the Father on a one-of-a-kind mission to save us from our sins.

But the entire time Jesus was being uniquely Jesus, he remembered God's terms and conditions. He was humble, selfless, and constantly obedient to the will of his Father. Paul summarized it well: **"[Jesus], being in very nature God, did not consider equality with God something to be used to his own advantage; rather, he made himself nothing by taking the very nature of a servant, being made in human likeness. And being found in appearance as a man, he humbled himself by becoming obedient to death—even death on a cross!"** (Philippians 2:6-8).

You and I need a Savior like that. It's hard to be yourself, even harder to remember to be humble and selfless, but Jesus' life and death are our constant source of forgiveness and hope. Thank God that Jesus was always Jesus!

Kiss the King
Daron Lindemann

A kiss is an intimate thing. I kiss my wife and not many others except my mom and granddaughters.

I kissed my dad's forehead during his final days of life when he was discomforted and confused by dementia.

I've seen people kiss championship trophies.

A kiss says that someone or something is very special. Everything else going on in the world cannot interrupt that moment and the importance of the relationship.

"Kiss his son, or he will be angry and your way will lead to your destruction. . . . Blessed are all who take refuge in him" (Psalm 2:12).

God invites you to kiss Jesus, his Son. Jesus wants an important relationship with you. He wants to look into your eyes, you to look into his, and for you to know that everything going on in the world cannot interrupt what he wants to do—with you.

Jesus is the King of the universe, yet sinners can and should kiss him in faith and love. If anyone turns away from Jesus, then they choose their own lost path and ultimate destruction.

A sinful woman, whom I believe was a prostitute, kissed Jesus' feet and poured expensive perfume on them (Luke 7). And in the Garden of Gethsemane, Judas betrayed Jesus with a kiss—a familiar form of greeting in that culture and time. For Jesus it was the kiss of death (Luke 22).

What do these two kisses have in common, as Jesus comes close to both people?

That's entitlement!
Jan Gompper

A senator on the reelection trail was at a luncheon sponsored by some of his constituents. He was very hungry, so when the woman handing out the chicken put two pieces on his plate, he asked her for a third. She said no. He pressed further, "Do you know who I am? I'm the senator." She retorted, "And I'm the woman handing out two pieces of chicken, so move along."

Have you ever felt entitled to something because of who you are or what you've accomplished? We live in an age of entitlement. Many people feel they are entitled to special treatment because of their celebrity status, wealth, education, nationality, race, etc. Sometimes even church people think they can rest on their laurels of being lifelong members of a certain denomination.

Entitlement isn't new. Some New Testament Jews who came to check out John the Baptist felt they were privileged because they were "followers of Abraham." But John called them a brood of vipers, instructing them to **"produce fruit in keeping with repentance. And do not begin to say to yourselves, 'We have Abraham as our father.' For I tell you that out of these stones God can raise up children for Abraham"** (Luke 3:8).

John understood that one's heritage, accomplishments, wealth, church membership . . . do not impress God in the least. But when we humbly recognize our sinfulness and place our trust in Jesus as our one and only Savior, **"he** [gives] **us the *right* to become children of God"** (John 1:12).

Now that's entitlement!

You are the fulfillment!
Linda Buxa

In the Bible book of Acts, after the disciples watched Jesus rise into the clouds, an angel came to ask them why they were still standing there. (Um, I'd probably be standing there too.) The disciples went back to Jerusalem, and all the men and women gathered together to pray. After all, a lot had gone on in the past few months—Jesus was crucified, died, came back to life, and then returned to heaven alive!

For all the times the followers seemed a little dense before, they were incredibly clear thinking at this moment. Peter stood up and said, **"Brothers and sisters, the Scripture had to be fulfilled in which the Holy Spirit spoke long ago through David concerning Judas, who served as guide for those who arrested Jesus. He was one of our number and shared in our ministry. . . . Therefore it is necessary to choose one of the men who have been with us the whole time the Lord Jesus was living among us"** (Acts 1:16,17,21).

That stopped me in my tracks. The disciples knew they were the group the Scriptures were talking about; they knew they were being used to fulfill God's plan and promises. That's amazing!

Then I realized that for believers now, *we* fulfill God's promises too (even though we're also often a little dense). Just because the Bible is done being written doesn't mean the Acts are done. God placed each one of us at this moment in time to continue to fulfill his promises to this generation. You are the fulfillment! That's amazing!

Seeming contradictions
Andrea Delwiche

Psalm 90 reflects Moses' lifetime of both dark and sweet movements as he followed the Lord. **"All our days pass away under your wrath; we finish our years with a moan. Teach us to number our days, that we may gain a heart of wisdom. Satisfy us in the morning with your unfailing love, that we may sing for joy and be glad all our days"** (verses 9,12,14).

Agony and joy. Regret and longing.

Moses knew God. He had spent weeks alone with the Lord. He had *seen* God after God had passed in front of him. God called Moses his friend. Moses had a role in the incredible parting of the Red Sea. But Moses had also observed families swallowed alive by the ground and snakebitten people crying for help. Moses himself would not enter the Promised Land of Canaan.

These seeming contradictions can be hard to hold in our hearts.

When we allow Jesus to tell us about God, we see God's love shining as it burns away everything that holds us back from the life he longs to give. Remember Jesus' familiar explanation to Nicodemus: **"For God so loved the world that he gave his one and only Son. . . . For God did not send his Son into the world to condemn the world, but to save the world through him"** (John 3:16,17).

Similarly, the apostle John's confident words: **"God is light; *in him* there is *no darkness* at all"** (1 John 1:5).

Lord, life is hard. Help us trust your workings and follow your way of love. Amen.

The most sufficient book ever
Mike Novotny

While there are plenty of books I *like* to read and many others I *want* to read, there is really only one book I *need* to read. **"All Scripture is God-breathed and is useful for teaching, rebuking, correcting and training in righteousness, so that the servant of God may be thoroughly equipped for every good work"** (2 Timothy 3:16,17). Notice that final phrase—If you have the Bible, you are "thoroughly equipped for every good work." You're not mostly equipped for every good work. You're not thoroughly equipped for some good works. No, you are thoroughly equipped for every good work!

In other words, the Bible is the most sufficient book ever. It is all you need to do everything God wants. Our Father knows it's easy for his children to forget both his commands and his promises, so he made the brilliant choice to write them all down! You need to know where you came from, where you are going, who you are, and who God is. You can't live well without identity, hope, forgiveness, and an answer to death. Thankfully, the Bible specializes in all of life's essential questions.

So before you scroll through the latest words written by flawed humans, turn your attention to the words written by our flawless God. His Word is what your heart most needs. No wonder the psalmist said of God's words, **"They are more precious than gold, than much pure gold. . . . By them your servant is warned; in keeping them there is great reward"** (Psalm 19:10,11).

Stronger for tomorrow
Nathan Nass

Are you going through a difficult time? Are you asking why God is putting you through this? Is it hard to trust that God is in control? All of us have those moments. "God, why do I have to go through this?"

David in the Bible faced some difficult times as a young shepherd. His flock of sheep was attacked by a lion and then by a bear. Sound fun? Having to fight a lion and a bear—without a gun? That's a difficulty I hope I never have to face! How could lions and bears be a good thing used by God?

Later in life, David understood. He later faced an even greater enemy: the giant Goliath. Yet David wasn't afraid. Here's what he said: **"The LORD who rescued me from the paw of the lion and the paw of the bear will rescue me from the hand of this Philistine"** (1 Samuel 17:37).

Do you see what David recognized? God used those past challenges to prepare him for what was to come. God gave him strength and faith in one difficulty to prepare him for another.

What is God preparing you to face? I know it's hard. I know you can't see it now, but God is using your current struggles to prepare you for the future he's planned for you. May God's strength and grace in Jesus give you hope for today, and may he use this struggle to make you stronger for tomorrow.

Dealing with "NO"
Katrina Harrmann

Have you ever gotten a "no" from God?

It knocks the stuffing right out of you, doesn't it? Especially if you're praying about something BIG: a sick loved one, an amazing new job, or a deadly war.

Sometimes we pour hours of prayer into really big asks . . . stuff that—at least to us—matters a LOT. This makes it hard to understand when God says no.

It can really sting. In fact, for many people, it stings so badly that they turn their backs on God.

But that is never the answer.

It helps to look at it through the eyes of a parent. Do you have kids or nieces or nephews? If so, then you've said no. What are some of the reasons you don't say yes? To teach them patience? To help them set correct priorities? To enable them to take action? Because you know something they don't?

All these are *sometimes* the reasons we don't get the answer we want from our heavenly Father. Also, there is sin in this broken world, and—even as Christians—we're not guaranteed an easy life, getting everything we ask for.

We might not always understand why we don't get the things we ask for. But our heavenly Father promises to always look after us and to provide the ONLY good things we'll ever need: forgiveness and saving grace.

"Pray continually, give thanks in all circumstances; for this is God's will for you in Christ Jesus" (1 Thessalonians 5:17,18).

Who or what owns you?
Clark Schultz

A quarterback once shouted to the rival crowd, "I still own you!" While amusing, it actually got me thinking. Who or what owns me? Who or what owns you?

It's been said that whatever you live for owns you. Is it property or possessions? Your smartphone? Sports? Your family? None of these blessings in and of itself is bad, but the tough part is not to let them own you.

If you teach children it's okay to skip church to chase a club sport trophy, what owns you? If social media posts determine your mood or a few less likes to your post send you into a downward spiral, what owns you? If you over-spend on your credit card to keep up with the Joneses, what owns you?

Friends, I'm guilty of putting many things above my God, but none of these things can go with me when I die. Solomon said it best: **"'Everything is meaningless.' What do people gain from all their labors at which they toil under the sun?"** (Ecclesiastes 1:2,3). Again, I stress it is not wrong to have or do nice things. In fact, it is en-couraged. But take a moment to focus on who it is you are living for.

While you ponder that question, listen to some good news. Despite your sins of ownership, **"You are not your own; you were bought at a price. Therefore honor God with your bodies"** (1 Corinthians 6:19,20). Christ gave his life for you! He puts you first always. So yes, Christ can say, "I own you."

Baptism is a big deal
Mike Novotny

I'm not sure if you've been baptized, if you celebrate your baptism, or if you have thought at all about baptism this week (or month or year), but I do know this—baptism is a big deal.

Just ask John the Baptist. John wasn't called John the Pray-er or John the Preacher or John the Leader. Instead, he went down in history as the Baptist, that guy who baptized people. Based on what his baptism offered, I bet John wouldn't have minded that title one bit. Luke records, **"[John] went into all the country around the Jordan, preaching a baptism of repentance for the forgiveness of sins"** (Luke 3:3). What was the point, according to this verse, of being baptized? The forgiveness of sins. Greedy tax collectors and abusive soldiers couldn't earn forgiveness from God, so John offered them baptism, where God promised the forgiveness of sins.

That's what the Nicene Creed says. Back in the year A.D. 325, the Roman Emperor Constantine invited church leaders to a council at the city of Nicaea (think church conference) in order to unify the church, and they left with a creed, a statement of what they believed, which has now been used around the world for over 1,600 years. Guess what shows up in its closing lines? "We believe in one baptism for the forgiveness of sins." For the forgiveness of sins. That's why baptism is such a big deal.

When God doesn't fight
Daron Lindemann

"**The L**ORD **is a warrior**" (Exodus 15:3). I love that verse. God is a fighter, and he never loses a battle! His undefeated record still stands today and will continue forever.

So when God fights, is he fighting for you or against you?

Does he ever hurl thunderbolts at you because he is burning mad? Does he concoct a witch's brew of circumstances to curse you because you've been bad? Will Jesus' nostrils flare, eyes squint, and fists squeeze tight for another fight against you today—a fight he'd rather avoid, but you leave him no choice because you're a dirty, disobedient sinner after all.

Let me be clear. God has plenty of enemies, but as a believer you are not one of them. God is not your enemy.

You are God's child. You are a saint. You are a new creation. At your baptism, God moved into your life and the Spirit of Jesus Christ lives in you. He comes to save and not to condemn.

God is on your side. He conquers your sins. He fights your fears. He defends you against all evil. He puts the devil in his place. But he doesn't fight you. He helps you.

"**The L**ORD **is with me; he is my helper. I look in triumph on my enemies**" (Psalm 118:7).

Your Lord fights for you, not against you, and he never loses a battle. He wants you to fight too, but never against him. For the victory!

May our victory not be hollow!
Jan Gompper

For pro-lifers, the Supreme Court's decision to over-turn *Roe vs. Wade* was a historical triumph. Personally, I thought this day would never come.

Of course, the court's decision will not end abortion. Individual states still have the right to decide whether or not to protect the lives of unborn children. Some have already chosen to do so; others vow they never will.

While the pro-life/pro-choice debate has always been contentious, a new surge of increased divisiveness has begun. So what's the next step?

Many Christians are proudly flying the victory flag, but victory will be hollow if women facing an unwanted pregnancy are treated like enemies for contemplating an abortion or like criminals if they make that unfortunate choice. Now more than ever Christians need to reach out to such women, as well as to adamant pro-choicers, with the love and grace of Jesus. Only when a woman sees her own worth as a redeemed child of God will she recognize the worth of her unborn child and be able to confess:

"You made all the delicate, inner parts of my body and knit me together in my mother's womb. Thank you for making me so wonderfully complex! Your workmanship is marvelous—how well I know it. You watched me as I was being formed in utter seclusion, as I was woven together in the dark of the womb. You saw me before I was born. Every day of my life was re-corded in your book. Every moment was laid out before a single day had passed" (Psalm 139:13-16 NLT).

May God grant this victory!

The fullness of grace
Nathan Nass

As I was scrolling recently, a Facebook meme jumped out at me: "The people Paul killed welcomed him into heaven." That's an amazing statement.

If you were a Christian in Israel after the time of Jesus, Paul was your worst enemy. Paul zealously persecuted Christians, threw them in jail, and killed them. He was directly responsible for the deaths of believers in Jesus.

But then Jesus did something unexpected. He changed Paul's heart and life. Jesus turned Paul from being a persecutor of Christians into the greatest Christian missionary. In fact, after sharing the good news of Jesus all over the world, Paul was executed for his faith. Paul's life shows the fullness of God's grace—God's undeserved love for sinners.

What do you think happened next? When Paul went to heaven by faith in Jesus, what do you think the Christians he had executed did? I bet the people Paul killed welcomed him into heaven.

Because they understood God's grace too. We're all saved by grace. It's that grace that led Paul to write: **"Here is a trustworthy saying that deserves full acceptance: Christ Jesus came into the world to save sinners—of whom I am the worst"** (1 Timothy 1:15). God's grace can reach into the sinful heart of a violent persecutor and melt it. God's grace can reach into the hurt heart of an executed martyr and heal it. The people Paul killed welcomed him into heaven. That's the fullness of grace!

People without peace make Jesus weep

Mike Novotny

According to the historian Josephus, who lived around the time of Jesus, nothing could wow your heart quite like a glimpse of Jerusalem. He said the sun's reflection off the gold of the temple was amazing—like looking into the sun itself. This is why Jesus' disciples marveled as they sat on the Mount of Olives and looked down on the sacred city and the temple.

But not Jesus. **"As [Jesus] approached Jerusalem and saw the city, he wept over it"** (Luke 19:41). Why would such beauty move our Savior to tears? **"[Jesus] said, 'If you, even you, had only known on this day what would bring you peace—but now it is hidden from your eyes'"** (Luke 19:42). The people of Jerusalem didn't know where to find true peace, a fact that made Jesus weep.

Jesus cares that much about people. He cares that much about you. It moves him to see you searching for peace in ways that won't work—more money, more success, the perfect body, the perfect family. He knows that no matter how momentarily good those things are, they won't last. That's why he's offering you something better. He's offering you himself.

Find peace in Jesus alone. That kind of faith will make your Savior weep . . . for joy.

God's love never changes
Clark Schultz

The mother with the grocery list said, "Do you want to stay in the car with Dad?"

The child yelled, "No! Yes! Wait! No! OK, I'll go into the store with you, Mom."

The father was dumbfounded that in 3.2 seconds the child changed his mind so many times so quickly.

Change . . . Our world is ever changing; smartphones, cars, clothing trends, and hairstyles all change. To some, change is frightening. "We've always done it that way" becomes our mantra to stop change.

Change can be good. New clothes, new worship music, and a new coat of paint all have their places.

I get through tough times like tax season, holding the hand of someone who is about to meet Jesus, or hugging someone who is at the end of their rope with this: our Father does not change. Now that's comforting!

"God is not human, that he should lie, not a human being, that he should change his mind. Does he speak and then not act? Does he promise and not fulfill?" (Numbers 23:19).

Our world can change drastically, but God's love for us will not. Nothing you do will make God love you more, and nothing you do will make God love you less.

Jesus had authority

Jason Nelson

I guess this is how we're doing it now. People with even modest name recognition, or no name recognition at all, can post a blog or host a podcast and offer their opinions on just about anything. Another voice of influence is born. Other people tune in and kind of pay attention. They follow and share what they read or heard with others.

I guess I'm old school, but I still believe in the value of expertise. Expertise is validated by degrees, certifications, and other emblems of completing a program of rigorous training. I don't want my doctors to only have opinions. I want them to have diplomas from recognized medical schools.

Even as a young man, Jesus demonstrated respect for scholarship when he went to the temple and engaged in dialogue with the teachers of the law. Later in his life he taught the Beatitudes, and those who had the privilege of listening to him commented that he taught as one having special authority compared to the teachers they were used to hearing. Critics wondered by what authority he could perform miracles and drive out demons. Jesus insisted he had authority to forgive sins and could summon thousands of angels to his aid if he needed them. Jesus' authority came from God. His teaching was way beyond just another rabbi's opinion. His authority was endorsed from on high: **"A bright cloud covered them, and a voice from the cloud said, 'This is my Son, whom I love; with him I am well pleased. Listen to him!'"** (Matthew 17:5).

Jesus' sequel
Clark Schultz

The number-one movie at the box office recently was a sequel to a movie that came out 36 years earlier. Many will argue the sequel is better, and I tend to agree. Most movies that do well at the box office are immediately green-lit for another installment, and that installment is rushed, not thought out, and not that good. Many tend to fizzle and lose the luster of the original.

When Jesus originally appeared on this earth, angels flew in faster than an F-18 and said, **"Today in the town of David a Savior has been born to you; he is the Messiah, the Lord"** (Luke 2:11). Jesus played the part we could not; he became our substitute. Jesus knew every line of the law, and unlike us he kept it all with pinpoint precision.

What is better will be Jesus' sequel return. Jesus comforted his disciples with these words: **"If I go and prepare a place for you, I will come back and take you to be with me that you also may be where I am"** (John 14:3).

Jesus has a home waiting for you—heaven. When will that sequel drop? Will it be 3, 6, or 36 years from now or tomorrow? It is easy to let our hearts be troubled, to let our faith fizzle, or to allow our love to lose luster. Still, Jesus loves us. He flew into the danger zone of sin and death for you and me! And when our final credits roll, he will return. He is coming to take you to be with him forever.

Finding strength in the wait
Katrina Harrmann

Isaiah 40:31 reads: **"But they who wait for the Lord shall renew their strength; they shall mount up with wings like eagles; they shall run and not be weary; they shall walk and not faint"** (ESV).

In Hebrew, the word for "wait" in Isaiah 40 is "Qavah." It is such a fantastic word with so much hidden depth.

The word *qavah* is a verb that means "to twist fibers together," like you would to make a cord or rope . . . binding smaller, weaker fibers into something strong and useful.

How many of us have been "at the end of our rope" or "hanging by a thread"—all examples of what happens when we don't have a very strong rope. Maybe we're only clinging to one little fiber!

But this verse implies that the longer we wait, the stronger we get as we're twisted up in the fibers of faith and our connection with God. God makes us stronger as we wait, transforming us from a lonely fiber into a ROPE! *Qavah!*

So the next time you feel frail and frayed, remember this. If you're in an exhausting season of waiting and just don't see the point, remember that God is using this time to strengthen and build you up so that you are stronger for whatever comes next.

I wasn't there when they died
Daron Lindemann

It is one of the most haunting regrets people can have—being absent at the moment a loved one dies. Let me encourage you in two ways.

Those who are dying often choose to take their last breath when a loved one is not present. Why? To provide a final, caring gesture protecting the loved one from the grim reality of death. It is offered as a gift.

Also, a dying loved one, if you weren't there when they passed, probably didn't need you there. There was only One your loved one needed to be present at the moment of his or her death, and it was not you. It was Jesus.

Jesus is their Savior, not you. Jesus conquered death at his resurrection, not you. Jesus is ever present as the true God, not you. So it's okay. Give yourself some grace (and truth) if you weren't present when your loved one died. Jesus was.

A man whose daughter was dying left her side and traveled to find Jesus. While he was away, she died. **"Don't be afraid; just believe,"** Jesus told him (Mark 5:36). That's what your loved one needs from you.

Believe that Jesus has been raised to life and that he offers eternal life to all who trust in him. While your loved one is still alive and alert, assure them of this. And when the moment comes, whether you are there or not, Jesus is their eternal, kind, present, powerful, and life-giving Savior.

God provides
Katrina Harrmann

It's amazing how God provides in moments when we feel bleak and hopeless. This happens in both big and small ways. Sometimes it's the small ways that astonish me the most.

One afternoon my dryer stopped working. I was stressed, as it was the third large appliance to quit working in our house that week.

Looking forlornly into my busted dryer full of sopping clothes, I sighed and raised my eyes heavenward, unsure what to do. As I looked up, I noticed something I'd never seen before, despite having lived in my home for over a dozen years.

Several plastic cords were running from one end of the 20-foot-long basement to the other—four or five times, back and forth. It was a built-in clothesline. Someone had installed it in the rafters and joists of the ceiling, and I had never even noticed it!

God provides for us in a thousand small ways each and every day. Most of the time we are ignorant of these blessings and don't even say thank you. But he's always providing for our needs.

This doesn't mean we always get what we want. But God's timing is perfect. He sees your hurts, and he cares for you along the way.

"'For my thoughts are not your thoughts, neither are your ways my ways,' declares the Lord. 'As the heavens are higher than the earth, so are my ways higher than your ways and my thoughts than your thoughts'" (Isaiah 55:8,9).

Serve like Rambo

Liz Schroeder

The people I have the privilege of working with in area sober living homes remind me of the movie *Rambo*. In *Rambo: First Blood Part II*, John Rambo (Sylvester Stallone) is a Vietnam vet who returns courageously to prisoner of war camps to free other POWs.

The residents I meet are tasting the freedom of life outside of prison walls. They are working on how to walk on the shaky ground of newfound sobriety. Free from the bondage of serving their drug and alcohol addictions, their big question is, So now what?

Take Marco, for example. Marco didn't want to go back to his old way of life. He had used people, abused substances, and damaged relationships with friends and family—some beyond repair. But that's not who he was anymore.

Marco eventually graduated from the program and moved out of the house. But he came back—not because he had relapsed but because he wanted to help free more prisoners. He wanted to use the freedom he'd been given to help others break the cycle of homelessness, drug abuse, and crime.

"You, my brothers and sisters, were called to be free. But do not use your freedom to indulge the flesh; rather, serve one another humbly in love" (Galatians 5:13).

What about you? You were a slave to the accuser, your secret sins, and the appetites of your flesh. But through Christ, that is not who you are anymore. You have been set free. Like Marco (and Rambo), use your freedom to free more prisoners.

FEBRUARY

Do everything in love.

1 Corinthians 16:14

Forgiveness for him?
Nathan Nass

A man opened up to me about his past. It wasn't good. Actually, it was really bad. He had broken laws. Committed crimes. In his own words, he deserved to go to hell.

But Jesus found him. Through his Word—and a girlfriend—Jesus reached out to him with grace and forgiveness. To the man's surprise, he found himself going to church, Sunday after Sunday.

But every time he went, one man at church kept staring at him. Week after week, the man would spend the service staring at him. Do you know who that man was? He was the judge who had sentenced the man repeatedly for all his previous crimes.

Can you imagine that? If you were that judge, could you forgive that repentant criminal? Could you welcome him to your church? Do you forgive the people who've sinned against you?

There's only one way—through Jesus. The Bible encourages us: **"Bear with each other and forgive one another if any of you has a grievance against someone. Forgive as the Lord forgave you"** (Colossians 3:13). How much has the Lord forgiven you? Everything. Every time. Isn't that amazing? With our past? With all that we've done? Jesus took it to the cross and died for every single sin. Forgiven!

So the next time you see that "sinner" sit down in your church, don't just stare at him. Smile! Is there really forgiveness for *him*? Absolutely. And for you and me too. Thank you, Jesus!

God gives what you need
Mike Novotny

When our two girls were younger, there were three songs my wife, Kim, and I sang constantly in our home in order to teach them the message and values of our Christian faith. The third most popular song was "I Am Jesus' Little Lamb." The second was "Jesus Loves Me, This I Know." But the most frequently heard song in the Novotny home was, by far, "You Can't Always Get What You Want" by The Rolling Stones.

If you're a parent, you know why we sang that song. Because our kids were addicted to "I want!" We could give them everything they needed—food, clothing, love, safety—but if they didn't get what they wanted, they turned into little demon-possessed emotional terrorists who punched, scratched, and hated their parents! So Kim and I kept singing that song: "You Can't Always Get What You Want."

That's even more important to remember with your relationship with God. It isn't bad to want good grades, good friends, good health, good weather, a good government, and a good life. But it is essential to remember the difference between what we might want and what we truly need. What we need is God's love, God's forgiveness, and God's mercy. Thankfully, whether we get some/most/all/none of what we want, in Jesus we always get what we need.

"'Martha, Martha,' the Lord answered, 'you are worried and upset about many things, but few things are needed—or indeed only one'" (Luke 10:41,42). You need God. Through Jesus, you always get him.

Not my problem
Daron Lindemann

"Not responsible for gravel projectiles smashing your windshield."

That's what the sign on the back of the dump truck read. Or something like that. Every time I read those warnings on trucks hauling gravel, I have this discussion with myself:

Is it really true that if gravel from that truck damages my car, the owner of the truck would not be responsible? Maybe I should slow down (or zoom past)? Wait. Maybe I could hang a sign on my backside when I'm having a bad day that says, "Not responsible for sarcastic put-downs or rude behavior caused by anger, irritability, or stress."

As unfair as we think it is for a gravel trucker to claim that we are responsible for his unsafe hauling, we do the same thing when we make others responsible for our bad behavior.

Nobody is responsible for your sins, your mistakes, and your problems except you. The sooner you admit that you caused them, the sooner you'll be free from them. But that's not all.

Jesus does promise that he is responsible for your problems. Not that he caused them, but he has cured them.

Jesus **"bore our sins in his body on the tree . . . 'by his wounds you have been healed'"** (1 Peter 2:24). Jesus is the only one who makes your sins his responsibility.

Whether gravel, pebble, or big boulder of guilt, Jesus will take it. And break it. Just like his tomb when he burst out of it alive.

Soul reform
Jan Gompper

In the wake of each tragic school shooting, our country debates whether to have restrictions on the ownership of assault weapons. Second Amendment legalists argue that "guns don't kill people; people kill people." Yet I don't think even *they* would argue against the truth that mentally ill people *with* assault weapons can more readily and quickly kill a greater number of people.

Anti-gun advocates want stricter regulations regarding who can purchase a gun and what types of guns should be available to the general public. These same people, however, say nothing about the graphic violence that daily infiltrates our lives in the form of "entertainment." Some of Hollywood's biggest stars speak the loudest for gun reform yet have appeared in countless films or TV series where gun violence is the norm.

The problem of gun violence (or any violence) goes deeper. A culture of violence (real or imaginary) seems to grant permission to be violent. At the very least, it desensitizes us to violence.

God knew this when he warned, **"Do not envy the violent or choose any of their ways"** (Proverbs 3:31). The Lord further pinpointed the root cause of violence: **"From the fruit of their lips people enjoy good things, but** *the unfaithful have an appetite for violence"* (Proverbs 13:2).

Whatever side of the gun battle we're on, what our world needs even more are advocates for "soul" reform, which can only occur when someone experiences the grace and love of Jesus.

Let's be part of the *real* solution!

The tightrope of salvation
Mike Novotny

One of the reasons so many people miss out on heaven is they think that getting to God is like shooting free throws instead of walking a tightrope. If you're playing hoops, shooting 99 percent is NBA All-Star good. But if you're walking a tightrope across the Grand Canyon, hitting 99 percent of your steps leaves you . . . well . . . dead.

The problem with "free throw theology" is that you focus on yourself instead of running to Jesus. Just do your best. Try harder. Learn from your mistakes. Be a good person, and you'll make it to a better place. But that's not true. Jesus said, **"Be perfect"** (Matthew 5:48). Paul wrote, **"The wages of sin is death"** (Romans 6:23). James said that someone who stumbles just once and violates God's law is **"guilty of breaking all of it"** (James 2:10). Sin just once, and you are in danger.

Unless you have a Savior. Two thousand years ago, Jesus stood at one end of the tightrope and offered you a ride. This is why we put our faith entirely in him, relying on his steps to save us. And this is why we read Luke 4:1-13 with intense interest. I encourage you to open your Bible to those verses, picture yourself on Jesus' shoulders, and celebrate as he takes step after obedient step in order to get you to the presence of God. When the tempter tempted, your Savior resisted.

Salvation is a tightrope. Thankfully, Jesus walked it for you.

God's protection
Andrea Delwiche

"Whoever dwells in the shelter of the Most High will rest in the shadow of the Almighty. I will say of the Lord, 'He is my refuge and my fortress, my God, in whom I trust'" (Psalm 91:1,2).

Words like *refuge* and *fortress* in Bible passages can sometimes slip past us. Perhaps we've heard them so many times that they are nearly *too* familiar, or perhaps we've never taken the time to define them and really consider what it means to call God "my refuge" or "my fortress."

A refuge is a place of shelter. People fleeing violence in their homes or countries need a safe place to go. A wildlife refuge is an area of land or water that has been set aside so a variety of species of animals can live in safety.

A fortress can be thought of as a castle. It could also be a secure geographical spot like an island or a secluded spot hidden in the mountains.

What happens if you and I take the time to personalize these pictures of God as a refuge or a fortress? How do you relate to these pictures of God? Do you see God providing refuge like a warm, dry home, or can you picture yourself resting along the quiet shores of a lake—a refuge from all that would harm you? How about a fortress? Take time and sit with God in prayer, asking his Holy Spirit to open these words to you, to help you see all the protection that God offers you today.

Fix your eyes
Katrina Harrmann

My husband is an avid cyclist. As he was teaching our kids to ride their bikes, he offered a piece of wisdom I've never forgotten: "If you see something in the road that you want to avoid, don't look at it or you'll ride right through it."

I thought he was crazy. But as I learned to navigate a narrow road bike tire down the shoulders of busy roads littered with sticks and rocks—and sometimes big chunks of glass—I was shocked to find that he was quite right!

If I saw a big rock in my path, for instance, the more I stared at it, the more my bike seemed to veer directly for it! In fact, my bike would unerringly lean toward whatever hazard had caught my eye. But when I looked through it to the safest path, I sailed through free and clear.

Life is like that too sometimes. We tend to follow what we keep our eyes on.

Sometimes this is not great stuff. It's stuff that is bad for us or can cause addictions. There are many things we shouldn't be looking at or investing our time or efforts in. But when we focus on Christ, we tend to veer in his direction, which is a lovely way to veer!

Remember. In life (and in cycling!) . . . you tend to follow what you keep your eyes on.

"Let us run with perseverance the race marked out for us, fixing our eyes on Jesus, the pioneer and perfecter of faith" (Hebrews 12:1,2).

Recognize how God reaches you
Mike Novotny

One of history's more jarring moments happened around A.D. 70 when Roman soldiers surrounded the city of Jerusalem, starved the Jewish rebels inside, and eventually crushed the crown jewel of Israel. Listen to how Jesus predicted and explained the coming destruction: **"The days will come upon you when your enemies will build an embankment against you and encircle you and hem you in on every side. They will dash you to the ground, you and the children within your walls. They will not leave one stone on another, because you did not recognize the time of God's coming to you"** (Luke 19:43,44).

That last line got my attention. "Recognize the time of God's coming to you." Be aware of how and when God himself is reaching out to you. Although most of us live far from Jerusalem and long after the fall of the temple, those words are worthy of taking to heart.

God comes to us in his Word. Although it might just seem like a book (or a quote in a digital devotion) or a mediocre preacher or another Sunday service, when the Bible is read/heard/preached, God is coming to us. Ignore his voice, and your spiritual destruction is sure to come. Pay attention to his warnings and promises, and you will end up in the new Jerusalem, the city where the Most High God dwells.

Recognize how God reaches you. He reaches out to you through his Word.

Jesus cleaned up our mess
Clark Schultz

My wife and I did something crazy, something we have not done in over six months. Get ready for it . . . we moved our couch in the living room.

When sending this devotion to the editor to be approved, I included a photo, but let me give you the rundown of the junk we found under the couch: one flip-flop, a few partially eaten goldfish crackers, a plethora of potato chips, the head to a Lego figure, balls from a pump-action toy gun, and a deluge of dust bunnies. Gross is an understatement. What's even more disgusting is that we and others sat on that couch not knowing what lurked beneath it.

As I sat there emptying the vacuum into the trash for the third time, I realized that this mess is a picture of you and me. We look perfect on the outside, nice and cushy. We dress up and cover the messes we make. But Ezekiel 18:4 reminds us that **"the one who sins is the one who will die."**

We can hide it all we want, but we can't escape our fate. Thank God we have something and someone more powerful than a Dustbuster. We have the Sinbuster in our Savior Jesus. He took on the messes we make and swept them all away. **"The blood of Jesus, his Son, purifies us from all sin"** (1 John 1:7). We are forgiven. So relax. Sit down. Take a load off, and be comforted that the biggest load has been taken care of by Jesus.

Keep reading
Linda Buxa

Many people who love Jesus love to quote Romans 8:28: **"And we know that in all things God works for the good of those who love him, who have been called according to his purpose."** I mean, why wouldn't we love words that bring so much comfort and peace and remind us that God is working for us. Sometimes, though, we might need just a little more encouragement. That's why we should keep on reading verses 29 and 30 too—slowly and with a little explanation. (After all, some of these are churchy words; it's easy to gloss over them.)

"For those God foreknew he also predestined"—He determined to do whatever it would take to get you close to him.

"to be conformed to the image of his Son, that he might be the firstborn among many brothers and sisters"—Because of Jesus' payment for sins, your status is transformed and you are now God's child.

"And those he predestined, he also called"—He chose you and made sure that you would be found and belong to him forever.

"those he called, he also justified"—You are no longer God's enemy, but instead he sees you as being holy and set apart.

"those he justified, he also glorified."—All blessings from Jesus are poured onto you. Your victory is so certain; your place is prepared. You get to radiate his glory to everyone around you.

Well, that's even better news!

God doesn't give what we want
Mike Novotny

After a few years of marriage, Kim and I decided that we needed some counseling. With two kiddos in diapers, we were running on fumes and kept fighting about the same thing every few weeks. So after a frustrating stretch, we reached out for help and booked a session with a counselor in town. Honestly, what I wanted was for the counselor to say those three simple words: "Kim, Mike's right." (For $100/hour, I thought that was reasonable . . .) But sometimes you don't get what you want. You get what you need. And I got what I needed, a long look at the sin in my own heart.

One of our biggest spiritual problems is that we tend to think that 99 percent of the problems in the world are because of "those people." If only the liberals/conservatives/old white guys/young black men/fundamentalists/progressives/etc. would change, everything would be better. But God, like my old counselor, prefers to start with you. With your heart. With your level of love for others, including the amount of patience, compassion, and grace you have for "those people."

Long before my counselor said it, Jesus taught the importance of focusing on our own faults. Read Luke 18:9-14, the parable of the tax collector and the Pharisee. Relate to the Pharisee who thought he was better than **"other people"** (verse 11). Imitate the tax collector who humbly cried, **"God, have mercy"** (verse 13). And celebrate the Jesus who exalts everyone who humbles himself in honest confession (verse 14).

Surgery-free transformation
Liz Schroeder

An affluent city near us is known for its plastic surgery. It's such a blessing for cancer patients, burn victims, or people who have been disfigured in car accidents. However, it's very tempting for those with disposable income to use it to turn back time, erase wrinkles, lift that which sags, give where the Lord has taken away, and take away where the Lord (or the all-you-can-eat buffet) has given.

"Now the Lord is the Spirit, and where the Spirit of the Lord is, there is freedom. And we all, who with unveiled faces contemplate the Lord's glory, are being transformed into his image with ever-increasing glory, which comes from the Lord, who is the Spirit" (2 Corinthians 3:17,18).

Father, you are love. You are loving. You have made us in your image, so we are lovely—and all the more so as you change us to look more and more like Jesus.

Forgive us for making our [flat] stomachs an idol and for worshiping smooth skin and toned tushes—as if those things will last, as if those things will satisfy the aching in our hearts. What we really want is approval, and we have that in Jesus, through his perfection. What we really want is acceptance, and again, through Jesus we already have it. What more could the world give us?

Cultivate a gentle inner beauty in us that draws others to seek you. Not for our admiration and glory but for yours. Amen.

A level of decency
Jason Nelson

Jesus spent time in Bethany with his friends Mary, Martha, and Lazarus. One time he placed himself in the middle of a squabble between sisters. Martha was busy preparing dinner, but Mary chose not to help her. Instead, she sat at Jesus' feet to learn from him. Jesus didn't take sides but did make a point about priorities.

"'Martha, Martha . . . you are worried and upset about many things, but few things are needed—or indeed only one. Mary has chosen what is better, and it will not be taken away from her'" (Luke 10:41-43).

I hear kindness in his voice: *I understand you are a person who feels responsible for many things, including getting a nice meal together for us. You are frustrated that you are doing the work and it seems like Mary is being lazy. I get that. But I would like you to recognize there are things even more important than food for the body. That is food for the soul. And right now, Mary's soul is hungry.*

Jesus didn't ridicule people for being human. He understood that his followers would express devotion to him in ways compatible with their dispositions. He could empathize with all of them. He always redirected them to the spiritual priorities of love for God and for one another.

We are in a season of unprecedented rudeness enabled by multichannel platforms of personal expression. But being created in the image of God implies we show a level of decency animals don't possess. We just don't eat each other.

I love you more
Katrina Harrmann

One afternoon I was feeling particularly crafty and started making a string/friendship bracelet for my then seven-year-old daughter. It was extremely complicated, but I was getting the hang of it and was nearly done. However, after an hour of working, I made one wrong move, lost track of where I was, and messed it up beyond hope.

It upset me so much that I sat quietly with my head in my hands. Then, a small hand slid a note across the kitchen counter. "I love you more than a bracelet." My daughter had scribbled this on a scrap of lined notebook paper. I hugged her as my heart overflowed with gratitude.

Boy, did that note put things in perspective! It made me stop and realize how often I get busy with things that I *think* are SO important when really, the thing that actually matters is sitting right in front of me.

Which begs the question: How many times in our lives are we busy with things that don't matter while God waits quietly on the sidelines, waiting for us to pay attention to him?

"I love you MORE," he whispers in our ears, pushing his note (the Bible) into our hands. Do we see? Do we notice? Do we even look up from whatever we're doing?

Take a moment to focus on what's most important the next time you feel caught up in the whirlwind of stress and life.

"For where your treasure is, there your heart will be also" (Luke 12:34).

Made for eternity
Nathan Nass

"You only live once!" How often do you hear that? We're bombarded with encouragements to seize the day because our end could come at any time. "You only live once!" Do you believe that?

Isn't that empty? If you've bought into the lie of evolution, I suppose it makes sense. If this world is all there is, you better treasure today, because when you're dead, you're dead. It makes sense, but isn't that sad? Even if you seize the day today, if your end is just a pile of ashes, who cares? Isn't that empty?

But God tells you something so much better: **"He has made everything beautiful in its time. He has also set eternity in the human heart"** (Ecclesiastes 3:11). While we are blessed with beautiful moments on earth, God made you for more than this earth. God made you for more than this life. God made you for eternity. "He has set eternity in the human heart." Deep down, you don't long to live for one hundred years; you long to live forever!

God didn't just set eternity in our hearts. He provided a way to live forever: Jesus. Jesus died on a cross and rose again to open the gates of heaven for us. Everyone who believes in Jesus doesn't just live once. For a Christian, life doesn't end at death. We get to live for eternity with Jesus.

So don't set your heart on anything in this world. You were made for eternity!

Motives matter
Mike Novotny

Motives matter, don't they? Sometimes a man tells a woman she's beautiful because he's a nice guy; other times it's because he wants to take her back to his apartment. Sometimes a teenage boy gives his mom a big hug because he's a kind kid; other times it's because he wants 20 bucks for pizza. The reason we are wary of a salesman with a big smile is because we know that motives matter, that a person's inner intentions matter as much, if not more, than their outer actions.

That's true with God too. Since God is love, his desire is to love us and to have us love him back. He doesn't want to use us for our praise, and he doesn't want us to use him for his presents. God is not a vending machine. He's a Father. And he wants to have a genuine relationship with us.

This is one of the strangely beautiful parts about pain. Jesus' friend Peter wrote that your suffering, grief, and trials prove the **"genuineness of your faith"** (1 Peter 1:7). In other words, your pain proves it. If you were using God for a good life, then you wouldn't praise him when life wasn't good. If God was just a vending machine who exchanged the coins of worship for the candy of blessings, then you wouldn't worship when God held back blessings.

Pain is anything but fun. Yet it has a grand purpose in our spiritual lives. It proves to the devil and the watching world that we genuinely love God.

Jesus' baptism is a big deal

Mike Novotny

When Jesus asked to be baptized, John the Baptist hesitated. Baptism is for the forgiveness of sins, but Jesus was sinless, so something seemed off. But Jesus insisted because he knew that his baptism was a big deal.

Luke tells us why: **"And as [Jesus] was praying, heaven was opened and the Holy Spirit descended on him in bodily form like a dove. And a voice came from heaven: 'You are my Son, whom I love; with you I am well pleased'"** (Luke 3:21,22). Heaven was opened—the barrier between the physical and the spiritual world was temporarily opened. The Holy Spirit came down like a dove—a sign that Jesus was pure, innocent, and beautiful and that he would be the sacrifice for poor sinners, just like poor Mary and Joseph brought a dove to the temple for their sacrifice. The Father's voice boomed with pride: "You are my Son, whom I love; with you I am well pleased." No one has ever loved anyone more than the Father and the Spirit love the Son (and vice versa!).

This baptism was the Trinity's chance to declare the identity of Jesus. After 30 years on the earth, Jesus was still as pure as a dove and absolutely deserving of the Father's love. He was no mere man. He was, and is, the only Son of the Father. That declaration is why Jesus' baptism is a big deal. So as the Father said, **"Listen to him!"** (Mark 9:7).

Fresh and green
Andrea Delwiche

"It is good to praise the LORD and make music to your name, O Most High, proclaiming your love in the morning and your faithfulness at night. For you make me glad by your deeds, LORD. . . . The righteous will flourish like a palm tree, they will grow like a cedar of Lebanon; planted in the house of the LORD, they will flourish in the courts of our God. They will still bear fruit in old age, they will stay fresh and green" (Psalm 92:1,2,4,12–14).

Look at the image of a flourishing tree. In Psalm 1 we are told that those who delight in the Lord and follow his will are like "a tree planted by streams of water, which yields its fruit in season" (verse 3). In Psalm 92 the righteous are described as bearing fruit in old age and being "fresh and green" in the last season of life.

This is a worthy goal, to model our lives along the pathways of God so whatever age we attain, we continue to grow younger as we grow in the joy and peace of Christ.

How is this youthfulness possible? The words of the apostle Paul come to mind: "I have learned the secret of being content in any and every situation, whether well fed or hungry, whether living in plenty or in want" (Philippians 4:12).

No matter what our age, through God's artesian well of grace, we can begin again each moment.

Holy Spirit, guide us and renew us that we may stay fresh and green! Amen.

Prove the devil wrong
Mike Novotny

Satan's annual resolution is to erase the love out of our relationship with God. He is more than okay with us believing that God exists (even demons believe that). He is cool with a contractual view of God (do good works and God will do you good). What he can't stand, however, is when we believe that God is love and when we love him in return. He himself doesn't believe it, and he doesn't want you to believe it either.

This is why Satan slandered the loving relationship between God and Job, claiming Job only used God to get a good life. **"But now stretch out your hand and strike everything he has, and he will surely curse you to your face,"** Satan hissed (Job 1:11). Strangely, God allowed that very thing to happen to Job. Wonderfully, Job didn't do what the devil assumed he would. Job fell down in worship. He praised the name of the Lord.

I wonder if Satan gnashes his teeth when hurting people go to church. Or when arthritic hands fold for another dinner prayer. Or when widows read devotions like this one. Just when Satan assumes we will curse God in our pain, we instead turn to him in praise. We thank him for being with us. We ask him for healing but then say, "Your will be done." We worship him for giving us heaven, an eternal home where pain is extinct.

Praise God today even if you're in pain. The devil will hate it. But the God of love will love it.

Grab a towel
Liz Schroeder

Since the dawn of time, man's most "Frequently Asked Questions" have been 1) Who am I? 2) Where am I going? and 3) What should I do? Or, if you've ever heard these questions asked by your mom, it may have sounded like this: 1) Who do you think you are, mister? 2) Just where do you think you're going? and 3) What on earth are you doing?

Valid questions. Deep questions. Have you ever wondered how Jesus would answer these questions?

"Jesus knew that the Father had put all things under his power, and that he had come from God and was returning to God; so he got up from the meal, took off his outer clothing, and wrapped a towel around his waist" (John 13:3,4).

In other words, he knew who he was and where he was going, so he served.

We can copy his answers. You know who you are because you know whose you are. You are a dearly loved child of God. You know where you're going because Jesus went to hell and back so you could be with him—now and forever. And you know what to do. If Jesus lowered himself to serve, so can you. You don't need to scramble for worldly prestige. There is so much to be gained through the self-forgetfulness of service.

I've heard the story of Jesus washing the disciples' feet summed up like this: "The insecure grab titles; the secure grab towels." Secure in your answers and identity, you can grab a towel.

God doesn't care
(and that's good news!)
Mike Novotny

Does God want you to rent an apartment or buy a house? Does he prefer you stay at your current job or look for a new one? Is his will that you retire at 65 or 75? There are a thousand questions that fall into this same category, that is, personal decisions the Bible doesn't exactly tell you how to make. I know people who agonize over these moments, asking, "Pastor, what does God want me to do?"

Here's the odd but comforting answer—God doesn't care! He's cool either way. He won't be mad if you choose A or B. While I know you would love some inside scoop on the will of God, there isn't one. And that is really good news. That means you don't have to sit and nervously wonder if God is mad at you for not purchasing a home/having another kid/etc. You can live with the confidence that God is with you, God is for you, and God has great plans to bless you. Our perfect Father will be with you, whatever path you choose.

I love the simple words of Moses: **"The secret things belong to the Lord our God, but the things revealed belong to us and to our children forever, that we may follow all the words of this law"** (Deuteronomy 29:29). What belongs to us—our business and focus—isn't some secret plan in God's head but rather the words he has revealed in the Bible. Pay attention to them, and you'll know exactly what God cares about.

The Lord reigns
Andrea Delwiche

"**The floods have lifted up, O Lord**" (Psalm 93:3 ESV). Water is a force. If you have stood by an ocean or one of the Great Lakes, you have perhaps witnessed the power of water. If you've been caught in floodwaters, you've experienced helplessness in the face of surging water.

It's hard to save yourself from water, whether real water or the waters of hardship. It's a lot of pressure to figure everything out, even if you are blessed with many resources. It's even harder to deal when you have no power and resources.

But what held true in the days of the psalmist is still true today: "**The Lord reigns; he is robed in majesty. . . . The world is established; it shall never be moved. . . . Mightier than the thunders of many waters, mightier than the waves of the sea, the Lord on high is mighty!**" (93:1,4 ESV).

There is both comfort and instruction in this psalm. Perhaps you need reassurance that there is someone who will bear you through the floodwaters of tragedy that are rising and threatening your life. Perhaps you need a reminder that God is far greater than you or the earthly powers upon which you rely. Only God controls the waters.

God reigns, and we ourselves are not God. God is actively ruling. He is strong to help. Consider sitting with this psalm today, and let the reality of God's dominion wash over you and bring his peace.

Choices
Jason Nelson

The mind of Christ was in Old Testament believers who trusted that God had a plan of salvation. Leaders like Joshua reflected that hope. He ushered the people of Israel into the Promised Land. When they were ready to settle it, he gave them something to think about. He made no threats but reminded them they had decisions to make. First among them would be renewing their commitment to the God who got them there. He set the example and spoke for his family: **"As for me and my household, we will serve the Lord"** (Joshua 24:15).

Christianity is not a *decision-less* religion. Here is an inconvenient reality. No one has to do anything they don't want to do. Even Adam and Eve had the choice to obey God or give in to temptation. Why do people do the right thing? It seems to me they are following one of two protocols: the enforcement protocol or the education protocol. The enforcement protocol taps into fear—fear of punishment and unpleasant consequences. The education protocol taps into love—love for God or parents or neighbors. The enforcement protocol is swift and heavy-handed. The education protocol takes a while because good character develops over time and is an outcome of persistent teaching. There are examples in the Bible of God using both. But there is no doubt which one he prefers. "God so loved the world that he gave his one and only Son" (John 3:16).

Blessing our socks off
Katrina Harrmann

We have a big dog who is about seven years old and loves nothing better than to beg for scraps of food at our little breakfast table. No matter what we are eating, she sits patiently at our elbows, staring up at us through doleful eyes . . . forever hopeful.

When we cook bacon or gravy, my husband will spoil the dog by pouring a tiny bit of bacon grease or gravy over the kibble in her bowl.

One afternoon he did this. But she was so obsessed with begging from me that she didn't even notice the amazing treat he had left for her in her food dish.

"You're so obsessed with other people's food that you didn't even notice the good treats I gave you!" My husband remarked, exasperated. "I blessed your socks off, and you didn't even notice it!"

I laughed because humans are the same way, don't ya think?

I wonder how many times a day the good Lord throws up his hands and sighs at us, saying, "I blessed your socks off! Why didn't you notice?"

Truly, our heavenly Father gives us SO many good things. We can hardly keep track! Yet it's so easy to become distracted by our "wants" that we fail to show gratitude. Let's remember to say thank you today!

"And my God will meet all your needs according to the riches of his glory in Christ Jesus" (Philippians 4:19).

I am the worst
Linda Buxa

I want people held accountable when they are not following the rules that I believe are good. You know, like when they steal things or abuse children. But if I'm honest, I don't want to be held accountable for my sins—even "little ones" like slightly breaking the speed limit. (Obviously, I know I'm breaking the rules, but I'm breaking them just enough that it won't get me in trouble and will still allow me to get there *this much* faster.)

Sometimes I pray for God to expose corruption and provide justice, but then I stop for a minute because I get a little afraid to pray that prayer. See, I don't want him to expose the corruption in my heart. I want justice for other people and mercy for myself.

This hypocrisy is why I need to remember what a man named Paul wrote thousands of years ago: **"Here is a trustworthy saying that deserves full acceptance: Christ Jesus came into the world to save sinners—of whom I am the worst"** (1 Timothy 1:15).

When I remember that I should be the one writing those words, I can take the plank out of my own eye before I remove the speck from someone else's. (That's a churchy way of saying that I need to be honest about my flaws before I point them out in others.)

When I remember that, then I can remember that Christ came for me. Then I tell all the other corrupt rule breakers that this good news is for them too.

But Jesus resisted
Mike Novotny

Seeing the homeless men who hang out near our church makes me appreciate just how intense Jesus' temptation must have been. **"The devil led him up to a high place and showed him in an instant all the kingdoms of the world. And he said to him, 'I will give you all their authority and splendor; it has been given to me, and I can give it to anyone I want to. If you worship me, it will all be yours'"** (Luke 4:5-7).

Imagine you had spent the last six weeks homeless, scraping by with an empty stomach and a shiver trapped in your bones. One day you walk past a hotel and see a gourmet buffet spread out inside. As you're fogging up the window, a voice says, "Hungry? I can get you all that food, a king-sized bed, and a hot shower. All you have to do is bow down, and in 30 seconds, it will be yours."

How tempted would you be to cut a moral corner? But when the tempter tempted, Jesus resisted. **"Jesus answered, 'It is written: "Worship the Lord your God and serve him only"'"** (Luke 4:8). "Not today, Satan. I worship God," the fully human, very hungry Son of God insisted.

And because he resisted, you have hope. No matter how hard this life might be, you have the hope of something better than all the splendor of this world. You have a place in the Father's house, a seat at the feast in the kingdom of God.

Thank you, Lord, for sending a perfect Savior!

Impractical preaching
Mike Novotny

I try to be a practical preacher. After I unpack a section of Scripture, I like to suggest a simple next step to help God's people put that truth into practice. But there are certain texts and certain times where it doesn't feel right to leave people with something more to do. Because sometimes (perhaps many times), the most biblical thing to leave people with is what has already been done for them.

It makes me think of Charles Spurgeon's death. When the great 19th-century preacher was drawing close to his last breath, he didn't leave his friends with five tips to be stronger Christians. Instead, he quoted the words of a now-famous hymn called "Before the Throne of God Above." The lyrics point to the sinless and perfect Lamb who died to save us.

The song doesn't give any next steps or things to do other than to behold Jesus. Fixing your eyes on his unfailing love might help you in ways that all the works in the world cannot.

"The next day John saw Jesus coming toward him and said, 'Look, the Lamb of God, who takes away the sin of the world!'" (John 1:29).

Doubt or belief
Linda Buxa

When it was almost time for Jesus to be born, the central figures in his birth story got some news.

Here's how it went with old Zechariah. The angel Gabriel told him Elizabeth, who was also old, would become pregnant with a son who would prepare the way for the Lord. He replied, "I doubt that." (That's not a literal translation.) Because Zechariah doubted, Gabriel said he wouldn't be able to speak until the baby was born.

Then, Gabriel visited Mary to tell her she would be the Savior's mom. When she said, "But I'm a virgin," she wasn't expressing doubt but a practical question. After Gabriel explained it, she said, **"I am the Lord's servant. . . . May your word to me be fulfilled"** (Luke 1:38).

Mary quickly went to visit Elizabeth, and one of the first things Elizabeth said was, **"Blessed is she who has believed that the Lord would fulfill his promises to her!"** (Luke 1:45).

Though I'm not a physical part of the Savior's line, I'm part of his family through faith. If you are too, then we get to ask ourselves if we doubt or believe God's promises to us. And he's got a lot of promises: hard-to-hear promises—we will have trouble; reassuring promises—God's peace guards our hearts and minds; hope-filled promises—Jesus has made us part of God's family, and now we have a whole, full life.

Do you doubt or do you believe?

Blessed are you when you believe the Lord will fulfill his promises to you.

Paying tribute to you
Jason Nelson

I might be wrong, but I'm guessing that few of you reading this have a statue of your likeness erected in a park named in your honor. I'm guessing you never received the keys to your city or pressed your hands in wet cement on a walk of fame. I'm guessing no one can look you up on Wikipedia. In a world that seems filled with people clamoring to get noticed, it's easy to feel insignificant. Even God featured the headliners in the Bible. We all know their names and name our children after them. I think only my mother knew of my namesake (Acts 17). But I do know this. A lot of good in this world would never be done without you. So I am dedicating this devotion to you.

The Bible does lump folks like us together when it refers to **"many others"** (i.e., Luke 8:3) who followed Jesus. In this case, here are some good women who supported the famous disciples out of their own pockets. They made a big difference in God's kingdom and were too many to name individually.

Being anonymous does not mean you're insignificant. Every day that you get up to be who you are and do what you do, you keep God's world spinning. God has made himself dependent on routine means to do extraordinary things that are easily taken for granted. He uses words, water, bread, wine, and many, many people like you. Thank you.

MARCH

For even the Son of Man did not come to be served,
but to serve, and to give his life as a ransom for many.

Mark 10:45

The most useful book ever
Mike Novotny

Americans, for the most part, are practical people. I've noticed that when I preach a message at church, my listeners (mostly, but not all, American) appreciate something they can apply practically to their lives. Thankfully, the Bible loves to do just that.

Look at the practicality of Christianity according to the apostle Paul: **"All Scripture is God-breathed and is useful for teaching, rebuking, correcting and training in righteousness, so that the servant of God may be thoroughly equipped for every good work"** (2 Timothy 3:16,17). The Book that God "breathed" out for us is— don't miss this word—*useful*. You can use it. It's helpful, handy, and practical.

Don't know what God is like, how you can be sure you're going to heaven, or the signs of the end times? The Bible is useful for teaching you. Know someone who is making dumb life decisions and needs to get back on a better path? The Bible is useful for rebuking and correcting. Feel unprepared for the challenges of raising kids or sense that you are unworthy of seeing God face-to-face? The Bible is useful for training you in righteousness.

Think of God's Word like your personal trainer. Every time you open it, God is speaking personally to you. He might get in your face to call you out, or he might put an arm around you to comfort you, but you can always be sure that the God of love is speaking to you. That's what makes the Bible the most useful book ever.

The heavenly Father's got this
Linda Buxa

If you have children, are you a fretting parent? I'm mainly chilled out, but I've also been known to—as I call it—panic pray. As my children got older, I started worrying about all the things they might face, all the things I hadn't taught them, all the ways I'd need to apologize to society because we probably don't wash our towels often enough, or—far more seriously—that they wouldn't make it home.

Then I read an excerpt from *How to Raise an Adult: Break Free of the Overparenting Trap and Prepare Your Kid for Success* by Julie Lythcott-Haims. She asked, "Why did parenting change from preparing our kids for life to protecting them from life, which means they're not prepared to live life on their own?"

While that gave me a bit of perspective, another question from God, the author of the Bible, kept popping into my mind: "Do you really think you love them more than I do?" (see Matthew 18:10).

Oh. That's right. These children are just on loan to me from God, their heavenly Father who promises that he has good plans for them, that he will be with them always, that he will guard them with his angels. My job is to teach them about God and about life. To remind them they are fully qualified to handle the challenges that each stage of life presents, that I'm excited to see God's plans for them unfold, that I can't wait to see how they will be lights in their slivers of this dark world.

How to suffer well
Mike Novotny

How do you hold on to your faith in God when life is falling apart? When you feel alone at school or devastated after your husband's death or confused by all the suffering God is allowing, how do you worship him still?

Job knows. After losing all 11,500 of his animals and all 10 of his precious children, Job fell to the ground in worship. He said: **"Naked I came from my mother's womb, and naked I will depart. The Lord gave and the Lord has taken away; may the name of the Lord be praised"** (Job 1:21).

Job didn't accuse God of being unloving, because Job believed that he was just a guy living between two naked days. He didn't come out of his mother's womb with 3,000 camels (that would have been something!). He wasn't a kid born with 10 of his own kids. He came into the world with nothing. Which means that God had given him everything. That belief allowed Job to suffer well.

Do you believe that too? Do you believe that everything good in your life is a gift from God, a gift he has every right (in his kindness) to give and every right (in his wisdom) to take away? Your home, your health, your family, your friends, your plans, your dreams. You didn't come out of the womb with anything, which means God is the true owner of everything.

Believe that and you will be ready to suffer well, holding on to the name that is worthy of all your praise.

My foot is slipping!
Andrea Delwiche

"When I said, 'My foot is slipping,' your unfailing love, LORD, supported me. When anxiety was great within me, your consolation brought me joy" (Psalm 94:18,19).

Do you remember your last "my foot is slipping!" moment? Maybe you were trying to step over a puddle or standing on rocks along a lake or heading down the basement stairs. There was one opportunity to grab ahold of something to prevent a wet foot, a soaked self, or serious injury.

How about emotional "my foot is slipping!" moments in the realities of making ends meet? When you feel yourself slipping, do you reflexively reach out, trusting that God will grab you before you hit the ground?

The apostle Paul, speaking of the sure hope of the resurrection, famously said, **"If only for this life we have hope in Christ, we are of all people most to be pitied"** (1 Corinthians 15:19). He was worried that people would forget that faith in Christ has *everlasting* consequences and hopes. But sometimes, *we* forget that faith in Christ makes a difference for our *daily lives.*

Through faith in Christ, we have the assurance of heaven. Through faith we also have resources for life on earth. Our Father God is our help in the present moment. Our brother, Christ Jesus, walks with us and supernaturally works all things here on earth for our good. Our Comforter desires to help us this very day. Our sure hope is for eternity. Our sure hope is for the present moment as well.

An encounter with the living God
Linda Buxa

You caught the player's jersey when he threw it into the crowd. The movie icon was out for a run, crossed the street in front of you, and briefly made eye contact. Or maybe you were on the same flight, recognized him, tweeted about it, and he replied. I remember standing along the side of the road as a child and waving as President Reagan's motorcade passed by.

What is it that makes us remember—for the rest of our lives—one brief brush with a celebrity when the reality is that the celebrity doesn't really even know we exist?

What if we consider that every moment spent with God is an encounter with a celebrity? However, this celebrity not only knows you exist; he has **"loved you with an everlasting love"** (Jeremiah 31:3). He says he rejoices over you with singing. He promises that he is Immanuel, which means "God-with-us." That means he isn't God-drove-passed-us or God-glimpsed-at-us or God-threw-us-a-jersey. He is the God who took on flesh and promises to never leave us. He promises that nothing can separate us from his love. He promises to bless us, to smile on us, and to give us peace. And instead of giving us his autograph, he's engraved us on the palm of his hand and written our names in the book of life.

These are the things we remember our whole lives.

Government according to Jesus
Daron Lindemann

Caesar, a pagan politician who claimed divine powers for himself that belong only to God, deserved obedience from Christians according to Jesus: **"Give back to Caesar what is Caesar's, and to God what is God's"** (Matthew 22:21).

Now here's some irony. Three days after Jesus said these words, Caesar's government pronounced Jesus a traitor and crucified him. Why didn't Jesus revolt against this injustice and pronounce his own authority over the Roman Empire before they killed him? Because Jesus trusted in his Father's authority over all government. With firm faith in his Father, Jesus could endure the injustice.

He explained it to Pontius Pilate during his trial: **"You would have no power over me if it were not given to you from above"** (John 19:11).

More than that, Jesus loved you enough to restrain his powers and die for you. He became a willing sacrifice to pay God for all sins.

Jesus loves everybody and saved us by his death at the hands of a dishonest, disobedient government. Then he rose from the dead and now lives with all authority.

With trust and love, Jesus overpowered the Roman Empire. Government soldiers guarding his tomb couldn't contain him. Government persecution of his followers couldn't stop them. And today, no government can stop Jesus or his believers.

Trust in Jesus. Love Jesus. He rules over all governments for the good of all believers.

Tired and frozen to the sword
Liz Schroeder

Eleazar might be one of the most famous warriors in Israel whom we've *never* heard of.

"As one of the three mighty warriors, [Eleazar] was with David when they taunted the Philistines gathered at Pas Dammim for battle. Then the Israelites retreated, but Eleazar stood his ground and struck down the Philistines till his hand grew tired and froze to the sword. The Lord brought about a great victory that day. The troops returned to Eleazar, but only to strip the dead" (2 Samuel 23:9,10).

Eleazar is given the distinction of being one of King David's "three mighty warriors," the best of the best. When all the other soldiers fled, Eleazar stood his ground, defending—of all things—a field of lentils. There was no time to stretch his sword-wielding hand between kills, and his hand froze to the sword.

Who can relate to Eleazar? Are you too tired to even raise your hand? Then I want you to know that you're not alone and you're in the right place.

Maybe you feel like you're the only one putting in the effort to save your marriage. You're the only one who struggles with ethics in your workplace. No one else in your classroom seems to be fighting for the biblical definition of sexuality.

Listen, Eleazar: Stand your ground. When you are fighting a battle that aligns with God's will, the Lord will bring about the victory. Keep fighting because the battle belongs to God.

Your baptism is a big deal
Mike Novotny

Do you think your baptism is a big deal? Big enough to stand up and clap for, to shed a tear over, to annually celebrate? I do. While Baptism is outwardly very simple (just some water and some words), what Baptism does for us is profound.

I think of Baptism like my phone charger. It doesn't seem like a big deal. It's a cord so skinny it can get lost in the bottom of a backpack or slip between the seats of my car. Compared to the smartphone in my hands or the power source in the wall, the cord seems insignificant. Until you remember that the cord connects one to the other, a way to get all that power in the outlet over to the device that needs it. No wonder we never go on vacation without bringing a charger!

I love that picture of Baptism. Baptism is one of God's ways of connecting you to Jesus. This is why many Baptism passages use words like *through Baptism* or *in Baptism*. Here's a classic example: **"We were therefore buried with him through baptism into death in order that, just as Christ was raised from the dead through the glory of the Father, we too may live a new life"** (Romans 6:4). How was the old, unsaved you buried with Jesus? Through Baptism!

So celebrate your baptism today! Because your baptism, according to the Bible, is a big deal!

No exclusions on grace
Nathan Nass

There are always exclusions, right? Everything comes with fine print. You go to the doctor and have to sign forms—lots of forms! You rent a car and have to sign forms—lots of forms! Your insurance policy comes with pages and pages of paperwork. Why? Because there are always exclusions. Always exceptions. That company is always there for you, except when . . .

But not God. Listen to his promise: **"So in Christ Jesus you are all children of God through faith, for all of you who were baptized into Christ have clothed yourselves with Christ. There is neither Jew nor Gentile, neither slave nor free, nor is there male and female, for you are all one in Christ Jesus"** (Galatians 3:26-28). God offers you new life through faith in Jesus. He makes you his own child! Through Baptism, God washes your sins away. He clothes you with Jesus' perfection! Doesn't that sound great?

So what are the exclusions? Just for Jews, right? Nope. God's promises are for all nationalities. Just for men, right? Of course not. God's promises are for men and women alike. Just for the wealthy, right? No way. Economic status doesn't matter. There are no exclusions on God's promises to you in Jesus.

Why? It's called grace. Grace is God's undeserved love. You can't earn it. Nobody does! Grace is God's gift to you in Jesus. The next time you see all the fine print, remember this: There are no exclusions on grace!

The end of "fake news"
Jan Gompper

Are you as tired as I am of hearing the term *fake news*? It seems we've been bombarded with this idiom ever since the 2016 political campaigns. Sometimes I wonder if those who like to bandy the term most have become a bit like the "boy who cried wolf."

Given our easy access to widespread information and disinformation on the internet, it is getting harder to differentiate between truthful and "fake" content. People will say anything to make a buck or sway people to their way of thinking, and even those designated as "fact checkers" can be accused of being biased.

All the while Satan smiles at the distrust that continues to grow in our country and world. After all, he **"does not stand in the truth, because there is no truth in him. When he lies, he speaks out of his own character, for he is a liar and the father of lies"** (John 8:44 ESV). His goal is to get us to distrust each other, our leaders, our institutions, and ultimately God.

But there's one piece of information that Satan will never be able to taint or change, and that's the good news of Jesus. No matter how hard he tries, he can never alter the *fact* that Christ's death and resurrection defeated Satan and his lies for all eternity.

Try as he may in this life, Satan's days of propagating lies and distrust are numbered, and we will one day bask in the glory of that *absolute* truth.

The masks we wear
Clark Schultz

When I was five, my eight-year-old brother would play "Scare Clark." This game consisted of him wearing a hockey mask and jumping out of the shadows to scare me. My all-time, not-so favorite was when he would hide with said mask under my bed and wait until I was almost asleep. Then he would reach his hand up and touch my arm. Yup, that got my heart rate up!

You can laugh, but admit it. You and I don't need a holiday to put on masks; we wear them every day. School stress, a rocky marriage, piles of bills, health issues, anxiety. Someone asks, "Hey, how are you doing?" To avoid the conflict, we simply answer, "I'm fine." We reason that no one would want to hear our problems. They have enough of their own.

What can we do about it? Go it alone? How's that been working for you? Permit James to encourage you: **"Therefore confess your sins to each other and pray for each other so that you may be healed. The prayer of a righteous person is powerful and effective"** (James 5:16).

Confess and pray to whom? That's why I love my church family. As one author noted, church is not a hotel for saints but a hospital for sinners. Fellow believers help us take off our masks to reveal that our current circumstances do not take away from who we are in Christ.

Things may not always be "fine" this side of heaven, but we don't have to go it alone.

The beauty around you
Jason Nelson

It may be in the eye of the beholder, but this beholder sees beauty in the world God created. The colors, shapes, and birdsongs of nature are templates for artists to follow.

I've never liked horror movies. They are ugly to me. I don't need to watch hideous creatures rise from the deep to destroy civilization. I'm not entertained by grotesque violence.

When I was lying in an ICU with my chest cracked open—sedated, intubated, and on a ventilator—I had very disturbing hallucinations. One was a descent into hell. It was a spiked ball with a light barely flickering inside speeding down a narrow corridor. It accelerated on the way down, careening from side to side with no bottom in sight, and it was taking me with it. Eventually something brought me out of it, and I could see the light of day outside my window. I could see beauty.

Streaming platforms push the limits to produce "original" content and gain subscribers. People seem to like this stuff. No one seems too concerned about the degradation of our society.

Jesus taught us to take a thoughtful look at the flowers in the field. He said that not even Solomon at the height of his glory was as impressive as the lilies in full bloom. The Bible encourages us: **"Whatever is noble, whatever is right, whatever is pure, whatever is lovely, whatever is admirable—if anything is excellent or praiseworthy—think about such things"** (Philippians 4:8). Beauty is praiseworthy like a sunrise.

Just like Job

Mike Novotny

Moments before the tragedy, Tia Coleman's family was just another group of tourists, smiling for a picture before the tour. Soon after, they boarded the boat that would sink, ending 17 lives, including 9 members of Tia's family. She survived, but her husband did not. Nor her 9-year-old, her 7-year-old, or her 1-year-old. The lightning bolt of suffering struck suddenly, leaving Tia with a life she never planned on living.

She had always been a churchgoing woman, lifting up her hands at the precious name of Jesus, but what would she do now? As she sat in the front row at the funeral, how would she react to the name of the God who had enough power to create the universe but had not chosen to calm the storm that killed her family?

Answer—She praised him. Surrounded by her pastor, her friends, and her church family, Tia frequently rose to her feet to praise God during the three-hour service. She closed her eyes to pray. She lifted her arms in worship. She didn't know why this had happened, but she did know who was worthy of worship. Like Job, her faith confessed, **"The Lord gave and the Lord has taken away; may the name of the Lord be praised"** (Job 1:21).

Sooner or later in life, we will feel the sharper edges of this broken world. When we do, I pray that our faith imitates Tia, a woman who imitated Job. May the name of the Lord be praised!

Follow mentors through fear
Daron Lindemann

Mike helped me ride a Harley. Ron taught me how to handle a gun. Bryan invited me to preach in front of—gulp—a thousand people. We need others to invite us into our fears with faith in the Lord.

Remember going to the amusement park and seeing a ride that looks fun but also seems scary? So you wait while your friends go on the ride. They have a blast and run back to you, "Let's go. Come with us!" You're still scared but you follow them, go on the ride, and it's awesome! You're enjoying freedom from fear because your friends led you instead of fear leading you. With their help, you led your fears.

Paul and his friends did this for other Christians. He wrote, **"You became imitators of us and of the Lord, for you welcomed the message in the midst of severe suffering with the joy given by the Holy Spirit"** (1 Thessalonians 1:6).

Do you see what happened here? Paul and friends had suffered persecution, and these other Christians were now suffering it too. Not with fear but with joy!

Find a mentor now. Connect with someone who can show you the way, open up the message of Scripture, and serve as an agent of the Holy Spirit.

Dear God, you gave Paul and the apostles to other Christians. Direct me to Christian models and mentors who can help me through my fears. And help me also help others. Amen.

Despair or prayer?

Jan Gompper

For 430 years the people of Israel had been slaves in Egypt until God heard their cries and used Moses to lead them out of captivity. It didn't take long, however, before they threw their hands up in despair, forgetting God's faithfulness and blaming Moses for leading them into the desert to starve to death.

Perhaps our country's current economic state has you feeling as if you've been led to a desert place. Housing costs have skyrocketed, interest rates are climbing, fuel and groceries have reached levels many of us can't afford. Certainly our complaints are justified, aren't they?!

Though history has repeatedly shown us that God sometimes allows his children to wander in the "desert of difficulties" to test their trust in him, it's easy to fail that test.

Over eight hundred years after being freed from Egypt, the Israelites were again conquered—this time by the Babylonians. Once again, they had forgotten God's faithfulness, but thankfully the prophet Daniel pleaded on their behalf: **"Lord, the great and awesome God, who keeps his covenant of love with those who love him and keep his commandments. . . . Give ear, our God, and hear; open your eyes and see the desolation of the city that bears your Name. We do not make requests of you because we are righteous, but because of your great mercy. Lord, listen! Lord, forgive! Lord, hear and act!"** (Daniel 9:4,18,19).

Lord, help us like Daniel. Turn our despair into prayer!

It's not (always) your fault
Mike Novotny

Sometimes our suffering is self-inflicted. As the book of Proverbs frequently warns us, gossips lose friends, hotheads increase drama, and adulterers get burned by the fire of their own passions.

But sometimes our suffering isn't our fault. While the devil would love for us to assume that God must be punishing us for our past sins, that isn't always/often the case. The death of your loved one wasn't God's payback for those years you didn't prioritize your faith. Your infertility isn't God's judgment for your premarital sexual behavior. And cancer is just cancer, not God's way of evening the score for what you did last summer.

How do I know this? Because of Job. Job suffered unspeakable pain (the death of his children, brutal health complications, etc.), yet the very first verse of the book tells us, "[Job] **was blameless and upright; he feared God and shunned evil**" (Job 1:1). Just in case you thought the author was exaggerating his character, God himself says the same things about Job in both chapter 1 and chapter 2—Blameless. Upright. God-fearing. Evil-shunning. The point? Job's upcoming pain wasn't God's payback.

I won't claim to know why you suffer in the way you do. But I do want to free you from the false belief that all suffering is connected to personal sin. Sometimes the world is just broken. Sometimes God uses the pain that you didn't cause for a higher purpose. It's not always your fault. That was true for Job. And it is true for you.

Jesus never twisted Scripture

Mike Novotny

Do you ever take a snippet of Scripture and make an unscriptural application?

God made you. That's true. God doesn't make mistakes. That's true too. So whatever you feel or want or desire in your heart must be from God, right? God forgives. That's true. God forgives us for everything. That's true too. So when you're tempted, just do it. God will forgive you no matter what, right? The devil is so good at taking half a truth and making it seem like the whole truth.

But Jesus never twisted Scripture for his own pleasure. **"The devil led him to Jerusalem and had him stand on the highest point of the temple. 'If you are the Son of God,' he said, 'throw yourself down from here. For it is written: "He will command his angels concerning you to guard you carefully; they will lift you up in their hands, so that you will not strike your foot against a stone."' Jesus answered, 'It is said: "Do not put the Lord your God to the test"'"** (Luke 4:9-12).

Jesus wasn't jumping to the devil's conclusion. He knew the text and the context, and his perfect knowledge and obedience are the reason why his death on a cross means something for you today. Jesus was the perfect Savior, the spotless Lamb of God, who took away the sins of the world.

Take a moment today to thank Jesus for resisting the tempter so that he could be your Savior.

I know the Planner
Nathan Nass

I don't know the plan. I really struggle with that. I don't know what's going to happen next in my life. I don't know why my plans don't work out. I don't know why it's all happening this way. Do you struggle with that too? Life so often doesn't make sense at all. I don't know the plan!

When I complained about that to a friend, he said, "But you know the Planner!" Long ago, God's people didn't know the plan either. The Israelites were stuck as exiles in a foreign country. But God gave them this promise: **"'For I know the plans I have for you,' declares the Lord, 'plans to prosper you and not to harm you, plans to give you hope and a future'"** (Jeremiah 29:11).

There is Someone who knows the plan: God does! You might not know the plan, but you know the Planner. He's the same God who created you and me. The same God who sent his Son, Jesus, to die on a cross for our sins. The same God who's prepared a home in heaven for everyone who believes in Jesus. God knows the plan. In fact, God has a perfect plan for you and me.

So let's practice saying this: "I don't know the plans, but I know the Planner! I don't know the plans, but I know the Planner!" May you find peace in God and in his plans for you today.

Following means listening
Andrea Delwiche

Psalm 95 begins, **"Let us sing for joy to the Lord"** (verse 1). In the joyful words of praise that follow, we are invited to join in spontaneously with the sea, the land, and all creatures of the earth to praise God.

If God is worthy of praise, it follows that he must be worth *listening to* as well. **"We are the people of his pasture,"** the psalmist says (verse 7), and yet unlike a flock of sheep who listen to and trust the voice of their shepherd, expecting safety and good, we tend to pick and choose as we hear God's voice, displaying a lack of trust in or respect for our Shepherd.

Listening implies not only hearing someone but acting appropriately on what they have said. We feel gratified when someone listens to us—to our advice, or request, or words of warning. Their attention shows respect. Psalm 95 pleads that we would listen to the Shepherd in the same way that we want to be heard: **"Today, if only you would hear his voice, 'Do not harden your hearts'"** (verses 7,8).

Jesus himself echoed the fervent cry of the psalmist, reenforcing how people who claim to love and follow God conduct their lives: **"My sheep hear my voice; I know them, and they follow me"** (John 10:27).

Does your praise of God extend to following him, *listening to* him? Do you follow Jesus as a sheep listens to a shepherd?

When stuff owns you
Daron Lindemann

I remember the garage sale of garage sales. The big day came. After people came and went, most of my stuff was still sitting in my garage.

My wife gently pointed out that I had priced things too high. A garage sale where things don't sell is a sign that you don't own your stuff. Your stuff owns you. This is hard. Jesus says so.

"How hard it is for the rich to enter the kingdom of God! It is easier for a camel to go through the eye of a needle than for someone who is rich to enter the kingdom of God. . . . With man this is impossible, but not with God; all things are possible with God" (Mark 10:23,25,27).

We're just too big with all our stuff. We can't fit through the door of God's kingdom. It's like a camel fitting through the eye of a needle. So Jesus comes through the door to us. Keep in mind how big Jesus is!

He's bigger than the mountains. He created them. He's bigger than the most powerful empires of the world, which crumble under the power and glory of his kingdom. He's bigger than time, bigger than your problems, and bigger than sin and death.

How could he fit through the eye of a needle? Jesus became small by giving up his bigness and beauty and by dying on a cross. Then he rose from the dead.

What you cannot ever do by yourself, what is impossible, Jesus did for you.

My mom's moment
Mike Novotny

As I was studying the book of Job recently, a thought moved me to tears. It was about the moment my mom stuck with Jesus.

Soon after I was born, my mom got pregnant with a third son, a little guy my parents would name James (a.k.a. Jimmy). But I don't remember him, because Jimmy didn't make it. Born sick, my little brother survived six weeks before he left this earth and joined Jesus in heaven.

While I knew the basics of my brother's death, I had never considered the temptation my mom must have faced to walk away from Jesus. She was a churchgoing woman, the one who took (and occasionally dragged ☺) me to worship every Sunday. The reason I grew up with the gospel was because of my mom. The reason I came to love my Bible was because of my mom. The reason I read Mark 8 and decided to become a pastor was because of my mom. And the reason I sat in my office that day preparing to help people deal with their pain was, in essence, because of my mom.

She could have walked away. She could have gotten angry and turned her back on God, assuming he had first turned his back on her. But she didn't. She stayed. Even though her faith was severely tested, she stayed.

Job said, **"The Lord gave and the Lord has taken away; may the name of the Lord be praised"** (Job 1:21). I'm so glad my mom agreed with Job.

Avoid extremism
Linda Buxa

It's easy to be extreme these days, isn't it? We see people (ourselves included sometimes) believing in something so strongly that we think the "other side" is full of idiots. (Did you just picture social media or politics or sports teams? Me too.)

The book of Ecclesiastes has some advice about religious extremes too: **"Do not be overrighteous, neither be overwise—why destroy yourself? Do not be overwicked, and do not be a fool—why die before your time? It is good to grasp the one and not let go of the other. Whoever fears God will avoid all extremes"** (7:16-18).

When it comes to faith, we want to be *all-in*, yet it's pretty clear that God is cautioning us about getting over righteous or legalistic. That's when religion is more about rules than a relationship with Jesus. We also don't want to be fools and act as if God's grace gives us blanket permission to sin.

Instead, with the Holy Spirit's coaching, discernment, and wisdom, you and I make informed decisions about what our lives look like as believers. You and I can be loud, opinionated, and still have fun with friends. We are allowed to read more books than just the Bible. We can listen to more than just Christian music, and we don't have to stop watching every single movie out there.

Whoever fears God will avoid all extremes.

P.S. To be fair, there is some extremism in faith. Only one way to get to heaven? Yes. But that's another devotion for another time.

Jesus didn't camp
Mike Novotny

Have you ever thought of how tempting it must have been for Jesus to go camping? At the mountain where Jesus revealed his glory, Luke tells us, **"Peter and his companions . . . saw [Jesus'] glory and the two men** [Moses and Elijah] **standing with him. As the men were leaving Jesus, Peter said to him, 'Master, it is good for us to be here. Let us put up three shelters— one for you, one for Moses and one for Elijah.' (He did not know what he was saying.)"** (Luke 9:32,33).

Even though Peter didn't know what he was saying, it made sense. "Jesus, it is good for us to be here. Down in the valley are the critics who nitpick your every word and the crowds who refuse to let you rest. But up here on the mountain are Moses and Elijah and your stunning glory. Let's stay here. James, John, and I can set up the tents."

But as tempting as those tents must have been, Jesus didn't take Peter's suggestion. Instead, he chose you. He left behind Moses and Elijah so that you could one day be with Moses and Elijah. He walked away from the fresh mountain air so he could gasp for breath on a cross. In other words, he chose you.

If you ever wonder if God notices you or loves you, just think of that moment when Jesus waved goodbye to Moses and Elijah so that you could receive mercy. That kind of love is the most glorious thing about Jesus.

Enemies
Katrina Harrmann

I was trying to play a video game with my son (and not doing a very good job) when I started to get overwhelmed by enemy fire.

"Ack! I think I went the wrong way! I'm getting attacked!" I groaned.

"No! That's good!" my son explained. "If you're running into a lot of enemies, that means you're going the right way."

I almost dropped my controller in astonishment. What a life lesson! What a peach of a teachable moment!

I can't begin to count the number of times in my life when bad things have happened, one after another, and I thought to myself, "Wow, I must be doing something wrong!"

I never even thought to think, "Wow, I must be doing something *RIGHT*!"

Because when we're doing right—when we're walking with God the way we should or doing good things in his name—we're wearing big targets on our backs, and Satan has us in his crosshairs.

In answer, God offers countless reassuring verses in Scripture that we can turn to when we feel overwhelmed by the enemies of this world.

"The Lord will grant that the enemies who rise up against you will be defeated before you. They will come at you from one direction but flee from you in seven" (Deuteronomy 28:7).

Enemy fire means we're on the right path. But God's right there with us!

Light drives away the shadows
Nathan Nass

I recently read a children's book to my kids about a bear who wanted to get rid of his shadow. He didn't like having this dark, shady thing following him around everywhere. So he tried chasing his shadow away. It didn't work. He tried digging a hole and burying it. Somehow, the shadow slipped out. He tried nailing it to the ground and drowning it in a pool. But there was no way to get rid of his shadow.

That reminds me of something: our sin. Each one of us has shadows we carry around. Darkness. Sin. We try to hide it. We try to ignore it. We try to chase it away. But it clings to us. The guilt. The shame.

Bear finally found one thing that made his shadow go away. Know what it was? If he stood outside at noon on a sunny day, the powerful light of the sun finally drove his shadow away.

Just like there's one thing that can drive your sins away. Like bear found, it's light. The Light. Jesus promised: **"I am the light of the world. Whoever follows me will never walk in darkness, but will have the light of life"** (John 8:12). Jesus' forgiveness wipes away every sin. Jesus' promises give hope and peace. Like the noonday sun, Jesus' presence drives away our fears.

Do you want to get rid of your shadows? Then come to Jesus. His light drives away the shadows.

Faith at a funeral
Mike Novotny

Our church held a Christian funeral service for a faithful member named Dave. His kids, grandkids, friends, and extended family gathered together to remember him and, even more, to remember what Jesus had done for him. We came not so much to celebrate Dave's life but to celebrate the One who is life, the Jesus who came back to life so we could have life after death.

But there was one moment I will never forget, something that had never happened to me in all my years of attending and leading funerals. We were singing "In Christ Alone," a song about finding hope and strength and light in Christ Jesus, but when we got to the stanza about Jesus' resurrection, one of Dave's kids stood up to worship. You should know that most people at our church are pretty reluctant when it comes to spontaneous expressions of worship, so we all noticed this woman as soon as she stood. But there was something about that moment and, even more, about the lyrics we were singing that made it perfect. Maybe that's why people started to join her. He stood. Then they stood. Then I stood. And we sang about the power of the empty tomb, about not fearing death, about putting our hope in Christ alone.

Death and grief are rarely easy. But there is something irreplaceable about having faith at a funeral. **"Jesus said to [Martha], 'I am the resurrection and the life. The one who believes in me will live, even though they die'"** (John 11:25).

Do not fear
Katrina Harrmann

Everyone is afraid of something, right? I'm afraid of sharks, financial planning, and clowns (not necessarily in that order). I'm also afraid of death and debilitating sickness. (Who isn't?)

What are you afraid of?

I bet you were afraid of different things when you were small! (Okay, sharks and clowns were still on my list when I was 10.)

I live in a 108-year-old home in Michigan. Like all old homes, it has its quirks . . . most notably, a "Michigan basement" that is old and creepy enough to scare even the most stalwart of intrepid youngsters.

Several years ago when my son was five years old, he came up to me and said, "Mom, can you turn on the light in the monster room?"

"Sure! Wait . . . what room is *that*?"

It was the basement, of course. His mind had built up an irrational web of fear—all centered on the darkest, most mysterious room of our old home and what he thought might be lurking there.

Many times our fears are totally irrational. Sometimes they seem a little more rational (our adult fears never seem like something to laugh at, do they?), but God still has the same message for all of us.

Do not fear. In fact, the phrase "do not be afraid," or some form of it, is written 365 times in the Bible. One for every day of the year.

"The Spirit God gave us does not make us timid, but gives us power, love and self-discipline" (2 Timothy 1:7).

News fatigue?

Daron Lindemann

Who's feeling a bit burned out on bad news? God wants you to hear his good news. There's a bunch of it in Isaiah chapter 40.

"Comfort, comfort my people, says your God" (verse 1). God communicates with you for your comfort, not to exploit you and enrage you.

"And the glory of the LORD will be revealed, and all people will see it together. For the mouth of the LORD has spoken" (verse 5). God's glory is blazing and brilliant. Nobody can look at him and live. But he has packaged his glory for us in things we can see, touch, and enjoy—his Son, Jesus; the water of Baptism; the bread and wine of the Lord's Supper, the pages of a Bible. Look for him there. Who is able to see it? "All people." And that's you.

"The grass withers and the flowers fall, but the word of our God endures forever" (verse 8). The daily news can't decide whose truth is true. God's good news has no limits, cannot be cancelled, and is always good.

"Do you not know? Have you not heard? The LORD is the everlasting God, the Creator of the ends of the earth. He will not grow tired or weary, and his understanding no one can fathom. He gives strength to the weary and increases the power of the weak" (verses 28,29). God isn't fatigued as he watches our world. He isn't frustrated. We haven't exhausted his kindness. He wants to help and save.

Ready?
Nathan Nass

Are you ready? My boys and I weren't. We were sitting on our beds at a hotel, watching sports highlights, when suddenly the fire alarm went off. Has that ever happened to you at a hotel? I'm ashamed to admit it, but we panicked. The boys yelled. I didn't know what to do. "Do I grab my keys? My clothes? Do we go outside? Do we just wait for the alarm to stop?" We weren't ready!

Thankfully, the cause of all that chaos was burnt toast in the breakfast room. But that experience stuck with me. We weren't ready, and it was terrifying, at least for a second.

Are you ready? Not just for a fire alarm. How about for the biggest event in the future of the world: Jesus' return? He's coming back. He's going to judge the world. There are only two final destinations: heaven or hell. That's a big deal, isn't it? That's why Jesus says, **"You also must be ready, because the Son of Man will come at an hour when you do not expect him"** (Matthew 24:44). Are you ready?

Thankfully, Jesus tells us exactly how to be ready for his return: repent and believe in him! The way to heaven is faith in Jesus our Savior. So don't put Jesus off. Today is the day to hear God's Word. Today is the day to confess your sins. Today is the day to believe in Jesus. Today is the day to be ready.

Bucket list
Mike Novotny

The other day I stumbled across a 2008 version of my bucket list, a document of 71 things I wanted to accomplish before I died. Most of the list, however, was laughable. "Learn how to moonwalk" or "See Billy Joel in concert." What?! Out of all the joys that life can offer, I chose dancing like Michael Jackson and singing with Billy Joel?

As humans, we are crummy at anticipating what will make us happy. We think the house and the money and the trips and the devices will create a satisfying life, but time often reveals these moments to be, well, momentary. They do make us happy for a bit, but they are not enough to fill up the bucket of our hearts.

But God can. **"You, God, are my God, earnestly I seek you; I thirst for you, my whole being longs for you, in a dry and parched land where there is no water. I have seen you in the sanctuary and beheld your power and your glory. Because your love is better than life, my lips will glorify you. I will praise you as long as I live, and in your name I will lift up my hands. I will be fully satisfied as with the richest of foods; with singing lips my mouth will praise you"** (Psalm 63:1-5).

Think long and hard today about the unfailing love of God. The Holy Spirit will remind you that your Savior's love is better than anything on your bucket list, because his blessings endure forever.

Let's bring back Easter

Mike Novotny

I feel bad for Easter. They say that Christmas and Easter are the two biggest days for Christianity, but compared to Christmas, Easter is pretty missable. When's the last time you had an office Easter party? or fought for a parking spot at the mall on Easter weekend? or argued about whether you could play Easter music after St. Patrick's Day? Every pop artist from Elvis to the Pentatonix puts out a Christmas album, but zero stars are dropping hits about the empty tomb. Easter is pretty missable.

But not in the Bible. Recently, I copied and pasted all the passages about Jesus' birth, and my computer's word counter told me that they added up to 633 words. When I did the same with the Easter story, I got 986 words . . . in just the book of Luke! Add Matthew, Mark, John, and Paul's resurrection chapter to the Corinthians, and you end up with 3,575 words! The Bible seems to be begging us: "Don't miss Easter!"

At Easter, death was knocked out. At Easter, your sins were verified as fully forgiven. At Easter, Jesus proved to the world who he truly is—God in human flesh. No wonder when Jesus appeared to John in the final book of the Bible, he said, **"I am the Living One; I was dead, and now look, I am alive for ever and ever!"** (Revelation 1:18).

Don't miss Easter. The empty tomb is history's best news ever.

APRIL

If you declare with your mouth, "Jesus is Lord,"
and believe in your heart that God raised him
from the dead, you will be saved.

Romans 10:9

How do you know God loves you?
Mike Novotny

When you are in unspeakable pain, it is natural to question the love of God. If God has the power to end your pain, then why doesn't he do something? Your mom dies young or you battle depression for years or your marriage ends despite your desire to keep fighting or you can't conceive after all those prayers or you live with the scars of abuse from your childhood. Given what you've been through, how can you *really* be sure that God loves you?

Here's my simplest answer—because pain proves it. You know that someone loves you when they are willing to suffer for you. Selfish people run from suffering, while those who genuinely care stick around because of love.

Now think of God. If he stayed in heaven, distant from pain, you would always have to wonder about his love. But if he himself was willing to suffer for you, that would say something. In fact, that would say everything.

This is why Jesus' pain proves it. Despite being God in human flesh, filled with almighty power to avoid suffering altogether, Jesus endured pain. The flogging, the thorns, the nails, the cross, the tomb. His pain said something profound about what our God is actually like. He is love. He must be.

"This is love: not that we loved God, but that he loved us and sent his Son as an atoning sacrifice for our sins" (1 John 4:10). Don't let the devil use your pain to deceive you. God is love. Jesus' pain proves it.

Jesus is the King we need
Mike Novotny

Jesus must have seemed like the perfect king for the average first-century Jew. Frustrated by suffocating taxes and the Roman occupation, most Jews begged God for a king who could conquer the Romans. That's what made Jesus so exciting when he rode into Jerusalem on Palm Sunday.

Jesus could read people's thoughts, meaning he could anticipate every strategy of every Roman general. Jesus could defeat a legion of demons with a word, meaning he could take on legions of Romans by himself. Kill a Jew, and Jesus could bring him back to life. Surround and starve Jerusalem, and Jesus could multiply a few loaves and fishes. Jesus was the king they had always wanted.

Much to their surprise, Jesus insisted on being the King they needed. They needed someone to forgive their sins, not fight the Romans, so Jesus didn't march into the Fortress Antonia and threaten the soldiers. Instead, he flipped tables in the temple, preached fearlessly about religious hypocrisy, and dealt with sin as he hung on a cross.

While Jesus could have cured our cancer, erased our anxiety, and solved our earthly problems, he instead chose to do something better. He gave us what we needed most, a way for sinners to be saved. **"One thing I ask from the LORD, this only do I seek: that I may dwell in the house of the LORD all the days of my life"** (Psalm 27:4). Ask God for that "one thing" you most need, and he will always answer as promised. In Jesus, you get what you need.

Rejoice in the Lord!
Andrea Delwiche

The world has seen something of royal pomp and circumstance in recent years. In the passing of Queen Elizabeth, many of us got a taste of the wealth and dazzling splendor of an earthly kingdom; immense crowds waited for hours to pay honor to the woman they admired.

Psalm 97 gives an account of heaven and earth honoring and worshiping God as sovereign: **"The Lord reigns, let the earth be glad; let the distant shores rejoice. Clouds and thick darkness surround him; righteousness and justice are the foundation of his throne"** (verses 1,2).

Can you see yourself in that rejoicing crowd?

How can we get in a celebratory spirit? Sometimes observing the dark sky with the distant moon and stars is enough to help us rejoice in our Creator. Sometimes we rejoice in the physical and spiritual gifts we receive.

We live under a wise and gracious Monarch, part of the royal family. Gifts of salvation and new life in Christ are renewed for us each day.

As you think about praising God, the Spirit wants to help navigate the hard questions. How have you been preserved by your Father-King? Can you see that light has been sown by him for you? Do you know the reality of God's joy? What does it look like right now in your heart, home, place of worship to celebrate his rule?

"Rejoice in the Lord, you who are righteous, and praise his holy name!" (Psalm 97:12).

Praise the Lord!
Linda Buxa

I really like the way Psalm 106 starts: **"Praise the Lord. Give thanks to the Lord, for he is good; his love endures forever. Who can proclaim the mighty acts of the Lord or fully declare his praise?"** (verses 1,2).

I'm not such a fan of the middle of the psalm though. (If you haven't, pull it up on your phone or read it in your Bible.) If you don't have a Bible handy, I'll summarize. It's basically an entire recounting of how awful God's people were. And it's not simply a quick, "Oh, we messed up." It's over 550 words of how egregiously despicable and rebellious they were.

My initial reaction is simply being grateful that your and my sins, failures, rebellion, and stubbornness are not written down in a song form for everyone thousands of years later to read and shake their heads about! But it does make me realize that being honest about (but not celebrating) our sins is a good thing. It's not to bring up guilt and make us feel shameful. Instead, it's to show how God is faithful even when we are not and that it is his grace—not our behavior—that saves us. We need that reminder every single day. Then we give him all the glory and all our praise, which is how this psalm ends: **"Praise be to the Lord, the God of Israel** [and us!], **from everlasting to everlasting. Let all the people say, 'Amen!' Praise the Lord"** (verse 48).

Say it with me: "Amen! Praise the Lord!"

When your outsides and insides don't match
Liz Schroeder

We saw Harry Styles at Chipotle. Well, it could have been Harry Styles. He looked an awful lot like him, and confidence oozed out of his perfect pores, just as it does out of the famous British singer/songwriter.

However, in the parking lot, my daughters and I witnessed this doppelganger blowing his nose *without a tissue* onto the blacktop. *Eww!*

As it turns out, "looks a lot like" and "is" are not the same thing.

Jesus had harsh words for people whose outsides did not match their insides. He called them hypocrites, blind guides, and snakes. His words were especially harsh because these people were in position to lead others astray.

"Woe to you, teachers of the law and Pharisees, you hypocrites! You clean the outside of the cup and dish, but inside they are full of greed and self-indulgence" (Matthew 23:25).

As parents, teachers, managers, coaches, and older siblings, we are also in positions that could potentially lead others astray. Our outsides haven't always matched our insides. We've served, but begrudgingly. We've parented, but out of pride. We've worked diligently, but it was so we could gratify our lust for pleasure and status.

Like Paul, we lament, **"What a wretched man I am! Who will rescue me from this body that is subject to death?"** (Romans 7:24). And like Paul, we rejoice, **"Thanks be to God, who delivers me through Jesus Christ our Lord!"** (Romans 7:25). Through Christ, our outsides *and* insides are clean.

Ten ways to help people through pain
Mike Novotny

What do you do when a loved one is in pain? When a friend is grieving a miscarriage, a buddy just got dumped, or you make it to the front of the line at a funeral, what do you say? What do you do?

I bet it is some combination of these ten things: (1) Just be there. Sometimes your presence is enough. (2) Say sorry. Express your sympathies for their loss. (3) Share a story. Have you been through something similar? (4) Offer help. Bring over a dinner to stick in their freezer. (5) Offer hope. Share how you, over time, got through it. (6) Offer a silver lining. Point out how many people are here to show their support. (7) Preach God's plans. Romans 8:28 is a classic. (8) Preach God's presence. Psalm 73:26 is my favorite. (9) Preach God's sympathy. Hebrews 4:15 is a go-to. (10) Preach God's salvation. Revelation 21:4 is golden.

I won't lie to you. Pain is messy. Any of these ideas can backfire with someone who is suffering (especially #6 and #7). But we all need community in the midst of personal tragedy. Show up, pray for wisdom, and do something. You just might be the glimpse of Jesus that your loved one needs.

"Therefore, as God's chosen people, holy and dearly loved, clothe yourselves with compassion, kindness, humility, gentleness and patience" (Colossians 3:12).

Smart as a worm
Nathan Nass

Are you as smart as a worm? At my church in Oklahoma, I've learned what to expect after a heavy rain. When I walk into the church entryway, it will be filled with earthworms. Big, foot-long Oklahoma night crawlers. I can't explain it. I have no idea how they get inside. But after every rain, there they are. Somehow, they know where to go to find refuge. They get into church, even when the door is locked.

Are you as smart as a worm? When life's storms hit, what do you do? I know what I do. I put my head down and pretend it's not happening. Or I dig harder and harder to save myself. Or I just simply give up and despair. Do you do the same? How foolish.

Learn from the worms. When storms hit, where can you find refuge? In church. More than that, in whom we hear about at church: Jesus Christ our Savior. **"God is our refuge and strength, an ever-present help in trouble. Therefore we will not fear, though the earth give way and the mountains fall into the heart of the sea"** (Psalm 46:1,2). You have a refuge in the storms of life—Jesus!

Jesus endured the storm of God's punishment on a cross for our sins so that we can have forgiveness and peace. No matter what storms you are facing today, there is strength and help in Jesus. When storms come, find your way to Jesus!

Empty!

Clark Schultz

An empty stomach gurgling during a silent prayer at church is embarrassing. Empty milk containers left in the refrigerator are quite annoying. My wife's game of how many miles she can drive with the "empty" light on her vehicle is quite nerve-racking for her passengers. And the cream of the crop is when you dream of going to the cupboard and having a delicious Oreo only to find the package still on the shelf, emptied of all its contents.

There's also the empty feeling you get when looking at photos of your spouse who is no longer standing by your side or the emptiness of a home that was once filled with children.

Empty stinks.

But there is one empty that means so much more: **"'Don't be alarmed,' he said. 'You are looking for Jesus the Nazarene, who was crucified. He has risen! He is not here. See the place where they laid him'"** (Mark 16:6).

What is alarming you? What emptiness creeps into your thoughts when you rise in the morning or keeps you awake at night?

The empty tomb means Jesus wins, and so do we. Because Jesus emptied himself and became fully human, he is our substitute. Sin can no longer empty us of happiness because our Savior sees us as clean. Death is now a sleep, and the empty pain we feel is replaced with hope because we will see our loved ones again. This is the one empty that means and gives us everything!

God's gifts
Linda Buxa

When God tells me he's the Giver of every good gift, it's easy for me to think of tangible blessings—family, friends, house, job, and my awesome chicken shoes. Sadly, I often forget the intangible blessings that he pours out too. So today, join me in focusing on God's gifts that don't include footwear. **"Now may the God who gives endurance and encouragement grant you to live in harmony with one another, according to Christ Jesus"** (Romans 15:5 CSB)

Gift 1—Endurance: Satan messes with your mind to get you confused and worn out. This is when the Holy Spirit steps in to remind you that Jesus endured 33 years of temptation . . . perfectly, to be our stand-in and offer himself for the sins of the world. Because you get credit for Jesus' life, God doesn't say, "Work harder." He says, "Use my strength. I've endured it all, and I will help you endure."

Gift 2—Encouragement: Satan works hard to make you feel worthless and alone, especially because of what you did. Meanwhile, God says, "I will never leave you or forsake you." He loves you because he chooses to love you, not based on your performance. Every day you wake up encouraged because his love gives you unlimited value.

Gift 3—Harmony: Satan tries to keep us fighting. However, people filled with encouragement and endurance don't need to fight. With the Holy Spirit working in us, we live at peace, connected to a whole network of people who love each other.

Come as you are—live as he is
Jan Gompper

Many church websites today display the motto: *Come as you are!* This is an encouragement for people to understand that Jesus (and their church) welcome and love them, no matter what their past lives have been or their present lives are.

Jesus, of course, demonstrated his love for sinners and societal outcasts throughout his earthly ministry. He stayed at the house of Zacchaeus, a tax collector who was looked upon as pond scum by Jewish synagogue leaders. He stopped to drink from a well near an adulterous Samaritan woman. He healed a woman (Mary Magdalene) of demon possession. He chose a ragtag bunch of fishermen and another tax collector to be his first disciples.

Jesus' example should cause *every* church to boldly proclaim: *Come as you are whatever sinful baggage you carry with you!* But churches are remiss if they don't remind us that Jesus also said, **"Now you are well; so stop sinning"** (John 5:14 NLT).

Come as you are doesn't mean that Jesus loves us just the way we are. It means that he loves us *despite* the way we are. He loved the *woman* at the well (*not* her adultery) so much so that he offered her **"living water"** (John 4:10). And once she (and others who encountered Jesus) experienced his message of grace and forgiveness, they left desiring to change the way they would live going forward.

We can always come as we are to Jesus, but once we fully encounter him, we will want to live as he is!

Together is better
Katrina Harrmann

My family likes to hike—serious hikes with 50 pounds of gear on our backs and covering several miles before stopping for the day, setting up camp, and cooking our dinner over an open fire.

What I've noticed is that the first day on the trail is often quite rough. It is easy to romanticize a long walk in the woods, but when your feet and back are aching from a heavy pack and your water bottle is getting low around mile eight, you start to wonder why in the world you are out in the woods on a hot spring day.

That's when it helps to have people around you doing it too. You help each other, lift each other up, offer words of encouragement, sing songs to distract from the bugs and the aches and pains, and help each other with your packs when you take breaks.

Suddenly, all complaining ceases. Each of my family members is in line, marching together, and we are much tougher than we would be by ourselves.

It's much easier to do a tough job when we are surrounded by people doing what we're doing and encouraging us along the way, isn't it?

"God has put the body together, giving greater honor to the parts that lacked it, so that there should be no division in the body, but that its parts should have equal concern for each other. If one part suffers, every part suffers with it; if one part is honored, every part rejoices with it" (1 Corinthians 12:24-26).

Grace for real sinners
Nathan Nass

"At least I ain't killed nobody." We sure like to set the bar high for ourselves, don't we? Not. How often isn't this our proud accomplishment: "I'm a pretty good person. At least I ain't killed nobody!"

Are you sure? Even if the bar for being a good person was so low that all you had to do was not kill anybody, would you be considered good? Consider what God says: **"Anyone who hates a brother or sister is a murderer, and you know that no murderer has eternal life residing in him"** (1 John 3:15). Have you hated someone else? Have you ever been angry? I have.

The Bible points out something we'd rather ignore: To God, our thoughts matter. To God, our words matter. Sinning—even killing—isn't just something we do with our hands. That's why I can't say, "At least I ain't killed nobody." I have. Again and again. With angry thoughts and bitter words.

That's why I need Jesus. That's why you need Jesus. Just as much as any murderer does. Just as much as any "big" sinner does. Because the more you read the Bible, the more you'll realize just how sinful you are. But the more you read the Bible, the more you'll realize just how gracious Jesus is. He died for you and me!

"Jesus still loves me, just as I really am?" Yes, he does! When you realize you're a real sinner, rejoice in God's grace for real sinners.

The most important day of your life
Matt Ewart

Of all the days you've been on the earth, which one would you point to as the most important of them all? Your birthday? Your baptism? Your graduation day? The day you met the person who changed everything?

I am sure there are several days competing for the title of "most important," but what if you lived as if the most important day of your life is *today*? In many ways, it is.

Jesus cautioned people about missing the significance of today. No amount of anxiety about the future will extend your life. No amount of dreaming or ruminating about the past will change where you are right now.

The past is gone. God hasn't given you tomorrow yet. All you have is a series of "right nows" that accumulate to shape the trajectory of your life.

Today is a beautiful gift from your gracious Father in heaven. He wants his Word to soak deeply within your soul to transform you from within. Today his Spirit wants his fruits of faith to grow in you in visible ways. Today Jesus wants to apply his unconditional love to your sin in a way that leaves you in awe of his grace.

Live every today as if it is the most important day of your life. In many ways, it is.

"But encourage one another daily, as long as it is called 'Today,' so that none of you may be hardened by sin's deceitfulness" (Hebrews 3:13).

Love what God loves
Katrina Harrmann

We've all probably heard the age-old phrase, "You are what you eat." But have you ever heard the one that goes, "You are what you love"?

Oof! That's a tough one!

"Wait a minute," we might argue. "That's not fair!"

After all, there are so many things in life that we enjoy and—quite possibly—*love* that perhaps aren't what we really want to use as definitions of who we *are*.

But if you really take the time to sit down and think about the top two or three things you love *most* in this world, it has to be said that often those things generally define us—don't you think?

Which means that we have to be careful what we love—right?

We need to put a priority on our relationship with Jesus and our faith in his saving grace. After that, we need to put a priority on *others*, loving them *more* than we love ourselves. Loving others as Jesus loves, as much as we can.

If you've ever been confused about this, it helps to think about it through God's eyes.

The Bible advises in Ephesians 5:1: **"Follow God's example, therefore, as dearly loved children."**

The strategy is simple. Love what God loves.

A discipline of praise
Andrea Delwiche

Sing to the LORD a new song, for he has done marvelous things. . . . Shout for joy to the LORD, all the earth, burst into jubilant song with music" (Psalm 98:1,4).

As I look at the words of this psalm, it is tempting to say, "This is more of the same." Like in many psalms, the psalmist here calls upon each of us to sing and praise the Lord for his goodness.

Why does this sometimes seem tedious or even distasteful?

In moments when I'm turned away from God, I forget that I am a created being and praise seems like unnecessary repetition. Yes, I am precious to God and significant to him, but's that because he has *made* me significant. It can be hard to remember that praise *begins* with acknowledging God's role in my existence.

But there might be times when I don't give thanks for my existence. Perhaps then I can use David's prayer from Psalm 17:8: **"Keep me as the *apple* of your eye; hide me in the shadow of your wings."** It will help me rest in God's love, giving me space to rest and breathe in safety.

This is why a *discipline of praise* is so useful. As I repeat something each day, regardless of my current perspective, I become conscious of God's presence. By the work of the Spirit, my soul is brought into communion with God.

The psalms' repetition of praise is good medicine. Through it God slows me down, reframes my life, and nurtures me through humble praise.

Be careful, not forgetful
Mike Novotny

"Pastor Mike," the young woman said, "do you remember me?" I stared at her sort-of-familiar face, and my brain immediately cried, "Mayday! Mayday! This is about to get awkward!" As much as I wish I could remember everyone's name, face, story, and situation, I can't. I forget. And my forgetfulness seems to be increasing with every birthday.

Are you like me? Do you have a Snapchat brain that can forget a person's name just moments after meeting them? Did you ever forget your homework/lunchbox/jersey at home when you went to school? or your username/password on one of your many online accounts? Ever forget someone's birthday? or your own anniversary? I bet you would agree that remembering is really hard.

Even with God. Moses once told Israel, **"Be careful that you do not forget the Lord"** (Deuteronomy 6:12). Moses wasn't worried that people would forget the Ninth Commandment or the minute details of the sacrificial system. He was concerned that they would forget the Lord himself!

This is why your spiritual habits matter so much. Even if your weekly church service or daily Grace Moments devotion speaks of things you already know, those habits are God's ways of helping you remember. The repeated message that "Jesus lived. Jesus died. Jesus rose" will keep Jesus' glorious work in your long-term memory so your soul has a constant reason to rejoice and have peace.

Remembering can be hard work. But Jesus is worth remembering.

The dirty pot
Katrina Harrmann

My daughter is a big fan of homemade mac and cheese. Well, she's a fan of *any* kind of pasta, but mac and cheese is her absolute favorite.

Ever since she was young, she's known how to boil the noodles and mix up the ingredients just like her father taught her (using hot pasta water—NOT milk—and mixing it together over the warm stove so the cheese doesn't become stringy).

But then, she tends to throw the pot to the side of the sink and let it sit . . . and sit—without bothering to wash it—figuring that eventually Mom will get it. The problem with that is that the longer it sits, the more it becomes like cement and is just about impossible to clean. The longer it sits—the more the washing gets delayed—the grosser it becomes.

Kind of like sin, right?

How often do we set our messes to the side, too impatient to deal with the fallout because we want to enjoy life. Then when we finally get around to acknowledging our slipups, they've become a disgusting mess that's almost impossible to clean up.

However, if we would address our sin to begin with . . . if we would just own up to it and take responsibility . . . it might not be *pleasant*, but it would be better for our spiritual health and our relationship with our loving God who always forgives.

"Wash away all my iniquity and cleanse me from my sin" (Psalm 51:2).

Jesus holds on to you
Nathan Nass

"Just hang in there." How often has a well-meaning friend or family member given you that advice? "Just hang in there. Hold yourself together. You'll make it through!"

The truth is, those well-meaning comments are actually terrible advice. When it feels like you're falling off a cliff, when it seems like you are hanging by your fingertips, the last thing you need to hear is, "Just hang in there."

"Really? That's the best you can say? Because I can't! I can't hang in there. I can't hold myself together. Can't you see that I'm falling apart?" To be dangling by a thread, to watch life spin out of control, and to hear, "Just hang in there . . ." How?

Do you know who never says, "Just hang in there"? Jesus. Instead, the Bible says this: **"He is before all things, and in him all things hold together"** (Colossians 1:17). From before the creation of the world, there is someone who holds all of life together: Jesus! Everything from the course of the earth around the sun to the course of your life today is in Jesus' hands. Jesus is holding on to you!

And if you look down at those hands of Jesus that are holding on to you, you'll notice something: nail marks. Because the One who holds on to you loves you so much that he died for you. Whatever you're facing today, don't just hang in there. Trust that Jesus holds on to you!

If you don't get it, admit it!
Mike Novotny

When I tried to read the Bible for the first time in high school, I definitely did not get it. "Wait. Why did God put that tree in the Garden of Eden if he knew Adam and Eve would take the fruit? And why do all these guys have so many wives? And how is God cool with his children rolling up to the Promised Land and killing all the locals?" I didn't get it.

If you've ever tried reading it, maybe you didn't get it either. The Bible is a big book that was written multiple millennia ago that has names that are hard to pronounce and teachings that can be tough to wrap your head around. Even Peter, a first-century Bible writer, admitted that (2 Peter 3:16).

That's why the African man from Acts 8 is my hero. When a Christian put him on the spot and asked him if he understood the Scripture he was reading, the African replied, **"How can I . . . unless someone explains it to me?"** (Acts 8:31). That humility led to a conversation, which led to his heart's transformation.

Can I encourage you to do the same thing? If you don't understand the Bible, ask someone for help. If the Sunday sermon goes over your head, email the pastor on Monday morning. There are people in your life who know the answers to your questions, and they would love to help you grasp the height and width and depth of Jesus' love for you.

If you don't get it, admit it!

Single people and marriage sermons
Mike Novotny

I was preaching a sermon on Christian marriage when I asked the husbands and wives in church to raise their hands. A minority of the people in front of me moved, a reminder that our congregation is filled with plenty of unmarried people (a fact that married pastors often forget!).

But before I bailed on the marriage sermon, I thought about the guy who wrote most of the biblical teaching on marriage—Paul. First Corinthians 7, an epic overview of marriage, was written by Paul. Ephesians 5, with its famous encouragement to love and respect your spouse, was also written by Paul. In fact, most of God's words to wives and husbands came from Paul.

Do you remember Paul's relationship status? Single. I love that fact. Paul's passion for devoted husbands and respectful wives came from his love for his fellow Christians. He didn't only focus on what was relevant to his own stage of life (middle-aged, single, fatherless, man in ministry) but instead took time to help his brothers and sisters in the faith.

If you're not married, I hope you don't tune out sermons or devotions on marriage. The husbands and wives in your life need your help, your prayers, and your encouragement. In the beautiful/challenging calling of marriage, they will lean on your support to put this single man's words into practice: **"Each one of you also must love his wife as he loves himself, and the wife must respect her husband"** (Ephesians 5:33).

Anger management
Liz Schroeder

Do you know someone with a short fuse? a hot head? someone who might benefit from anger management classes? Ironically, what that person would learn at the first class would be that they don't, in fact, have an anger problem. That's because anger is actually a secondary emotion.

It would be like asking a doctor to treat your sudden loss of sight or speech. After performing an assessment, the physician would do very little to address the immediate sight/speech symptoms and EVERYTHING to address the fact that you are having a stroke.

Anger is a symptom. Anger bubbles up when we don't feel that it's safe to show our primary feelings. It would be way too vulnerable to say that we're feeling hurt, disrespected, or neglected, so we slam the cupboard door, go on a tirade, or punch a hole in the drywall.

"What causes fights and quarrels among you? Don't they come from your desires that battle within you? You desire but do not have, so you kill. You covet but you cannot get what you want, so you quarrel and fight. You do not have because you do not ask God" (James 4:1,2).

Rather than masking those scary primary emotions with angry outbursts, you can take your hurt, fear, and unmet needs to God. He will hold you.

The next time you're seeing red, stop and ask, "What am I trying to hide?" Then entrust yourself to the care of the Great Physician. He'll get to the heart of the issue.

Not guilty
Jason Nelson

God never asked us to suspend rational thought processes in order to be Christians. That's because there is a very close connection between logic and truth. Encouraging logical thinking is the influence of Paul, Augustine, and Aquinas on the Western church. The most important teaching in Christianity is a logical conclusion: **"If Christ has not been raised, your faith is futile; you are still in your sins"** (1 Corinthians 15:17). There is evidence for the resurrection. Jesus foretold it. The disciples witnessed it. The church has proclaimed it throughout its long history. We put our hope in it.

When people are irrational, the truth gets compromised. Children will deny sneaking a treat even though chocolate is on their faces. Their denials become hysterical, even to the point of tears. Beware of anyone who asks you to ignore the evidence you can see plainly.

In a court of law, lawyers are held to that burden of proof. The standard they must meet is *reasonable* doubt. Can they present enough evidence to the contrary to create reasonable doubt in the minds of a judge whether the accused is guilty as charged? **"We have an advocate with the Father** [in our defense]**—Jesus Christ, the Righteous One"** (1 John 2:1). And though the preponderance of evidence is against us, Jesus' death and resurrection made it reasonable for our perfect God to declare us not guilty. Because Jesus lives, our victory is won.

God's blessings
Matt Ewart

"God bless."

One day I realized I was using those words frequently without really thinking about them. It was the way I signed off on most emails. It was something I prayed would happen for people who were struggling. It was something I said every time someone sneezed, which is a weird way to acknowledge someone else's involuntary bodily action. I noticed I was using "God bless" without a lot of thought.

What about you? Does "God bless" have meaning, or has it become a pleasant platitude that means little?

Proclaiming God's blessing to people is something he wants us to do. It goes back to the Israelites when they were fresh out of Egypt. God commanded Aaron and his sons to say to the people: **"The Lord bless you and keep you; the Lord make his face shine on you and be gracious to you; the Lord turn his face toward you and give you peace"** (Numbers 6:24-26).

The Hebrew word for *bless* comes from the same Hebrew word for *kneel*. The idea is that even though God is infinitely greater than us, he bends to meet us at our level. He brings his powerful strength down to our level for our benefit.

Jesus fulfilled God's blessing for you and all people. The one called God Among Us brought the power of heaven into a human body so that he could defeat death once and for all.

The next time you give or receive God's blessing, remember that those words are a celebration of what God did for us through Jesus.

Read the signs
Linda Buxa

I live in a rural area, and as each season changes, we all see the signs. One of my farming neighbors says that as soon as you start seeing spiderwebs in the grass and in the trees, the first frost is about six weeks away. When farmers start cutting down the corn, we all say, "Watch out for deer." After all, the deer can't hide out quite as much in such a rich food source, so they move a little more.

God wants us to know about some other important signs too, ones that have implications about when Jesus will be coming back. **"At that time many will turn away from the faith and will betray and hate each other, and many false prophets will appear and deceive many people. Because of the increase of wickedness, the love of most will grow cold, but the one who stands firm to the end will be saved. And this gospel of the kingdom will be preached in the whole world as a testimony to all nations, and then the end will come"** (Matthew 24:10-14).

That's a hard and heavy section, but don't miss the good part: the gospel will be preached! And you and I have been called to be part of that! We have the privilege of sharing our testimony and bringing more people to know that they are loved by the eternal God.

Faith at the point of pain
Katrina Harrmann

You've likely experienced painful moments in your life.

But how do you relate to God when you're in that moment of pain?

A pastor recently brought this home to me by describing the thieves who were crucified on crosses near Jesus. Remember them? There were two.

Both of them, in their pain and suffering, mocked Jesus. But one changed and was meek and acknowledged Christ's godhood, begging only to be remembered by his Savior, Jesus.

These are two very common ways of reacting when we are in intense moments of pain and suffering: wrathful and bitter versus long-suffering and meek.

So how do YOU approach Jesus when you're at the point of pain? It's tough to remain calm and meek, isn't it? To bow your head and accept your circumstances rather than rant and rave for all your worth can be such a battle. When life deals us serious blows that we can't understand, it's very easy to act like the enraged and bitter criminal instead of the accepting, humble criminal.

Let us pray that we have the patience and fortitude to approach Christ in a way that acknowledges him as King of our hearts—and try to remember that our Father wants good for us.

"Come to me, all you who are weary and burdened, and I will give you rest. Take my yoke upon you and learn from me, for I am gentle and humble in heart, and you will find rest for your souls" (Matthew 11:28,29).

Judge Jesus' way (Part 1)
Mike Novotny

Imagine how great life would be if we all practiced what Jesus preached: **"Do not judge"** (Matthew 7:1)? Imagine if our world was a judgment-free zone. Imagine if all the students, teachers, and parents at your school supported and encouraged each other instead of criticizing and complaining about each other. Imagine if everyone in your church and community focused on their own behavior instead of pointing fingers at everyone else's behavior. Imagine what it would sound like to watch the news if everyone was passionate about finding people doing right instead of blaming everyone else for being wrong. Sounds refreshing, doesn't it?

Before you answer, let me give you some examples. Imagine if everyone at school supported and encouraged abusive parents instead of criticizing them. Imagine if everyone at church focused on themselves instead of pointing fingers at the church member stealing money from the offering. Imagine if every American was about finding people doing right instead of accusing people who are lying. Do not judge? *Hmm.* I guess we need to think more about this whole judging thing.

This is why Jesus had a nuanced teaching on judgment. There are times, as previously quoted, when Jesus doesn't want us to judge other people, even if they are doing wrong. But his overall teaching on the matter is best summarized when he said, **"Judge correctly"** (John 7:24). In the days to come, we will learn to do just that. Your world can't function without judgment, so let's learn how to judge Jesus' way.

Judge Jesus' way (Part 2)

Mike Novotny

If you hold a strong opinion about something, make sure God agrees with you. One day the Pharisees said, "Jesus! Your friends don't practice the rituals of our religion." But Jesus snapped back, "You hypocrites! Your **'teachings are merely human rules'** (Matthew 15:9). You judge my friends for not washing their hands the 'right way,' but your criticism isn't based on what God says. It's all about what you say!"

If you want to judge like Jesus, stick with God. Does God have an opinion that can be found in his Word? If so, read it, believe it, and judge according to it. If not, be flexible, gentle, and judgment averse. Start with God.

For example, think about going to church. Some people think we should dress in shorts, tennis shoes, and whatever shirt is on top of the pile because God loves us no matter how we look. Others think we should wear our "Sunday best" because God is a great King. Some Christians judge megachurches for being so big that people don't really know each other. Other Christians judge small churches for being so small that people know *everything* about each other.

But what does God think about that? Flip through your Bible, and you will find nothing. That means, if you want to judge like Jesus, take a deep breath, be humble with your personal preferences, and focus your attention on what God has revealed in his Word. Where else is Jesus calling you to calm down your judgments?

Judge Jesus' way (Part 3)
Mike Novotny

.

One of the hardest but most important parts of judging Jesus' way is to judge yourself before you judge anyone else. Jesus taught, **"First take the plank out of your own eye, and then you will see clearly to remove the speck from your brother's eye"** (Matthew 7:5). First judge your own sin with an open Bible. Then use the same Bible to judge theirs. There is a time and a place to judge another's behavior, but it should never be the first thing on your agenda.

Humility is essential for unity, but it is rare in our day. Think of the most popular podcasts, news anchors, and influencers. Do they follow Jesus' advice? Do they start their episodes with personal confessions and humble apologies? Or do they jump right to judging "those people" for their latest transgression? But as satisfying as it might feel to pounce on others' ugly behavior, guess what those "others" are doing right back? Pouncing on you!

Jesus knows a better way. Come to him with your finger-pointing addiction. He is full of grace and mercy and will point his finger to the cross, where he bled for such sins. Then, gently, he will teach you to judge a different way, a better way, a way that starts with humility and confession.

Judge Jesus' way (Part 4)
Mike Novotny

There is a little-known truth about judging Jesus' way that many Christians miss. **"What business is it of mine to judge those outside the church? Are you not to judge those inside? God will judge those outside. 'Expel the wicked person from among you'"** (1 Corinthians 5:12,13). Judging Jesus' way means focusing on those of us who claim to believe in the God of the Bible instead of on those who don't.

Jesus lived during the reign of the Roman Emperor Tiberias, who worshiped countless Roman gods. In fact, Jesus lived next to the city of Tiberias and walked on the Sea of Tiberias, but his sermons weren't scathing critiques of Tiberias. Even though Jesus knew that the pagans were lost, blind, and without true faith, his judgment was massively tilted toward those who claimed to believe in the God of Israel.

I wonder if our tendency to focus on the sins of the world instead of the sins of the church is connected to fear. It's fairly easy to blast "those people" who aren't in the room. But it's nail-biting to confront the people who are. The church elder who controls his kids with anger. The small group that gossips all too often. The pastor who thinks a bit too much of himself. Confronting the sins among us scares us.

But Jesus will help. He promised his presence when two or three gather in his name to deal with sin (Matthew 18:20). That means he will be present to help you judge correctly.

Judge Jesus' way (Part 5)
Mike Novotny

Grace makes your upcoming judgment great. Judgment day, despite its long delay, is still on its way. But the thought of standing before the all-knowing, perfectly just Jesus doesn't have to make you nervous or anxious. Because God's grace makes your judgment great.

Grace is God's undeserved love, the love he showed for you when he sent Jesus to this earth. Jesus came into this finger-pointing world and did the unthinkable. He chose to be judged. **"We all, like sheep, have gone astray, each of us has turned to our own way; and the** Lord **has laid on him the iniquity of us all. By oppression and judgment he was taken away"** (Isaiah 53:6,8). Jesus being judged in your place is what will make your judgment day great.

On his judgment day (Good Friday), Jesus was called horrific names—liar, blasphemer, sinner. On your judgment day, God will call you beautiful names—son, daughter, saint. On his judgment day, Jesus was accused of sins he didn't commit. On your judgment day, God won't accuse you of the sins you did commit. On his judgment day, Jesus was sentenced to death. On your judgment day, you will be promised life that never ends.

Judging Jesus' way doesn't just mean to focus on ourselves and our churches. It also means to focus on grace, the love that will make your judgment day great.

MAY

For as the soil makes the sprout come up and a
garden causes seeds to grow, so the Sovereign Lord
will make righteousness and praise
spring up before all nations.

Isaiah 61:11

I know hope

Liz Schroeder

Have you ever wanted to be Neo from the movie the *Matrix*—especially during exam season? In the movie, a plug is put into Neo's neck. It runs a program, and moments later Neo states, "I know kung fu." A whole new world opens up to him. How great would it be if we could just plug in, run a program, and understand a semester's worth of calculus!

In Baptism, we receive downloads that are even more amazing than kung fu (or calculus). By the water and the Word, we receive forgiveness of sins, faith, and new life in Christ. Whether you are sprinkled or dunked, you are immersed in the new language of that life: hope.

Hope sounds exotic to the ears of this world. It's like when I hear someone speaking French: I don't understand it, but I don't want them to stop either.

"Let everything you say be good and helpful, so that your words will be an encouragement to those who hear them" (Ephesians 4:29 NLT).

There is so much noise in the world, and precious little could be categorized as good or helpful. Your words of hope will stand out; they will attract attention. When you hear complaints but speak gratitude, hear gossip but speak encouragement, hear frustrations but speak solutions, you will change the world.

After Neo learns kung fu, his mentor, Morpheus, says, "Show me." Through the water and the Word, we are fluent in the language of hope. Our Mentor says, "Show me." Speak hope into a world desperate for it.

Seek justice for the defenseless
Andrea Delwiche

"The King is mighty, he loves justice—you have established equity; in Jacob you have done what is just and right" (Psalm 99:4).

Justice is important to God. In Scripture, God is *especially concerned* that the poor and defenseless are receiving justice because they do not have the resources to reach out and claim it for themselves. If it's important to God, it should be important to us.

Pay attention to these strong words from Deuteronomy: **"Cursed is anyone who withholds justice from the foreigner, the fatherless or the widow"** (24:17). Or these words from Isaiah: **"Learn to do right; seek justice. Defend the oppressed. Take up the cause of the fatherless; plead the case of the widow"** (1:17).

Read through the gospels and notice the words and actions of Jesus. Time after time he speaks and acts on behalf of those who cannot help themselves. He condemns followers of God who do seemingly perfect things without loving others: **"Woe to you Pharisees, because you give God a tenth of your mint, rue and all other kinds of garden herbs, but you neglect justice and the love of God"** (Luke 11:42).

Is seeking justice for people in all circumstances still a characteristic of the Christian church? Is it part of our individual churches? How about in our personal lives?

Lord, give us hearts filled with your love and willing bodies and minds to bring Christ-like justice to all people! Amen.

Can Christians live together before marriage?
Mike Novotny

That title deserves careful thought as we seek a biblical answer: **"Marriage should be honored by all, and the marriage bed kept pure, for God will judge the adulterer and all the sexually immoral"** (Hebrews 13:4).

"Marriage should be honored by all."—Even if your parents were bitterly divorced or you'd rather save for a beautiful wedding or marriage would cost you some social security benefits, God's primary concern is that you honor marriage as God's institution.

"And the married bed kept pure."—God invented sex. He loves you and has put a sign on the bedroom door— Reserved for marriage.

"For God will judge the adulterer and all the sexually immoral."—Sex before marriage is serious to God. If you stay sexually active without any remorse or repentance, God will judge you.

While I cannot find a passage that says, "Thou shalt not live together," these words are my primary spiritual concern for every cohabiting couple. If you live together, you are likely to bring impurity into your bed and the judgment of God upon your head.

I know that means you might have a decision to make. Reach out to a pastor (I know that will feel awkward) and talk through your options. If he knows his Bible, he will respond to your repentance with Jesus, grace, wisdom, and a path forward. Will it be easy? No. Christianity rarely is. Will it be worth it to honor marriage? Your Father promises it. Trust him.

A time for sadness
Linda Buxa

It's hard to know what to say in hard and tragic times, isn't it? What do you say when a child is back in the hospital for the umpteenth time? How do you express the sadness when you discover that your friend's spouse is verbally and emotionally abusive? Words are often inadequate in the face of heartbreaking tragedy.

Even though I'm not really known for being silent, I often refer to the story of Job (pronounced *Jobe*), a man who lived thousands of years ago who lost all his children and all his wealth in the blink of an eye. His friends came and sat with him for seven days without saying a word. Brilliant!

You see, too often we try to explain away grief or to minimize pain that isn't ready to be eased. That's why I like the reminder in Ecclesiastes 3 that there is **"a time to weep and a time to laugh, a time to mourn and a time to dance . . . a time to be silent and a time to speak"** (verses 4,7).

Even though believers in Jesus know that grief here on earth is nothing compared to the eternal glory of heaven, we still weep and mourn. There's a time for that.

Still need something to say? When a friend lost her young husband in a tragic accident, another friend told her, "I'm sorry this is part of your story." What a lovely way to express sadness over the reality of the situation without minimizing the hurt.

Bloom in God's time
Katrina Harrmann

One of my favorite flowers are the big, fluffy peonies that bloom in Michigan in May. They always look like puffy snowballs to me—so beautiful!

I've been getting braver with perennials, so a few years ago, I decided to purchase a peony plant at a local nursery. It was supposed to be a lovely shade of light pink.

Supposed to be.

Since that time (about four years ago), I've had plenty of luck with hydrangeas, several species of lilies and dahlias, hibiscuses, and gladiolas, not to mention astilbes and hyacinths. I've become competent with perennials. But ever since I bought that little peony—though the plant has gotten lush and green—not a single bud or bloom has ever graced its leafy greenery.

It's beyond frustrating that the flower I *most* want to see fails to show up every year.

People can be like that too sometimes. We often have specific ideas about when and how we should "bloom," but sometimes it doesn't work out that way.

We have to bloom in God's time and trust in his plan and timing for our lives, instead of relying on our own expectations.

I refuse to rip out my peony and throw it away. Every year I tend it, hoping that this will be the year! So if there's anything you're working hard on, don't give up. God's timing is always perfect.

"In their hearts humans plan their course, but the Lord establishes their steps" (Proverbs 16:9).

Finding Jesus
Nathan Nass

Even today, Abraham Lincoln is one of the most recognizable people of all time. His height. His hair. His hat. His beard. Even people with little interest in history can recognize Abraham Lincoln.

So here's a surprising stat: when Abraham Lincoln was running for president in 1860, it's estimated that only around 5 percent of voters knew what he looked like. With no internet and few photographs, Lincoln was nowhere near as recognizable as he is today. So how did people know whom to vote for? They had to read his words. They read the reports of his debates. They voted for him based on his word.

Doesn't that sound strange? Today, everything's a spectacle. Everything's got to be entertaining.

That's why it's so easy to miss Jesus. Here's the only way to know your Savior: through his Word. Just like with Abraham Lincoln in 1860, our knowledge of Jesus doesn't come from pictures or videos. It comes from reading Jesus' words in the Bible. Jesus himself said, **"You study the Scriptures diligently because you think that in them you have eternal life. These are the very Scriptures that testify about me"** (John 5:39).

Want to find Jesus? Read his Word. Hear him describe his love for you that led him to a cross. Hear him talk of his plans for you, both here on earth and forever in heaven. Hear his promises that, unlike any politician, he always keeps. If you want to find Jesus, read his Word.

The finish is worth it
Matt Ewart

The first generation of Christians was all but gone by the end of the first century. The apostle John was the only one remaining from the original 12. There weren't many others left who had witnessed Jesus personally.

This was also a time of intense persecution for many Christians. The Roman Empire was executing them. Public opinion of them was negative. It got to the point where many of them probably wondered, *"Is God even here?"*

If he was there, why was he not doing something to make things better?

There can be difficult times in life when it seems everything is working against you. Even if you do the right things, they lead to disaster and grief. There might be times when you wonder if God even knows where you are.

So at the end of the first century, God sent this message to his people through the apostle John—a message that he still wants his church to hear today: **"It is done. I am the Alpha and the Omega, the Beginning and the End"** (Revelation 21:6).

When Jesus offered himself as the sacrifice for your sins, he guaranteed that you and God would never be far apart. Nothing can separate his love from you.

No matter where you end up in life, God always knows where you are because he is already where you are going. He is the Beginning and the End. Keep your hope anchored to Jesus. The finish is worth it.

Shout for joy!
Andrea Delwiche

"Shout for joy to the LORD, all the earth. Worship the LORD with gladness; come before him with joyful songs. Know that the LORD is God. It is he who made us, and we are his; we are his people, the sheep of his pasture. Enter his gates with thanksgiving and his courts with praise; give thanks to him and praise his name. For the LORD is good and his love endures forever; his faithfulness continues through all generations" (Psalm 100:1-5).

What if you took some time today and followed the directives given in each verse of this psalm of praise?

Ask for the Spirit to give you some quiet time so you can focus on praising God. Picture yourself doing some version of all the directions given.

Shout for joy! (Maybe it's a whispered shout; maybe it's a loud shout that surprises those you live with.) Then picture yourself in a crowd of people all of whom belong to God, singing songs of gladness. Think about what it means to be part of God's flock of intentionally created people. Imagine yourself entering the gates of God's kingdom with joy. Take time to construct a prayer of thanksgiving.

You are part of an immense family here on earth and in heaven. It's your privilege to be part of a diverse flock that's lived, worshiped, and been blessed by God.

God is delighted by you. He enjoys the time you spend with him. May God increase your understanding of his loving care.

No cover-ups for evil allowed!
Linda Buxa

In November 2022, Harvey Weinstein was on trial—again—for raping women who originally met with him thinking the powerful Hollywood figure was simply going to help their careers. As the victims shared their testimonies, people were disgusted by Weinstein's abuse of power.

Mind if I'm depressing for a little bit? People have abused their power for as long as the world has had sin in it. About 450 years before Jesus was born, King Xerxes deposed his wife Vashti and searched for a new queen. That's how we meet Esther in the Bible. She was one of a number of young women given a year of training in how to be beautiful. Then each got one night with Xerxes. If he didn't like them, they went into his harem. The one he liked became queen. (Spoiler alert: It was Esther.)

These stories outrage us because we know it is wrong when "those people" use their power for evil, leaving victims in their wake. What about us though? We may not go to the extremes that Weinstein and Xerxes did, but it is easy to treat people poorly, to disregard them, to dismiss them as less valuable for any number of subjective reasons. That outrages God.

Today, let's remember to look at all people who were made in the image of God. Let's **"live as free people, but do not use your freedom** [or position of influence] **as a cover-up for evil; live as God's slaves. Show proper respect to everyone, love the family of believers, fear God, honor the emperor"** (1 Peter 2:16-18).

The most sacred Book ever
Mike Novotny

Few things get me quite as excited about my Bible as Paul's words to Timothy: **"All Scripture is God-breathed"** (2 Timothy 3:16). Break down that simple sentence and tell me that it doesn't take your breath away!

God-breathed—That unique phrase means that the Scriptures come directly out of God's heart. Just like the breath that comes out of your mouth starts deep within you, so also the Book that Christians love comes from deep within God.

Scripture—That word literally means "written things." Think of a script, the *written* document that actors follow, or a scribe, whose job is to *write* things down. Just like actors follow the script that comes from the heart of its writer, so also we believers follow the script that comes from the heart of the Spirit.

All—This might be my favorite word of all. The Bible isn't 10 percent God-breathed, like a kids' juice box that contains 10 percent real fruit. No, all the Scripture, from Genesis 1 to Revelation 22, is breathed out by God. Every chapter and verse comes not from mere men but from the God whose words are always true and always for our good.

Put it all together and you have a thrilling truth—the Bible is God speaking to you. Don't be deceived by that wrinkled cover or those standard issue pages. All Scripture is God-breathed!

If the cloud won't lift
Jason Nelson

As a counselor, I worked with depressed students, parents, and colleagues. It's difficult to live under a cloud. In some cases, talking helped and medication helped. In a few tragic cases, the person ended his or her life.

There is a bias that depressed people are flawed and emotionally weak. Or in the worst misunderstanding, their faith isn't strong enough. The insensitivity of others is a depression builder.

Was Jesus ever depressed? We can trace the course of it in the Bible.

- Jesus was tested in every way that we are. It's safe to assume bouts of depression were included.
- When he was drained from teaching the crowds, he went off by himself to pray in order to recharge.
- When his passion intensified on Holy Week, he announced it was time to go to Jerusalem where he would be handed over to those who would kill him.
- In the Garden of Gethsemane, Jesus prayed that he might be spared the suffering he could see coming.
- From the cross, he said in a loud voice, **"My God, my God, why have you forsaken me?"** (Matthew 27:46). It is the deepest depression to feel forsaken by God. Jesus endured being forsaken by his Father so we wouldn't be forsaken by him.

Have I ever been depressed? Have you ever been depressed? I think so. If the cloud of depression won't lift, seek the help of others.

Moment-by-moment praise
Andrea Delwiche

A 19th-century writer once wrote, "We never praise the Lord better than when we do those things which are pleasing in his sight."

That makes me think of Psalm 101. The psalm writer's intention is to live in commitment to the praiseworthy Lord: **"I will sing of your love and justice; to you, Lord, I will sing praise. I will be careful to lead a blameless life—when will you come to me?"** (verses 1,2).

Notice the ways the psalmist intends to do this: **"I will conduct the affairs of my house with a blameless heart. I will not look with approval on anything that is vile. . . . Whoever slanders their neighbor in secret, I will put to silence"** (verses 2,3,5).

Praising the Lord through our actions is a lot of work! God asks us to spend intentional time with him, avoid evil influences, and love our neighbors as ourselves, just to name a few. We're called to live lives worthy of our calling (Ephesians 4). Consider these words from the book of James: **"Suppose a brother or a sister is without clothes and daily food. If one of you says to them, 'Go in peace; keep warm and well fed,' but does nothing about their physical needs, what good is it? In the same way, faith by itself, if it is not accompanied by action, is dead"** (2:15-17).

Our faith expresses itself in loving actions—a form of praise to God. What commitments, with the Spirit's help, can you make to praise God with your moment-by-moment living?

Three goals for good friends
Mike Novotny

Despite their soon-to-be-seen flaws, I love what Job's friends did for their buddy who had hit bottom. **"When Job's three friends, Eliphaz the Temanite, Bildad the Shuhite and Zophar the Naamathite, heard about all the troubles that had come upon him, they set out from their homes and met together by agreement to go and sympathize with him and comfort him"** (Job 2:11).

Did you catch their three goals? (1) To go. (2) To sympathize with Job. (3) To comfort Job. These guys left their homes, beds, and lives to be with their friend, offer their sympathy, and to say something comforting. While they didn't exactly achieve all three (read Job 3 to 31), I love their intentions.

Some of my classmates did this. A while ago, we heard the shocking news that one of our college and seminary classmates died of COVID at the age of 40. That's when a few of his closest friends sprang into action. They left behind their beds in Wisconsin, packed into a couple of cars, and drove 600 miles to Kansas "to go" and "to sympathize" with his wife and "to comfort" his kids. They just went. That's what friends do.

Is there someone you know who's hurting today? These three goals are a good checklist for a powerful way to show Christian love. You don't have to fix it (nor are you able to), but you can be a glimpse of God's presence, sympathy, and comfort. That's what friends do, just like our friend Jesus did for us.

God's attributes
Andrea Delwiche

"Ascribe to the Lord, all you families of nations, ascribe to the Lord glory and strength. Ascribe to the Lord the glory due his name; bring an offering and come into his courts. Worship the Lord in the splendor of his holiness; tremble before him, all the earth" (Psalm 96:7-9).

My red dictionary gives the definition for *ascribe* as follows: *"1. to credit or assign, as to a cause or source. 2. to attribute or think of as belonging, as a quality or characteristic."* You can also notice the word *scribe* in the word. A *scribe* was someone who made manuscript copies.

So what are the characteristics and qualities of God that we are being asked to attribute to God? There are many laudable characteristics of God mentioned throughout this psalm: strength and glory unlike any other, good judgment, beauty, and splendor. We could each think of additional characteristics.

The psalmist also calls us to rejoice. Knowing who God is, we rejoice to be created and sustained by a God who **"does not change like shifting shadows"** (James 1:17). We are thankful that he will be equitable and faithful as he reigns over us all.

These truths are written in Scripture, in countless devotions, in poetry, and in works of art. We are called to be scribes and write them on our hearts and into each interaction of our lives.

In what personal way can you remember and mark God's goodness? The ways to live your praise are nearly as endless as God's goodness.

Biblical self-care (Part 1)
Mike Novotny

Four out of the five pastors at my church recently admitted (and gave me permission to tell you) that they almost didn't make it. "I was working at least 70+ hours per week (sometimes a lot more). I was tired, stressed, and constantly distracted." "I was overly committed, putting in 60–70+ hours. High blood pressure. Apathy toward work." "My wife and group of close friends had an intervention, which was the reason I'm probably still in ministry, by God's grace."

Can you relate? Maybe you're juggling a dozen responsibilities right now—trying to be a good spouse and a good parent and a good daughter and a good church member and a good friend and a good _____, leaving you so busy you fall asleep as soon as you sit down. Or maybe these feelings are foreign to you. You've never worked a 60-hour week in your life, and you prioritize your mental health to the point of keeping your distance from stressful jobs, tough bosses, and frustrating coworkers. This all falls under the modern idea of "self-care," the tension of caring for your own physical needs without becoming overly selfish and soft.

In the days to come, I want to help you balance the hard work that God wants and the needed rest that God gives, a rhythm that the Father made you for, Jesus saved you for, and the Spirit is working toward. As Jesus said, **"Come to me, all you who are weary and burdened, and I will give you rest"** (Matthew 11:28).

Biblical self-care (Part 2)
Mike Novotny

"If you find a job that doesn't feel like work, you'll never work a day in your life." Do you believe that? Jesus had the most important work ever, but he got tired, so tired he once fell fast asleep in an uncomfortable boat. The apostle Paul admitted his work of sharing Jesus was so hard that he experienced sleepless nights. This means that your work, even if it's good work, is going to feel like work.

Maybe I'm just getting older, but I'm noticing a lot of younger Christians who are quick to quit their work once it gets hard. Some say it is a necessary step for their mental health and that God doesn't want them to be stressed. While I agree there are times when it's good to find new employment, quitting after a hard week is a good way to stay weak. There are seasons in life when it's time to care about a greater good and start thinking about caring for others.

God promised Adam, **"By the sweat of your brow you will eat your food until you return to the ground"** (Genesis 3:19). You're going to sweat. The thorns and thistles and people are going to make work feel like work. But life isn't only about self-care. It's also about the work that cares for others. So ask God for the strength to stick with it, not to quit, to get up again, and to serve others in Jesus' name.

Biblical self-care (Part 3)

Mike Novotny

While God wants us to sweat, he also wants us to rest. Jesus did. **"Then, because so many people were coming and going that they did not even have a chance to eat, he said to them, 'Come with me by yourselves to a quiet place and get some rest'"** (Mark 6:31). That's Jesus Christ preaching and practicing self-care!

Have you experienced the blessing of regular rest? I have. I try to work hard from Sunday through Friday but then be blessed by a full day of rest. It's hard to protect that time, but every time I do, I can literally feel the relief of rest. My body and spirit start to sense it even on Friday—rest is coming. And rest I do! I spend extra time with my wife. I rarely shave, rarely shower before 10:00 A.M., rarely wear pants that aren't stretchy. I love it when my daughters come up with an idea—"Dad, can we?"—and the blank schedule makes me say, "Why not?" That's the kind of rest that I need.

I need to say this to those of you who are compassionate and selfless to a fault—You need rest. Your inner pharaoh will crack the whip and tell you that you're lazy for sitting down, selfish for sleeping in, sinful for not saying yes to another demand. Resist that slave driver. It is never sinful to be like your Savior. Even Jesus took time to rest.

Biblical self-care (Part 4)
Mike Novotny

So much of our work is about getting people to like us, isn't it? We work so hard on school projects because we want the teacher to notice our potential. We show up early or stay late at our jobs because we want to impress our managers. We have Pinterest birthday parties, filter our social media selfies, and volunteer for six things because we want people to think we are good moms, good people, and good church members. Getting people to like us is work!

That's not how it works with Jesus (thank God!). The good news of the Christian faith is that getting God to like you isn't based on how much you worked but rather on the work of Jesus. Instead of setting up a spiritual obstacle course to heaven and making you sweat, Jesus did the work for you.

Remember Jesus the night before he died? It was his season of suffering, and he loved you so much he didn't quit until the work was done. He didn't care about self-care or himself in that moment, because he cared about you. He finished his work of forgiving your sins so your relationship with God wouldn't be about works.

Getting people to like us can be exhausting, but Jesus offers us the grace of eternal rest. **"Come to me, all you who are weary and burdened, and I will give you rest . . . and you will find rest for your souls"** (Matthew 11:28,29).

Repent!
Nathan Nass

God sent someone with the specific job to prepare people's hearts for Jesus. That sounds pretty important, doesn't it? God wanted people to be ready for Jesus. How? Here was John the Baptist's message: **"Repent, for the kingdom of heaven has come near"** (Matthew 3:2).

How often do you hear that message today? "Repent!" I'm guessing not that often. Instead, we hear, "I'm free to do what I want!" Or, "To each his own!" Or, "If it feels good, do it!" That's not what God commanded John the Baptist to tell people. If they wanted to be ready for Jesus, they needed to repent. In other words, they needed to confess their sins, turn away from them, and look for forgiveness in God.

That sounds old-fashioned, doesn't it? Is that still God's plan for us today? Jesus isn't about all that repentance stuff, is he? Here's something surprising: when Jesus began to preach, do you know what he preached? **"Repent, for the kingdom of heaven has come near"** (Matthew 4:17). Sound familiar? It's exactly the same message! Jesus was a preacher of repentance, just like John the Baptist was.

Want a relationship with Jesus? Want Jesus' peace and forgiveness to fill your heart? It starts with this: Repent! Stop making excuses. Confess your sins. Turn away from them. Then look to Jesus and Jesus alone for forgiveness, love, and salvation. Jesus died to take your sins away. So here's how to prepare your heart for Jesus each day: repent!

Put in place for a purpose
Mike Novotny

Have you ever felt like your life lacks purpose? You're at a job you don't love, grinding out another shift and hoping for something better to pay the bills. Or you're the mom who spends all day with the kids and feel like you're not getting anything done. Or you're stuck at home with a disability that has no cure. It feels pointless. If there's a plan, you can't see it.

But here's a God-sized promise that I find all over the Bible—you were put in place for a purpose. You might not see it just yet, but God has you in this place at this time for a specific purpose.

Ever read the Bible book of Esther? The name of God isn't mentioned a single time throughout the whole story, yet you still see the hand of God using everything, even humanity's sinful things, for a bigger purpose. Paul would later put it this way: **"In all things God works for the good of those who love him, who have been called according to his purpose"** (Romans 8:28). In *all things*. That includes even your most boring, confusing, and painful things.

Brainstorm with me a bit. What might the purpose of this season be? To keep you aware of your desperate dependence on Jesus? To connect you with a certain person who needs your experience (or your Jesus)? To protect you from a certain temptation?

I don't know the specifics, but I do know that you were put in this particular place for a divine purpose.

You don't want to read this
Matt Ewart

Several times a year I sit down with different groups of people to talk about faith. We spend an entire meeting talking about how to read the Bible. One of the discussion questions goes like this:

What are some obstacles that keep people from reading the Bible?

Common answers have to do with busy schedules and difficulty making sense of the Bible. I validate those answers as we talk through some solutions. But one brave person recently admitted this:

"Sometimes I don't read the Bible because I feel guilty."

Those words immediately struck a chord in my heart. When I am feeling guilty, the accuser is quick to remind me that I do not deserve to sit at Jesus' feet.

When the seeds of the accuser sprout into guilt, you and I become like Adam and Eve in the Garden of Eden. We hide from God rather than pursue him. Guilt can lead us to drown out his Word with busyness or numbness.

That is why part of you did not want to read this devotion—just like part of me did not want to write it.

But here we are . . . right where God wants us to be.

It only takes a moment for the grace of Jesus to disarm your guilt when he says, **"Peace be with you"** (Luke 24:36).

You are free. You are washed. You are forgiven. You are loved. And your Father would love to remind you of these truths every day—especially on the days when you feel least worthy to receive them.

The calendar helps us remember
Mike Novotny

The average citizen of Israel, even if they are not at all religious, knows more about the Old Testament book of Esther than most Christians I know. They could, quite easily, tell you all about Esther, Mordecai, Xerxes, and Haman. How is that possible? Because it is in their calendar, and it is not in ours.

About 2,500 years after the events of Esther occurred, many Jewish people mark their calendars based on these words: **"The Jews took it on themselves to establish the custom that they and their descendants and all who join them should without fail observe these two days every year, in the way prescribed and at the time appointed"** (Esther 9:27). And that's exactly what most Jews do. Sometime in late February or March, they celebrate a holiday called Purim, where they read the entire book of Esther and celebrate their survival as a people.

Here's a powerful truth for your spiritual life—the calendar helps us remember. Since most of us don't have photographic memories, we are wise to leverage the power of our calendars. Those reminders—whether it's writing "church" every Sunday in our calendars or setting a morning alarm that reads, "read your Bible"—are blessings to our brains that communicate the grace of God down to our souls.

Do you have a calendar (paper or digital)? If so, how might you use it to help you remember the glory of our Savior-God?

A unique perspective
Andrea Delwiche

Psalm 102 is entitled: **"A prayer of an afflicted person who has grown weak and pours out a lament before the Lord."** With this in mind, read the psalmist's self-description: **"I am like a desert owl, like an owl among the ruins. I lie awake; I have become like a bird alone on a roof"** (verses 6,7). This cry begins a beautiful prayerful intercession with God.

Like a bird perched high on a roof, a person set apart by suffering has a unique view. This writer, torn by unique agony, is given unique perspective—a heart for God's hurting people. Listen to this intervention: **"But you, LORD . . . will arise and have compassion on Zion, for it is time to show favor to her; the appointed time has come. Let this be written for a future generation, that a people not yet created may praise the LORD: 'The LORD looked down from his sanctuary on high, from heaven he viewed the earth, to hear the groans of the prisoners and release those condemned to death'"** (verses 12,13,18-20).

As suffering outsiders, there is space to reflect not only on our *own* relationship with God but also to intercede for others. The Spirit gives perspective through prayer—*conversation* with God.

We aren't called to prolong our suffering. Yet during extended pain, are there ways we can intervene on behalf of others? May God bless our searching, our pain, and our prayers.

No ifs, ands, or buts
Jan Gompper

Do you suffer from Big But Syndrome? No, this isn't a devotion on weight loss or exercise plans— check the spelling.

The problem I'm speaking of goes something like this: "I'm sorry, *but* you just don't understand." "I'm sorry, *but* it's not all my fault." "I know cheating is wrong, *but* everyone else does it." "I know I should spend more time with God, *but* I'm just so busy all week." But . . . but . . . but.

Excuse making comes naturally to us because it started with us: **"The man said, 'The woman you put here with me—she gave me some fruit from the tree, and I ate it'"** (Genesis 3:12). Did you hear it? "I'm sorry, God, *but* it's really your fault."

"Then the Lord God said to the woman, 'What is this you have done?' The woman said, 'The serpent deceived me, and I ate'" (Genesis 3:13). Translated: "I'm sorry, God, *but* the devil made me do it."

Thankfully, God's forgiveness didn't come with a *but*. Sure, there were consequences for Adam and Eve because of their sin, just like there usually are when we sin, but God's forgiveness is unconditional. He doesn't say, "I forgive you, *but* you better be perfect going forward." Rather, he has forgiven us even though he knows we will *never* fully obey him. **"God demonstrates his own love for us in this:** *While* **we were still sinners, Christ died for us"** (Romans 5:8).

Jesus' death and resurrection say, "You are forgiven . . . no ifs, ands, or buts!"

Fight for the faith
Mike Novotny

A few months back, a stranger stopped me in the produce section of my local grocery store and said, "Pastor, you don't know me, but I want to show you this." He pulled out of his wallet a sermon I had preached on sexual sin, and I could see his personal notes scribbled in the margins. This man looked at me with an intensity in his expression and said, "It's about the fight, right? I'm still fighting."

I don't know much about that man's story, but I bet you can relate to it. You are far from perfect in your behavior, but you really do want to obey your Father. You are so grateful for the mercy of Jesus that you want to follow him. But sometimes following Christ is a fight against the comfortable ways of your own flesh.

Jesus' brother Jude has some encouragement for us today: **"But you, dear friends, by building yourselves up in your most holy faith and praying in the Holy Spirit, keep yourselves in God's love as you wait for the mercy of our Lord Jesus Christ to bring you to eternal life"** (Jude 1:20,21).

As you fight against those old temptations, take note of all the help that God is offering you. You are his *dear friend*. You have been given this *most holy faith*. When you pray, you have the Holy Spirit in your heart. You are kept in God's love, waiting on Jesus' mercy and longing for eternal life.

The fight may be fierce, but faith in Jesus is more than enough.

Very good
Andrea Delwiche

If you were to build a canoe, you would choose your materials carefully. As the boat's maker, you would best understand how to use the thing you have made. You would know what weather, water, and weight conditions it could handle. It would be a good canoe. It would have limits.

The same principle holds true when God looks at each of us. **"As a father has compassion on his children, so the LORD has compassion on those who fear him; for he knows how we are formed, he remembers that we are dust"** (Psalm 103:13,14).

At times I've read these words and felt that when the Lord remembers I am made from dust, he's disappointed. He thinks, "Why don't you operate like someone carved from marble or cedar? Why aren't you more resilient, more faithful, less prone to need my help?"

This isn't the case though. When the Lord created humanity, he chose the stuff of earth to be his creative medium. He formed us from materials of the universe and proclaimed us "very good."

Things aren't what they were back in the first days after creation, but the Lord knows what we are made of—he chose the materials—and he finds great joy and goodness in us. God didn't make a mistake when he crafted you. He knows where you will need help and where you thrive. He doesn't sit in heaven shocked and disappointed. His love is endless. He delights in you. He doesn't regret forming you, even on your hardest days.

Preach, Christian!

Liz Schroeder

I woke up this morning to a Snapchat video of one of my adorable great-nephews, Christian James. Christian just turned two, complete with a construction-themed birthday party ("I'm 2 and Digging It"). From the comfort of his dinosaur pajamas, Christian was preaching a construction-themed message this morning. With all the confidence and cadence of a Southern minister, Christian proclaimed, "Build your life on the *Lord* Jesus Christ!"

Preach, Christian!

Along with learning how to golf, how to fix a leak, and how to mow the lawn, Christian's dad is instilling in him how to be a man after God's own heart. In addition to using his words, eating his vegetables, and learning to share with his baby brother, Christian's mom is laying the foundation for a lifelong relationship with his Savior.

My husband and I have had the privilege of laying that foundation five times over, and we've also entrusted our children to pastors, teachers, and mentors to build on that foundation.

"By the grace God has given me, I laid a foundation as a wise builder, and someone else is building on it. But each one should build with care. For no one can lay any foundation other than the one already laid, which is Jesus Christ" (1 Corinthians 3:10,11).

How about you? Is there a "construction worker" you need to thank for investing in your faith journey? Maybe it's a coach from high school, a special teacher, or your grandma. Thank them. Thank God for them. And keep building.

It's not a show
Nathan Nass

I want people to notice. I bet you do too. When I do something good, I glance around to see who saw it. I hope other people notice. I crave people's praise and attention. "Wow. Great job! That was amazing!"

But that's not what Christianity is all about. Jesus says, **"Be careful not to practice your righteousness in front of others to be seen by them. If you do, you will have no reward from your Father in heaven"** (Matthew 6:1). Those words cut at my heart. It's not a show! Instead, **"when you give to the needy, do not let your left hand know what your right hand is doing"** (Matthew 6:3). **"When you pray, go into your room, close the door and pray to your Father, who is unseen. Then your Father, who sees what is done in secret, will reward you"** (Matthew 6:6). Get the point? Christianity isn't a big show.

That's because Christianity isn't about all the things we do. Christianity is about all the things God has done for us through Jesus. The message we want others to see and hear isn't, "Look how special I am!" It's, "Look at how gracious God is. Look at how Jesus died for us. Look at the promises God gives us!"

There's an old phrase that says that Christians live to the glory of God and the salvation of souls. Isn't that true? It's not a show. To the glory of God and the salvation of souls!

Think before we speak
Katrina Harrmann

A girl was getting ready for her first day of middle school. As her mother tucked her into bed that night, she held out a tube of toothpaste.

"As you start school, it's important to remember that your words have incredible power to build someone up or tear someone down." She squeezed out a big dollop of toothpaste onto her daughter's hand and handed her the tube. "Could you put that toothpaste back into the tube for me, dear?"

Her daughter tried to smear some of the paste back into the tube, making a mess. "Mom, that's impossible!"

Her mother grinned. "I agree. Always remember that your words are like toothpaste in a tube: very easy to come out but impossible to take back once they've been spoken. So be careful what you say to people. Hurtful words are hard to remedy."

How true! Throughout James chapter 3 in the Bible, we are reminded that what comes out of our mouths is capable of setting the world on fire! Taming our tongues is a daily battle for most of us. We need to remember that our words carry immense power to hurt or heal, to uplift or tear down. Let's strive to speak words of love!

"With the tongue we praise our Lord and Father, and with it we curse human beings, who have been made in God's likeness. Out of the same mouth come praise and cursing. My brothers and sisters, this should not be" (James 3:9,10).

Help! is a brave word
Mike Novotny

I recently met a young woman who just became a Christian. During our conversation, she told me of a book about a horse, a mole, a fox, and a boy who become friends and teach each other the most important lessons in life. One time, the boy asks the horse, "What's the bravest thing you've ever said?" The horse replied with a single word: "Help."

Straight from the horse's mouth, right? There is much biblical truth to what our four-legged friend said, because some of our most important spiritual moments happen when we set aside our pride and ask someone for help. Your brave "help!" might be admitting that you are caught in a sin (moodiness, lashing out, fear, etc.) and in desperate need of encouragement and accountability. Or it might be confessing that you don't really understand the Bible (What exactly is Communion? How can Jesus be both God and man in one person?) and need a mature Christian to disciple you. Or perhaps you realize that you can't battle anxiety, raise your son, or get through your grief without a helping hand from your Father and your brothers and sisters in Christ. A humble "help!" might be the wisest, bravest, most Christian thing you say today.

"Let us then approach God's throne of grace with confidence, so that we may receive mercy and find grace to help us in our time of need" (Hebrews 4:16). God loves to help his children. Ask him (and others) for help in your personal time of need.

Thieves, hired hands, and shepherds
Matt Ewart

According to Jesus, there are three types of people in your life: thieves, hired hands, and shepherds.

Thieves are people who only want something from you. You are the means to get money, fame, or fulfillment of a desire. Some thieves know exactly what they are doing, while other thieves might not understand the way they hurt you.

Hired hands are people who help you but only because there is something in it for them. They are not necessarily bad people. They just have limits. They can help up to a certain extent, but when it gets too costly, they withdraw.

And then there are shepherds. A shepherd invests in your life in a way that the return stays with you. This kind of person will often smell like your house because of the time they spend with you. Though they are often a person of higher standing, they leverage their resources for your sake.

Jesus taught about these kinds of people so you would be able to recognize them in your life. But then he took it one step farther. As great as it is to have shepherds, this is how Jesus referred to himself: **"I am the good shepherd. The good shepherd lays down his life for the sheep"** (John 10:11).

When you find your relationships lacking, remember there is one Good Shepherd who has given you all you need. Follow his voice, and invite others to join you too.

JUNE

"You did not choose me, but I chose you and
appointed you so that you might go and bear fruit—
fruit that will last—and so that whatever you
ask in my name the Father will give you."

John 15:16

Samson: Gifted from birth
Jon Enter

You are the answer to someone's prayer.

In the Bible's Old Testament, a baby named Samson was God's answer to the Israelites' prayers for deliverance from the Philistines. God appeared to the wife of a man named Manoah, saying, **"You are barren and childless, but you are going to become pregnant and give birth to a son. He will take the lead in delivering Israel from the hands of the Philistines"** (Judges 13:3,5). What an amazing message directly from God himself telling her that the son she had yearned for was gifted for deliverance and blessed from birth!

You don't need God to bust through the earth's atmosphere to personally, verbally tell you that you've been gifted and blessed from birth. God's Word declares you are. Ephesians 2:10 makes it obvious: **"For we are God's handiwork, created in Christ Jesus to do good works, which God prepared in advance for us to do."**

You are God's handiwork. You were created and purposed to bless others and to be the answer to other people's prayers for peace, guidance, and hope. God prepared good works for you to do.

Those good works don't always need to be grand gestures. Small things matter. Smiling at others matters. Complimenting someone unexpectedly matters. Buying someone a coffee or their favorite candy bar matters. Sitting by someone sitting alone at school or at work matters. You matter. What you do in the name of Jesus matters.

So who is it? Who are you going to bless next?

Samson: Follow the instructions
Jon Enter

In Judges 13, Samson's parents received special instructions on how to raise their soon-to-be-conceived son. **"You will become pregnant and have a son whose head is never to be touched by a razor"** (verse 5). Before he was even born, Samson was set apart by God as being different.

You aren't commanded by God to grow your hair out to be a real-life, long-haired Rapunzel. But God does have very specific instructions for you. Are you ready? Brace yourself. **"Anyone who loves me will obey my teaching"** (John 14:23). God's Word is not a choose-what-you-want buffet. If the Lord placed commands in his Word, he expects us to follow his instructions perfectly, not to ignore them.

What clear command of God do you struggle to follow? You sin. You repent. You keep failing and falling back into its tempting clutches.

That's why God sent his Son, our perfect Savior, to obey God's laws in our place.

The stakes were high. Our eternity and Jesus' eternity were on the line. If Jesus sinned, not only would we all be in hell, but so would Christ. He'd cease to be perfect. God took a colossal, eternal risk when Jesus came to this world. But he did it because that is exactly what you mean to him. Jesus fulfilled the law perfectly in our place, so that means I can tell you confidently that your sins, your failures, are gone, forgiven . . . forever. Have peace with God because God has peace with you.

Samson: Revenge knows no end
Jon Enter

Here's a riddle for you: The more you take of them, the more you leave behind. The answer? Footsteps.

Samson once challenged the Philistines to crack a riddle: **"Out of the eater, something to eat; out of the strong, something sweet"** (Judges 14:14). The answer? Honey eaten from the belly of a dead lion.

When the Philistines pressured Samson's wife for the answer and she gave it to them, Samson got revenge by killing 30 of them. They got revenge by giving Samson's wife to another man. Samson got revenge by burning their fields. They got revenge by burning Samson's former wife to death. Samson got revenge by killing 1,000 Philistines with a donkey's jawbone.

As this story illustrates, revenge doesn't make anything better. It destroys. It never satisfies. It multiplies hate and hurt. Hurt people hurt people.

Who hurt you? Who is bugging you, just begging you to unleash your anger?

God gives the answer to the pain you feel in Romans 12:17,21: **"Do not repay anyone evil for evil. . . . Do not be overcome by evil, but overcome evil with good."** Revenge knows no end; it never heals the original hurt.

Jesus could've retaliated when the devil attacked him. Jesus could've responded against the evil of the devil with evil in return. He didn't. Jesus overcame the devil with his goodness, with his perfection on the cross.

Revenge is ended when it's brought to the cross of Jesus; there you find peace. Hurt people hurt people, but forgiven people forgive.

Samson: Small is mighty
Jon Enter

How do you envision Samson? With a mountain of muscles? Taller than everyone? What if he just looked like an average guy?

In Judges 16, the Philistines tried to discover the truth behind Samson's impossible-to-understand strength. They bribed his girlfriend, Delilah, saying, **"See if you can lure him into showing you the secret of his great strength"** (verse 5). If Samson's strength was from Herculean-sized muscles, they wouldn't have bribed Delilah. Maybe Samson was 5 feet 6 inches tall and 135 pounds. With that small frame, you'd ask how Samson could do such mighty things!

What's your great strength? I doubt you can bench-press 782 pounds, which is the current world record. Your Samson-sized great strength is anything you do dedicated to God. In Matthew 10, Jesus declares that even giving someone a cup of water in his name is an act of great faith strength. The little things matter to God just as much as the big things.

The devil is good at convincing us that little acts of kindness are meaningless. When you feel that way, read these words: **"Let us not become weary in doing good, for at the proper time we will reap a harvest if we do not give up"** (Galatians 6:9). Don't listen to the devil! He's afraid of you shining your light of faith. Light scatters the darkness! Make him flee as you live your life of faithful service to others.

Samson: Don't compromise yourself
Jon Enter

When Samson's enemies bribed Delilah to discover the secret to his strength, Samson lied and said that if he was tied with seven fresh bowstrings, he'd be powerless. After Delilah tied him up, the Philistines attacked. Samson fought them off easily.

Delilah prodded again. Samson lied again. The Philistines attacked and failed again. This repeated and repeated **"until** [Samson] **was sick to death of it. So he told her everything"** (Judges 16:16,17). Samson compromised himself. Delilah wore him down.

That's how the devil works. He knows how to attack our hearts and wear us down. We lose our tempers at those who annoy us. We bad-mouth the professor who keeps dumping on homework. We mock our boss who is out of touch with reality. We get worn down by the devil's assaults, and we compromise ourselves. We sin. So did Samson.

But God still loved Samson, and he loves you. **"The Lord is near to all who call on him, to all who call on him in truth"** (Psalm 145:18). Call upon Jesus and know he loves you. Know he fully, freely forgives you. Know he is with you.

He was with Samson. Samson compromised himself, but God restored him and continued to do mighty things through him.

God has done the same for you. You are restored. You aren't broken; you're forgiven. God has mighty things planned for you in his name. So start praying and asking, "God, what do you have for me next?"

Take away the stone
Matt Ewart

Lazarus died. It seemed he died too young.

Mary and Martha—sisters of Lazarus—were heart-broken. The entire community gathered around them and mourned with them. Sorrow was in the air.

It was so heartbreaking that even Jesus was moved to tears when he saw all the people who were grieving. But rather than console the crowd or gather everyone together for prayer, he walked up to the tomb and gave an unusual order: **"Take away the stone"** (John 11:39).

Martha had an understandable objection. She was responsible for making sure that the remains of her brother were not desecrated, and everyone knew that opening the tomb would subject the mourners to an unpleasant smell.

But Jesus persisted. And finally, Martha consented. The stone was rolled away.

You can read the rest of the story in John 11:38-44.

What is behind your stone? What have you kept hidden out of the sight of others?

Maybe you worry that people will be appalled if you dare to open it up. Or perhaps you worry that what's hidden is even too much for God to handle.

Jesus invites you to take away the stone. He has the power to address the areas of your life that are sealed off. Trust him. Let him speak to the anger, lust, selfishness, or greed that is hidden away in your heart.

He mourns the affect these things have on you, but he can conquer them for you. Where his voice is heard, even those who are dead can walk again.

Flip the kayak

Katrina Harrmann

I have a kayak I don't use much, so it mostly sits upside down and ignored behind our garage.

Recently, we were doing some yardwork, and I decided to move it. I flipped it over, and all kinds of creepy-crawly bugs were underneath. Gross! I never noticed all the yuck until I flipped the kayak and let the light of day shine in the dark spaces.

Aren't there times in our lives . . . maybe even *years* at a time . . . when we think we're doing fine? We're holding tight. We're steady as a rock. We have not and will not be moved! But without realizing it, we've hunkered down in the wrong places. We've become stagnant by not moving. Our spiritual lives have lagged. And we might *think* we're fine, but if we let in a little light . . . Ohh! The creepy-crawlies go skittering for cover. Yikes!

God's Word has a way of "flipping our kayak" and exposing everything that needs looking at.

You might think all is well, and maybe it is! But it also might be time for action. It might be time to evaluate your spiritual life or take a look at any pet sins that may have gotten tucked into the darkness as you sit tight, thinking they'll go unnoticed.

Flip over that kayak! Get into God's Word.

"I am the light of the world. Whoever follows me will never walk in darkness, but will have the light of life" (John 8:12).

What about the people you don't like?

Linda Buxa

Jesus spent his life serving. The one who **"did not come to be served, but to serve, and to give his life as a ransom for many"** (Matthew 20:28) healed the sick, washed his disciples' feet, cried with the mourning, fed the hungry, comforted the hurting, and—ultimately— gave his life for them. When he went back to heaven, he gave us the privilege to serve others in his name.

So now it's our job. Serving the people I like is not a challenge. But I struggle when it comes to being kind to those who aren't near the top of my favorite people list. Maybe they hurt me in the past, perhaps we have opposite views on cultural topics, or maybe our personalities just don't mesh. Who is it for you? Maybe it's the person who is *so* vocal about politics, the neighbor who is mad because of homeowners' association issues, the coworker who's never held accountable for her poor work.

I've looked, but I haven't found a passage in the Bible in which God gives us a pass on loving and serving the people we don't prefer. Instead he says, **"If it is possible, as far as it depends on you, live at peace with everyone"** (Romans 12:18).

We don't live in heaven (yet), so peace may not always be possible. But when it is, if it's in our power, it's our job to serve, to love, to live at peace—even with the people we don't like.

Grace isn't our excuse
Mike Novotny

Every year I have the privilege of talking about biblical sexuality at a local Christian high school where many of the students have been blessed with years of prior Christ-centered education. But I've noticed, more now than ever before, questions like this one: The Bible says that every sin is forgiven, so doesn't that mean that an unrepentant gay person (or unrepentant straight person) is still going to heaven if they're Christian?

Are you following the logic? Since every sin was taken to the cross and since trusting in Christ is the way to heaven, does it really matter how we behave sexually? Does any behavior really matter if salvation is all about Jesus?

Jude has an answer: **"Ungodly people . . . pervert the grace of our God into a license for immorality and deny Jesus Christ our only Sovereign and Lord"** (Jude 1:4). Some people pervert God's grace and act like it is a free pass to sin, a choice that essentially denies the lordship of Jesus, that is, his right to decide how we should live.

This is not Christianity. Christianity, like Christ himself, insists on both repentance and belief (read Mark 1:15). That means repenting of whatever Jesus says is wrong and believing in what Jesus did to make us right with God. For biblical faith to exist, both truths must exist in a person's heart.

Grace isn't your reason to sin. It's your best reason not to.

Do look up!
Jan Gompper

In screenwriter David Sirota's political/social satire *Don't Look Up*, an astrology student and her professor discover that a comet, large enough to destroy the world, will hit earth in a little over six months. Both try to warn key political and media figures about the impending apocalypse, but no one takes them seriously.

Sirota's depiction of society is much like Paul's here: **"In the last days there will be very difficult times. For people will love only themselves and their money. They will be boastful and proud, scoffing at God, disobedient to their parents, and ungrateful. They will consider nothing sacred. They will be unloving and unforgiving; they will slander others and have no self-control. They will be cruel and hate what is good. They will betray their friends, be reckless, be puffed up with pride, and love pleasure rather than God. They will act religious, but they will reject the power that could make them godly"** (2 Timothy 3:1–5 NLT).

The ending of *Don't Look Up* took me by surprise. The student astrologist had met a lapsed evangelical who still believed in God. During a final dinner with the professor's family, as the comet's landing looms imminent, this believer offers a prayer for God's protection.

God wrote a better ending, for **"we are looking forward to the new heavens and new earth he has promised, a world filled with God's righteousness"** (2 Peter 3:13 NLT).

Because of Christ, the title of our script is *Do Look Up*, for our best role is yet to come!

80/20 is bad for all 100

Mike Novotny

In 1896 Vilfredo Pareto noticed something odd about his garden. As he picked his peapods, he noticed that some pods had more peas than others. A lot more, in fact. He estimated that 20 percent of the pods contained 80 percent of the peas; a small minority had produced the great majority. He discovered what some later named the Pareto Principle, the theory that 20 percent of a group produces 80 percent of the results.

Big question—Is Pareto's Principle true for churches? Do 20 percent of the church members do 80 percent of the serving, give 80 percent of the offerings, and invite 80 percent of the guests? Based on the data I have from my own congregation, Pareto's Principle seems sad but true.

But here's the whole truth—80/20 is bad for all 100. When only some serve, all of us suffer. The "vital few" volunteers get burned out and become bitter about ministry. And those who don't serve miss out on the personal connections, the congregational impact, and the blessing of giving that Jesus promised when he said, **"It is more blessed to give than to receive"** (Acts 20:35).

The Jesus who loved you enough to lay down his life wouldn't lie to you. When we move from 80/20 to 80/40 and then 80/60, we will experience God's blessing. If nothing else, we will regularly remember the Savior who came not to take but to give, laying down his very life as a ransom for many (Mark 10:45).

One day at a time
Nathan Nass

My mind often starts to race. I bet yours does too. I think of all the things I have to do today. Then I think of all the things I have to do tomorrow. And the next day. And next week. And next month. And next year. And then it's not just my mind that's racing. My heart races too.

How will I get it all done? How will I make it through all that? Life can seem so overwhelming.

So take a deep breath and listen to Jesus: **"Therefore do not worry about tomorrow, for tomorrow will worry about itself. Each day has enough trouble of its own"** (Matthew 6:34). Isn't that great advice? Don't worry about tomorrow. You already have enough trouble today. You're not meant to handle two days' worth of trouble in the same day. You're certainly not meant to handle a month's or a year's worth of trouble on one day. "Do not worry about tomorrow, for tomorrow will worry about itself." That's great advice! One day at a time.

But from the mouth of Jesus, that's more than just advice. That's power and strength to live each day without worry. The God who cares for the little birds and the wildflowers will certainly care for you. The God who gives you eternal life through faith in Jesus will certainly give you all you need today. So don't worry about tomorrow. Trust in God's grace, one day at a time.

Grievances
Jason Nelson

It didn't take too long after sin entered the world for people to start harboring grievances. Cain killed his brother Abel because Cain was brooding over God's acceptance of Abel's offering and rejection of his own. Cain could've prayed to God to search his heart and help him be more sincere. He could've asked Abel to teach him how to be more devoted. Instead, Cain murdered his brother in an act of violence. Violence escalated. Cain became a fugitive. One of his descendants, Lamech, became a gangster. He sang a song bragging that he killed a man for wounding him. For some social deviants, it is easier to kill someone than it is to talk to them.

We see violence increasing in this land we love. The instances vary from domestic disturbances to drug deals gone bad to payback for being bullied to random home invasions. People disagree on what to do about it.

In the Garden of Gethsemane, Peter thought he was justified in resorting to violence to protect Jesus. But Jesus told him, **"Put your sword back in its place . . . for all who draw the sword will die by the sword"** (Matthew 26:52). It was time for Jesus to redeem the world. And whoever lives by the sword will eventually die by it. The Bible gives us strategies for blunting others aggression toward us: Turn the other cheek. A soft answer turns away wrath. We walk in danger, but God will give his angels charge over us to protect us.

Do not share your faith
Matt Ewart

If you are hesitant to share your faith with others, I have some good news. When Jesus commissioned his disciples to go out into the world, he did not exactly tell them to share their faith: **"[Jesus] rebuked them for their lack of faith and their stubborn refusal to believe those who had seen him after he had risen"** (Mark 16:14).

Their faith was uncompelling, to say the least. It was lacking. It needed to grow. If their fumbling faith was all they had to share, they would have been better off staying at home.

Maybe you feel similarly. You believe in Jesus, but at the same time you are wrestling with some of the things he taught. Maybe you are trying to make sense of a theological truth. Or maybe you are just trying to sort out God in your heart.

Rather than calling us to share our faith, Jesus called his disciples to do this: **"Go into all the world and preach the gospel to all creation"** (Mark 16:15).

Jesus commissioned us to share the gospel, not our faith. What's the difference?

Bringing others to faith in Jesus does not depend on how well we understand God, nor does it depend on us being able to explain things perfectly. The good news of Jesus is powerful all by itself to both strengthen our faith and bring others to faith.

So take the pressure off yourself. Don't worry about having everything figured out. Focus on sharing the good news of Jesus, and let his gospel do the work.

It's not fair!
Katrina Harrmann

Has someone ever treated you unfairly or with a complete lack of respect? It happened to me recently, and it was baffling. It's not fair! And there was no one to report it to—no way to make it "right." I had to accept it and move on like nothing had happened. Ouch!

As human beings, we can barely tolerate someone on Facebook with a different opinion than we have, let alone someone who *willfully* treats us as less than human and then goes about their day acting like nothing has happened.

Sometimes that's life, though. And the more I got to thinking about it, the more I realized that I knew of someone who was treated in such a disgraceful manner all the time. In fact, he was treated much worse than me! And he never sat stewing about it or plotting revenge.

Jesus.

The cross is the ultimate example. Christ was not only insulted and humiliated by people who were disrespectful; he was *killed* by them. Wow!

What can we learn about Jesus's habit of not getting even, of remaining calm in the face of unreasonable hatred?

It's a tough lesson—are you ready? **"Love your enemies and pray for those who persecute you"** (Matthew 5:44).

That's a tall order! And you and I are only dealing with petty grievances compared to what Christ suffered. But there's no better way to let go of anger and hurt than to pray. If someone has treated you badly, try praying for them to find the peace that passes understanding.

You are the answer!
Linda Buxa

The people around me have been discouraged lately. (Wait, that sentence could be sorely misinterpreted. Let me try again . . .) The people around me have been discouraged lately because there seems to be so much division, so much discord, so much dissonance.

I get it. The current societal tone could easily weigh us down, but maybe we could instead see it as our personal mission. Paul, a man who went from creating discord among people to promoting peace with Jesus, issued this challenge: **"Finally, brothers and sisters, rejoice! Strive for full restoration, encourage one another, be of one mind, live in peace. And the God of love and peace will be with you"** (2 Corinthians 13:11).

Strive for full restoration—In Greek, this literally means to mend your ways. Repair what's broken in your life. Don't allow trash to litter your life, and don't give up on the transforming power of the Holy Spirit in your life or in the lives of others.

Encourage one another—Let your words be ones that build up others, cheering them on and building bridges.

Be of one mind—You won't be of one mind with unbelievers on eternal things. But, when it comes to other believers, be of one mind on things that matter.

Live in peace—Be a peacemaker and find more joy in reconciling than fighting. Then pass on the joy of love and grace to others.

And the best reward for doing that? The God of love and peace will be with you.

God loves celebration
Andrea Delwiche

Most of us celebrate and enjoy feasting at some point during the year, but I suspect that oftentimes we don't consider celebration as being an integral part of worship. Preparing the food, setting the table, lighting the candles, gathering, praying, and enjoying the delicious flavors of the meal and the conversation—all this is part of the overflow of goodness for Christ followers.

"He makes grass grow for the cattle, and plants for people to cultivate—bringing forth food from the earth: wine that gladdens human hearts, oil to make their faces shine, and bread that sustains their hearts" (Psalm 104:14,15).

Our triune God is joyful. Our God loves celebration. Our God gave us taste buds and a sense of smell and hunger that can be satisfied by good things. God planted the capacity for celebration in our hearts. Yes, there is a time for fasting and silence in worship, and there are feasting seasons.

God gave this instruction to the people of Israel for one of their yearly celebrations: **"Use the silver to buy whatever you like: cattle, sheep, wine or other fermented drink, or anything you wish. Then you and your household shall eat there in the presence of the Lord your God and rejoice"** (Deuteronomy 14:26).

Following Jesus guarantees us a full life. Will there be deep sadness? Of course. But goodness, wisdom, and celebration are part of our inheritance. When will you have a meal to celebrate all God's blessings to you?

Prediction or promise?
Clark Schultz

Prediction or promise? Decca Records once told the Beatles that their sound was on the way out. Thankfully the Beatles didn't take that prediction to heart.

Prediction or promise? There will be flying cars as in movies like *Back to the Future*. I haven't seen one yet.

What about the Bible? Prediction or promise? **"He will judge between the nations and will settle disputes for many peoples. They will beat their swords into plowshares and their spears into pruning hooks. Nation will not take up sword against nation, nor will they train for war anymore"** (Isaiah 2:4).

When this passage was written, Israel and Judah did not have much to look forward to other than captivity. All hope to them was lost. But don't read Isaiah's words as a prediction of future geopolitical peace. It's a promise of everlasting peace when Jesus returns.

When we are faced with a captive fear, what do we cling too—a prediction or a promise? Looking at God's track record in the Bible, we know that he does not make predictions. He makes promises. What's better— HE KEEPS HIS PROMISES.

The promise of a Savior, the promise to be with you always, the promise to make things work out for your good, the promise that you are a child of God through Baptism, the promise your sins are forgiven—are all promises that are kept by God. Don't take my word for it; take God's.

God's Word to married men
Mike Novotny

I recently typed *husbands* and *married* and *marriage* into a Bible search engine, and what I discovered were the "7 Commandments for Christian Husbands." If you're a married man (or know one who needs some encouragement), here's what our Father says to husbands: **"Be considerate** [of your wives]" (1 Peter 3:7). **"Treat** [your wives] **with respect"** (1 Peter 3:7). **"Do not be harsh with** [your wives]" (Colossians 3:19). **"Love your wives"** (Colossians 3:19). **"Love your wives"** (Ephesians 5:25). **"Love** [your] **wives"** (Ephesians 5:28). **"Love** [your] **wife"** (Ephesians 5:33). Apparently, we dudes depend on repetition!

I (obviously) am not a married woman, but I have counseled enough married couples to summarize most women's wants in this way—wives want a husband who acts without being asked. Such men cover almost all the above commands at once.

No, men can't read minds, but we can pay close attention to the data—to her schedule, to her goals, to her to-do list, to her frustrations, to her desires, etc. God will give a married man more than enough evidence to act on, and that action will mean the world to his wife.

Fellow husbands, marriage is work, but the work is worth it. When you fall short, run back to Jesus for mercy. When you need help, call on the Spirit for wisdom and your friends for encouragement. That's how you can lead the way to a happier, holier home.

God's Word to married women
Mike Novotny

I recently typed *wife* and *married* and *marriage* into a Bible search engine, and what I discovered were the "7 Commandments for Christian Wives." If you're a married woman (or know one who needs some encouragement), here's what our Father says to wives: **"Respect** [your husband]" (Ephesians 5:33). **"Love** [your husband]" (Titus 2:4). **"Be subject to** [your husband]" (Titus 2:5). **"Submit"** (Colossians 3:18). **"Submit"** (1 Peter 3:1). **"Submit"** (Ephesians 5:22). **"Submit"** (Ephesians 5:24).

Quite the list, huh? I know that many sinful men have weaponized these words for their selfish gain, so let me say two things. First, this is God's list. Those words weren't copied and pasted from The Patriarchy Club's "About Us" page. They came from the same God who gave you life and then gave you his Son so you could have eternal life. Read each command; then, in light of its trustworthy source, receive it with an open heart.

Second, seek to be a submissive wife. Just as Jesus submitted to his Father, out of love and respect for his will, your holy calling is to be like Jesus. After you have shared your heart and your mind like Jesus did with his Father, be willing to say with Jesus, "Not my will but yours be done."

When you fall short, run back to Jesus for mercy. When you need help, call on the Spirit for wisdom and your friends for encouragement. That's how you can do your part in creating a happier, holier home.

Where every great marriage starts
Mike Novotny

Recently, when I typed *wife* and *husband* and *marriage* and *married* into a Bible search engine, I discovered 14 specific commands for Christian spouses. What I noticed, however, was that all 14 of those commands came later in the New Testament letters and never in their opening chapters.

That's no accident. God knows great marriages don't start with us doing good things but instead with Jesus doing the greatest thing for us. That's why 1 Corinthians 1 says, **"Christ Jesus . . . is our righteousness, holiness and redemption"** (verse 30). The reason you are "right" with God isn't because you've been perfect in your relationships with others but rather because Jesus was perfect in his. The first chapter of Colossians explains, **"**[God] **has reconciled you by Christ's physical body through death to present you holy in his sight, without blemish and free from accusation"** (verse 22). Jesus' perfect life and innocent death did everything to make you flawless in our Father's eyes. That's why Paul, before he told spouses to love and respect each other, penned, **"Praise be to the God and Father of our Lord Jesus Christ, who has blessed us in the heavenly realms with every spiritual blessing in Christ"** (Ephesians 1:3).

If you or someone you love is struggling in their relationship, remember God's order of operations. First, he fills up our hearts with what Jesus has done. Then he urges us to pour ourselves out into others. Fuel up on Jesus, and you'll be ready to live out your faith!

A foundation in the storm
Nathan Nass

As I write this devotion, a hurricane is bearing down on the Gulf Coast. Winds of 100+ mph. Storm surge. Heavy rain. For people in the storm's path, life is being turned upside down. Schools are cancelled. Evacuations are ordered. Houses are boarded up. There's so much uncertainty in a storm.

You know that. Whether or not you've ever faced a hurricane, you've faced plenty of storms. Maybe you're facing a storm today. It could be a hurricane. It could be cancer. It could be waves of anxiety. It could be the weight of guilt or regret that envelops you. Storms turn life upside down.

So Jesus gives you a foundation in the storm: **"Therefore everyone who hears these words of mine and puts them into practice is like a wise man who built his house on the rock. The rain came down, the streams rose, and the winds blew and beat against that house; yet it did not fall, because it had its foundation on the rock"** (Matthew 7:24,25).

Notice something: Even if you believe in Jesus, even if you hear and follow the Word of God, there will be storms in your life. Everyone faces storms.

But you have a foundation—a Rock: Jesus Christ and his Word. Jesus' forgiveness can withstand the weight of every sin. Jesus' presence can strengthen you against every wave of anxiety. Jesus' promises give you hope even in the face of death. Remember: Jesus is your foundation in the storm.

Jesus is my vine
Matt Ewart

Jesus loved to use parables and metaphors to explain who he was. This is one of them: Jesus said, **"I am the vine; you are the branches"** (John 15:5).

After this seemingly odd comparison, he then shared an agricultural principle that everyone can understand. When a branch remains connected to the vine, everything is fine. When a branch is disconnected from the vine, it dies.

When we think about our lives, it's easy to confuse branches for vines and vines for branches.

We can mistake a branch for the vine when we turn to other people to give us what only Jesus can provide. For example, parents tend to overbook their schedules when they try to get their child involved in every possible way. Their child becomes their vine.

We can also get mixed up when we think of ourselves as the vine. We think that the world will stop spinning if we don't show up at work or if we're not there to help a loved one. That puts a lot of pressure on us.

But there is extraordinary peace when we let Jesus sort out who is who. He is the vine. We are the branches. We have all we need when we are connected to him.

When you begin to feel the pressure of impossible expectations, or when you feel that others aren't meeting your needs, just repeat these words to yourself: Jesus is *my* vine. I am *his* branch.

Community is messy
Mike Novotny

I wish community was less messy. I wish we could join a church with no people problems, sign up for a small group without any awkwardness, and find friends who always see eye to eye. But those wishes won't come true. Not in this world. Especially not when tragedy strikes.

Many millennia ago, Job had three friends who planned to comfort him after the tragic loss of his children and health. But their first week with Job was messy. **"They sat on the ground with him for seven days and seven nights. No one said a word to him, because they saw how great his suffering was"** (Job 2:13).

Bible commentators aren't sure what to make of their silence. Some say this was a loving choice, since no words would make Job's grief go away. Others point out that this must have been unbearably awkward. Imagine sitting in the same room with someone for an entire week without a word!

I appreciate this tension, because real community is messy. We show up in love, and then we say a less-than-loving thing. We have good intentions when we text, but then we end up being misunderstood. We bring up God's plans for our pain, but then our friend gets angry at plans that involve so much pain.

It's messy, but there's no other type of true community. So show up. Do your best. Ask for God's forgiveness and their forgiveness when necessary. Bear with one another in love. Do life together. We need each other, even if our community is messy.

Refreshed
Nathan Nass

A strange thing happens when you comfort someone else with God's Word: you get comforted. An unexpected thing happens when you encourage someone else with Jesus' promises: you get encouraged. Have you noticed that? Wise Solomon did. He wrote this proverb: **"A generous person will prosper; whoever refreshes others will be refreshed"** (Proverbs 11:25).

This is one of the upside-down truths of God's kingdom. When you generously share with others—whether it's time, money, comfort, or encouragement—you don't end up with less. You end up refreshed.

The opposite is also true. When I focus on me, when I spend my time thinking about me, when I fight for what's best for me, I don't end up fulfilled at all. I end up emptier than ever.

So take your eyes off you. Put them on Jesus. Think of his blessings to you. His grace. His forgiveness. His presence. His peace. Do you know how you'll feel? Grateful. Refreshed.

And then focus your eyes on the people God's placed in your life. Take what Jesus has given you and use it to refresh others. Give to those who are in need. Comfort those who are mourning. Encourage those who are despairing. Sit with those who are alone. Listen to those who are depressed. Help those who need a hand. And something surprising will happen. Not only will God refresh that person through your acts of faith, but you will feel refreshed. It's true! "Whoever refreshes others will be refreshed."

"Pastor, do you keep these commandments?"

Mike Novotny

One evening after teaching a classroom of teenagers about sex, marriage, and living together, a young man raised his hand and asked, "Pastor Mike, do you keep all these commandments?" (I wish there was camera footage of my facial expression after his question!)

Maybe thinking about love, respect, marriage, and sexual purity makes you feel tremendously guilty. Whether your selfishness imploded a previous relationship, your choices have damaged your current relationship, or your sexual history is messy and shameful, most of us wish we could go back and do things a better, more biblical way.

But since we can't go back, we run ahead to Jesus. We cling to the cross and make our confession, "We sinned. Jesus, we are sorry." Because (this is my favorite part) Jesus is eternally available to us. Even those of us who have sinned in sexual or relational ways. Your situation might be as embarrassing as the prostitutes who gathered around Jesus or the woman caught in the act of adultery, but please remember that Jesus saved them. And he will save you too.

"Jesus Christ is the same yesterday and today and forever" (Hebrews 13:8). The same Savior who opened his arms to messy souls back then is opening those same arms to you today. The cross of Jesus doesn't have an expiration date! So take all of yourself to Jesus. He can handle it. He is the perfect Savior for commandment breakers. Like me and you.

Don't sing songs to a heavy heart
Jan Gompper

Have you ever experienced a serious loss, setback, or disappointment and received cliché encouragement from friends or relatives? "It's always darkest before the dawn." "You just need to get back on the horse." "For every cloud there's a silver lining." (You get the picture.)

Sadly, even well-meaning Christians sometimes throw out Bible passages in clichélike fashion. While words from Scripture certainly have more merit, they can ring hollow to a person who isn't ready to receive them.

Solomon understood this when he wrote: **"Singing cheerful songs to a person with a heavy heart is like taking someone's coat in cold weather or pouring vinegar in a wound"** (Proverbs 25:20 NLT). He knew that hurting people need to be *allowed* to grieve in order to process their pain and eventually come through it.

It was this wisdom of Solomon that led pastor and psychiatrist Dr. Kenneth C. Haugk to create a lay caregiving education program called Stephen Ministries. Through this program, members of congregations, to whom God has given the spiritual gift of caregiving, receive training in how to walk alongside a hurting person without offering advice or direction. Stephen ministers are not counselors or therapists; they are simply *listeners* who allow hurting people to process their pain, however long it takes.

Not everyone who struggles with loss or pain needs professional help. They may just need a trained, caring listener who won't sing songs to their heavy hearts.

Love letters
Katrina Harrmann

A few years after we moved into our one hundred-year-old home, I was cleaning out the highest, most-hard-to-reach shelf in our bedroom closet when I came across a mysterious and dusty bundle of letters from the 1940s. What an amazing find! Even better, they were sweet, nostalgic love letters from a husband to his wife as one of them was staying with family in our house more than 60 years ago. I was so thrilled to find these relics of the past with their simple, yet endearing lines and honest expressions of love.

Not long afterward, I happened to post about the find on my personal blog, and the couples' remaining grandson—who was the only member of that family left—contacted me and received these priceless family heirlooms.

We too have a family heirloom . . . love letters written to us many, many years ago in the hope that we would continue reading and remember the great love our heavenly Father has for us. The Bible—his love letter to us—continues to instruct and comfort us daily, even thousands of years after it was originally written. And better yet, we can share these letters with others, hoping to reunite with other members of our extended Christian family. What a love story!

"The Lord appeared to us in the past, saying: 'I have loved you with an everlasting love; I have drawn you with unfailing kindness'" (Jeremiah 31:3).

Not no one
Nathan Nass

Sometimes it seems like there's no one. Do you know what I'm talking about? No one who listens. No one who cares. No one who's there. No one who understands. That's a terrible feeling, isn't it? There's nothing worse than no one.

You're not the only one who's felt that way. King David did in the Bible. Before he became king of Israel, there was a time when David had to hide in a cave as an army sought to kill him. In that dark cave, here's what he wrote: **"Look and see, there is no one at my right hand; no one is concerned for me. I have no refuge; no one cares for my life"** (Psalm 142:4). No one concerned . . . No one cares . . . No one . . .

But in the middle of his fears and doubts and sins, David realized something. Even though no one else was there, he wasn't alone. He wrote, **"When my spirit grows faint within me, it is you who watch over my way"** (Psalm 142:3). As bad as it seemed, there was not no one. There was God! God was watching over David's life every step of the way. So here was David's prayer: **"I cry to you, Lord; I say, 'You are my refuge, my portion in the land of the living'"** (Psalm 142:5).

When you're all alone, cry out to Jesus your Savior and know that there's not no one with you. There's always Jesus. He is your refuge. Always!

The potential is in the seed
Matt Ewart

At any given moment, there are two versions of you: the version that is and the version that could be.

There was a commercial that showed two versions of a man in old age. One version was healthy and active, playing with his grandchildren. The other version was sick and unhealthy, lying in a hospitable bed.

Each version was the result of the decisions he had made earlier in life.

Do you ever wonder how life would have ended up differently if you had made different decisions? For some readers, this engages your *wonder*. For others, it engages *regret*. Wherever you land, check out this parable from Jesus: **"This is what the kingdom of God is like. A man scatters seed on the ground. Night and day, whether he sleeps or gets up, the seed sprouts and grows, though he does not know how. All by itself the soil produces grain"** (Mark 4:26–28).

We can get so caught up wondering *what could be* that we miss what God is doing. His kingdom work is not limited by our potential. His Spirit is not subjected to our level of understanding. He works in ways we don't understand.

You might not understand the seeds that God has been planting in your life. He can even plant them in your mistakes. But they are growing, and it takes time to get from seed to sickle.

Whatever version of yourself you see in the mirror today, know that God is not finished with you yet.

JULY

But as for me, I watch in hope for the Lᴏʀᴅ,
I wait for God my Savior; my God will hear me.

MICAH 7:7

No coincidence. Just providence.
Mike Novotny

Why are you here? Out of all the things you could be doing or words you could be reading, why are you here right now? There are two answers to that question—coincidence and providence. This moment could be a coincidence. Totally random. Or it could be providence. It could be God's plan working all things for your good.

I'm not sure about your answer, but I am sure that people who strongly believe in providence end up with more praise and more peace. When life is good, you can praise the God who put you in this place for this purpose. And when life isn't good, you can have peace: "There's a reason I'm going through this. I don't know it, but I believe it—God didn't leave me." The good stuff is better and the bad stuff is bearable when you believe in providence.

That's why I love what Paul said to some intellectuals in Athens: **"From one man he made all the nations, that they should inhabit the whole earth; and he marked out their appointed times in history and the boundaries of their lands. God did this so that they would seek him"** (Acts 17:26,27). Notice how deeply Paul believed in providence, proven by his belief that we are in this place (lands) in this time (in history) because God had a plan.

What a promise! You are here for a reason. Even if you can't yet see it or don't totally grasp it, your life is part of God's plan. That's providence.

Death is not the end
Ann Jahns

I live about a block away from one of the largest and most respected medical systems in Wisconsin. It's where I held my dad's hand after the stroke that God used to call him home to heaven. It's where a family member kept a tearful, prayerful vigil by the bed of her gravely ill daughter until God spared her life with the gift of medical technology and the skill of her doctors. Countless other friends and family members have received care there, hearing news either elating or devastating. It's a sobering place.

Despite the billions of dollars spent at this hospital system—on technology, salaries, and infrastructure—it can't alter the inevitable. No matter who receives care there and no matter how revolutionary that care is, every person who walks through the doors of that amazing facility will someday die. Romans 6:23 is crushing in its finality: **"The wages of sin is death."** No wiggle room or space for misinterpretation there.

If you're still hanging with me, there is good news. The best news. For those who die in Jesus, death is not the end. It's not the final chapter in your story; it's only the beginning. Only through death can we enter into the glorious life that is waiting for us—life forever with Jesus, where there is no more death or tears or pain or grim diagnoses. Let's marvel at the remainder of Romans 6:23: **"*But* the gift of God is eternal life in Christ Jesus our Lord."**

Isn't that the most beautiful "but" you've ever heard?

Bringing Jonah back
Matt Ewart

God commissioned the prophet Jonah to deliver an important message. The message was designed to prevent judgment from falling on the city of Nineveh. But in a mixture of spiteful hatred and bitter vengeance, he decided that Nineveh was not worth saving. So he got in a boat and went the opposite direction.

There is a little Jonah in all of us. Maybe today you are thinking about an area of life where you've been turning a deaf ear to what God is telling you. You know what he wants you to do, but you're resistant to it.

The result is anguish. If Jonah's conscience was working at all, then maybe he did what we do when our consciences bother us. He was constantly looking over his shoulder, waiting for God's wrath to catch up.

God did catch up to him. But not with wrath.

"Then the Lord sent a great wind on the sea, and such a violent storm arose that the ship threatened to break up" (Jonah 1:4).

God did not send this storm to get back at Jonah. This storm was designed to bring Jonah back.

When hardships enter your life, you might come to the conclusion that God is getting back at you for something you did. But your God doesn't do that. Jesus' death proves how far God was willing to go to reach runaways like you and me. He can use anything to bring you back.

Your homeland is a gift from God

Katrina Harrmann

God has a long history of blessing people by giving them homes. The Israelites in Canaan . . . Joseph and Mary in Egypt . . . Jacob's son Joseph in Egypt after his brothers threw him down a well . . . Even Abraham was called away from Ur to the promise of a new home.

But homes aren't always nice. After all, for a few years, Joseph also called a jail cell home after he was wrongly accused. And Jonah lived for days in the belly of a big fish.

Your homeland is a gift from God. But the evil in this world sometimes thwarts and corrupts that. The devil diligently strives to destroy our homes. If he can disrupt our homes, he hopes to ruin our relationship with the Father. Remember what he did to Job?

The Fourth of July is an ideal time to thank God if you have a good homeland . . . or in the U.S., a free country. What a blessing! Just like Job or Jonah, this isn't the case for everyone. And we should continually pray for those whose homelands or countries are ravaged by war, politics, or disease.

Praise God for giving us a country where we can worship him and live our lives in relative freedom and peace.

"By wisdom a house is built, and through under-standing it is established; through knowledge its rooms are filled with rare and beautiful treasures" (Proverbs 24:3,4).

Faultless
Mike Novotny

For about 15 years of my life, I was a rabid collector of sports cards. Baseball cards, football cards, basketball cards, and hockey cards were stacked, boxed, and stored in my bedroom closet by the tens of thousands. A few of them were rather valuable, so I purchased some thick plastic cases to protect their tender cardboard corners from being crumpled, nicked, or torn. Because, as every hobbyist knows, something in mint condition can be priceless.

That's how God thinks of you. You are human, meaning that, just like me, you are all too easily crumpled by pride, stained by impatient choices, and torn by foolish behavior (likely done to impress your friends). In your natural condition, you wouldn't be worth anything to God.

But Jesus has changed your value. Jude wrote, **"To him who is able to keep you from stumbling and to present you before his glorious presence without fault and with great joy"** (Jude 1:24). Your God is able to present you "without fault," without a single flaw, even in the bright light of his glorious presence.

How is that possible? Only through Jesus. Jesus restored your soul to perfection and then promised to "keep you from stumbling," that is, to keep you in the protective case of the Christian faith. If you have Jesus, you have a blameless, flawless, faultless soul.

What is more valuable than that?

A day at a time
Jan Gompper

When I was growing up, my mother frequently reminded me to take it a day at a time. I wasn't good at doing so back then, and, truth be told, I still struggle with it. The problem is that my brain gets ahead of me. I think of all the what-ifs or project myself into the future while still in the present. Today that would be termed a form of anxiety disorder.

It is estimated that 15 million people suffer from some type of anxiety disorder. For some, their anxiety is so severe that they experience panic attacks or become unable to function altogether.

Thankfully, there is medication to help those severe cases. But for those of us who suffer from milder anxiety, listen to the wisdom of Holocaust survivor Corrie ten Boom: "Worrying is carrying tomorrow's load with today's strength—carrying two days at once. It is moving into tomorrow ahead of time. Worrying doesn't empty tomorrow of its sorrow; it empties today of its strength" (*He Cares, He Comforts*).

God understood anxiety disorder long before it had a clinical name. That's why he addressed the topic in at least 53 Bible verses. He reminds us that if he cares for the birds of the air and flowers of the field, he's got our backs (Matthew 6:26-34). He further counsels, **"Do not be afraid; do not be discouraged, for the Lord your God will be with you wherever you go"** (Joshua 1:9).

Ms. ten Boom and my mom wisely heeded God's counsel—Take it a day at a time!

What God values
Nathan Nass

Have you heard of Jeroboam II? He was probably the greatest king of ancient Israel. He ruled for 41 years; conquered Israel's enemies; and brought peace, prestige, and prosperity. But do you know how many verses of the Bible are dedicated to him? Just seven (2 Kings 14:23-29). But it's enough to tell us that Jeroboam II **"did evil in the eyes of the Lord"** (2 Kings 14:24). God doesn't value political accomplishments. He seeks faithful hearts.

In contrast, there was a poor widow who lived in Zarephath, which wasn't even in the land of Israel. This poor widow had nothing but one little son. She didn't accomplish anything great, except humbly and faithfully baking bread each day for God's prophet Elijah. Yet, do you know how many verses of the Bible are dedicated to her? Eighteen (1 Kings 17:7-24)! The Bible pays more attention to a poor widow than a conquering king.

Do you value what God values? Do you value prestige and prosperity and human accomplishments—like Jeroboam? Or do you value a humble trust in God's promises that looks to serve others—like that widow?

Jesus and his cross teach us what God values: **"God chose the lowly things of this world and the despised things—and the things that are not—to nullify the things that are, so that no one may boast before him"** (1 Corinthians 1:28,29). Jesus didn't come for the great in the eyes of the world. He came for you. Why? Because God values you!

Playing favorites
Jon Enter

In the book the *Sibling Effect*, Jeffrey Kluger says that most parents have a child that they favor and that they are liars if they claim otherwise. Were you the favorite child growing up? If you're a parent, is there a child who's just easier to get along with? It's hard not to play favorites. But when parents play favorites, everyone loses.

Sadly, in the households of the three Old Testament patriarchs, you find unapologetic favoritism. Abraham favored Isaac over Ishmael. **"Isaac . . . loved Esau, but Rebekah loved Jacob"** (Genesis 25:28). Jacob favored Joseph over his 11 other sons. This favoritism led to lying, fighting, jealousy, banishment, premeditated murder, and slavery.

It's natural to feel close to a person who has the same likes and passions as you. But when that's how someone parents, when favoritism happens, it destroys trust and rips families apart. Even the favored child grows up broken as no one can love that child to the level of their blinded-by-favoritism parent. If this is happening, confess it to God and to your children. Change before everyone loses.

This is not how God the Father treats us. **"God does not show favoritism"** (Acts 10:34). Your heavenly Father loves you fully, eternally, completely. He doesn't hold back. He forgives you with that same passion. If you're a parent, don't hold back your intentional, compassionate, and guiding love from all your children. May each child be absolutely convinced, "I'm the favorite!" It's possible because that is what you are to God!

Little by little
Linda Buxa

We all wish God would snap his fingers and make our lives easier. We wish nicotine cravings would simply disappear, depression would magically lift, or our broken relationships would be immediately restored. Instead, it can seem like God is taking too long to answer our prayers. We wonder if he's even listening.

The Israelites got it. After 430 years of slavery, they finally escaped Egypt and were making the trek *home* to Canaan. Even though the Israelites had waited a loooong time for this, God didn't snap his fingers and give them everything.

God told Moses, **"I will make all your enemies turn their backs and run. I will send the hornet ahead of you to drive the Hivites, Canaanites and Hittites out of your way. But I will not drive them out in a single year, because the land would become desolate and the wild animals too numerous for you. Little by little I will drive them out before you, until you have increased enough to take possession of the land"** (Exodus 23:27-30). They would have to be patient, because if they were successful all at once, they wouldn't be able to handle it.

Hmm. Maybe when we think God is acting at a glacial pace, he's actually working little by little to develop patience, perseverance, and wisdom in us. Maybe he's excited to bless us, but we aren't quite ready for it. Maybe we can learn to wait patiently as God works in us until we have "increased enough" to be ready for what he has in store for us.

Start with grace
Mike Novotny

If you grew up in church, what do you remember hearing about financial giving? Did it start with grace? Was Jesus the first part of the pastor's or priest's message? I'm sorry if it wasn't. Maybe you grew up with the pressure of "give, give, give!" but never got to enjoy, "He gave! He gave! He gave!"

The apostle Paul began his explanation of Christian giving with these words: **"You know the grace of our Lord Jesus Christ, that though he was rich, yet for your sake he became poor, so that you through his poverty might become rich"** (2 Corinthians 8:9). Paul didn't start with dollars but with grace. He didn't jump into what we can give to God but what God has given to us.

Although Jesus was rich, living large among the mansions of heaven, yet for your sake he became poor. Jesus spent 33 years camping on earth. You ever camped? Best night of sleep you've ever had? Um, no. Jesus had unending comfort in heaven, but he gave up that comfort to be with you. Why? God wanted to make you a billionaire with blessings, to give you so much love and forgiveness that you will never run out. No, you and I didn't deserve it, but Jesus still did it. That's grace.

There will be a time to pull out your budget and pray for a generous heart. But that can wait while you take time today to ponder the most generous heart of all, the One who gave his only Son so you could be saved.

Stick with grace
Mike Novotny

I took some unofficial measurements of the offering boxes in our church lobby and the cross that hangs in our sanctuary. I discovered that our offering boxes are a forearm wide, a hand deep, and a cubit tall (that's elbow to fingertips). Overall, each box is about the size of my torso. But our cross is far bigger—13 feet tall and 7 feet across. If the church decor is preaching a message, it is declaring that what God gave to us is far bigger than what we give to God.

That's a vital part of Christian giving. Does our Father want us to give generously to support Christian ministry? For sure. But our offerings are given with more joy and excitement when we start every gift with grace. Paul told the Corinthians, **"For you know the grace of our Lord Jesus Christ, that though he was rich, yet for your sake he became poor, so that you through his poverty might become rich"** (2 Corinthians 8:9). The generosity of Jesus was their constant motivation to be generous.

It can be easy to skim past the gospel and get to "paying the church bills" or cutting another check to St. _____ Church. But that repetition will become robotic without a long look at your redemption in Jesus. Maybe the next time you're ready to give an offering, pause, stare at a cross, and think about your spiritual bank account. Call to mind the heart of God, which deposited unending glory in your account so you could live large in his presence forever.

Just give it!
Mike Novotny

One of the biggest struggles that my congregation has is keeping its generous commitments. Whenever we open the Bible and preach on giving, people check a box/sign up to volunteer/make a verbal commitment . . . which they often don't keep. When our staff follows up to find the best time to volunteer, some emails never get opened. It's a common but frustrating situation.

Paul faced that challenge. His friends in Corinth had committed to giving to the poor in Jerusalem, but then they were dragging their feet. That's why Paul wrote, **"Last year you were the first not only to give but also to have the desire to do so. Now finish the work, so that your eager willingness to do it may be matched by your completion of it, according to your means"** (2 Corinthians 8:10,11). Finish the work! Paul wanted his friends' action to match their intention. God wants the same thing for all his children.

In my experience, giving is like going to the gym. I can find six dozen excuses why today isn't a good day to go, but then, once I make myself do it, I'm glad I chose it. If you're talking yourself out of generosity these days, maybe the simplest solution is just to give. Put God to the test (Malachi 3:10). See if it isn't more blessed to give than to receive (Acts 20:35). In so many ways, more spiritual than financial, our Father stands by his promise that **"a generous person will prosper"** (Proverbs 11:25).

Give what *you* can
Mike Novotny

The story of Jesus and the generous but poor widow in Luke 21:1-4 is worth your time. Jesus has a different way of determining generosity. He doesn't count the total dollars given or hours volunteered. Instead, he considers what each person is able to give.

Paul captured that same idea: **"For if the willingness is there, the gift is acceptable according to what one has, not according to what one does not have"** (2 Corinthians 8:12). Notice the repetition of the word *one*. Biblical generosity isn't dividing the total church budget by the number of members to determine a flat rate. It's about each "one" giving based on the unique amount that God has given them first.

We have different incomes, don't we? Some of you are so broke you can't afford to pay attention. Some of you are so broke you go to KFC just to lick other people's fingers. (I Googled "you so broke jokes" ☺.) If you're working part time or on a fixed income, you can't give $100/week. And that's okay. But some of you can give that much and more. You're so rich you buy Christmas gifts for your dog. You're so rich you throw food in the garbage every week. You're so rich you have Netflix and Hulu and cable. If that's you, you have the capacity to be an example of First-World generosity. Go big. Give big. You won't regret it.

In the kingdom of God, we are called to give what we can. So, child of God, what can *you* give?

Jesus' trip
Clark Schultz

Growing up, traveling to our cottage took FOREVER. Okay, it only took four hours, but in kid time that was an eternity. Suddenly we would see the exit sign for our cottage and the rundown gas station, and we knew we were close. We weren't there yet, because 20 more minutes of travel would ensue, but we knew we were in the homestretch. We knew the end was in sight, and soon we would be enjoying the north woods and relaxation.

In the first two chapters of Matthew, there's a genealogy of Jesus, the birth of the Savior, the wise men's visit, and the plot to kill young Jesus. But like an exit sign, the word *"Then"* appears in Matthew 3:13, and we can rejoice that the end of the story is near: **"Then Jesus came from Galilee to the Jordan to be baptized by John."**

It was a long trip from the fall in the Garden of Eden and the promise of a Savior to the time when Jesus came. But it was worth the wait.

Jesus came willingly without a, "Oh, Dad, do I have to go and die for those people?" No, he willingly journeyed on the road we could not. He traveled that road perfectly. And because he traveled that road for us, we are as impatient as kids as we wait for our final destination.

Believe him
Matt Ewart

"Lord, to whom shall we go? You have the words of eternal life."—Simon Peter (John 6:68)

Just because you know something doesn't mean you believe it. For example, you can know that eating an entire bag of chips is unhealthy, while at the same time believing that your situation justifies you eating an entire bag of chips. (I might have done that a few times in my life.)

If you have ever been frustrated by a habit or behavior that you were unable to change, there is a good chance that your beliefs were to blame.

If you get to the end of a stressful day and you decide to eat or drink more than you should, you might believe that the way to peace is through what you consume.

If you erupt in anger at your misbehaving kids, it might be because you believe that their behavior reflects your worth.

If you cheat or steal, it might be because you believe that the world is not treating you fairly.

If you try to conform your behaviors without transforming your beliefs, neither will happen. But if you transform your beliefs, your behavior will follow along.

This is where the power of Jesus' words comes in. His words do not just reveal knowledge. They connect with your heart in a way that creates and grows faith.

Your peace comes through him. Your worth was established by his sacrifice. His love is unconditional. Don't just know his words. Believe them.

Don't forget to look up!

Katrina Harrmann

I was several hours into a 25-mile hike with my family when I realized something odd.

I had stopped looking up.

Somewhere between mile 3 and 8, I had become so burdened down by my 40-pound pack that my gaze had become glued to the path to make sure that my feet didn't catch on any of the numerous roots and rocks along the trail. And while this was perhaps a wise choice, I made myself look up into the vaulting cathedral of white pines that were towering above me. It took my breath away.

I've noticed that people often fail to look up.

Making yourself do this often means seeing things in a whole new perspective and perhaps losing a little control of your feet. But many times I've been rewarded—once by a pair of bald eagles that were soaring through the tree-tops above my head.

Why do we stop looking up? We are all guilty of this in our lives when it comes to God. We stop talking to him, fix our eyes on earthly things, and go on autopilot through life, trying to manage everything on our own. To what end? Our good and gracious Father is right here, waiting for us to look up.

If only we looked up more often . . . what beauty we might behold!

"I lift up my eyes to the mountains—where does my help come from? My help comes from the LORD, the Maker of heaven and earth" (Psalm 121:1,2).

Do not be afraid of the future
David Scharf

When it comes to the future, it's like we are wearing blindfolds. We want a sign that everything will be okay. Does God give signs? The answer is yes, but not necessarily in the places we so often look, like everyday occurrences. That is NOT how God gives signs.

Here is God's sign that it will all turn out: **"*This* will be a sign to you: You will find a baby wrapped in cloths and lying in a manger"** (Luke 2:12). Do you want assurance of the future? Then you must look at the past. There *are* times in history when God lifted the blindfold off and said, "Go ahead. Take a peek." He doesn't ask us to read the stars but only to follow the star that leads to the Savior's manger. He doesn't ask us to climb to heaven into his mind but only to climb a hill called Calvary to see God's heart. He rips the blindfold off and says, "This is what I wanted to show you!"

Where do you see yourself in 5 or 10 or 25 years? Right where you are now, led by the Lord who loves you. So do not be afraid. When the blindfold is finally removed in heaven, your Jesus will say, "Look, my child, this is what I was leading you to." For now, be thankful that God has given you a peek from beneath the blindfold!

You are royalty
Ann Jahns

On September 8, 2022, Queen Elizabeth II, Britain's longest-reigning monarch, passed away at the age of 96. The world watched in fascination at the pomp surrounding her funeral proceedings.

Did you watch? If so, did it make you feel . . . average? I'm going to guess you don't live in a palace. When Jesus calls you home, thousands of people won't shuffle respectfully past your casket, and your funeral procession won't stretch for a mile. History books won't record your life.

But guess what? You *are* royalty. Your royal status is higher and deeper and more eternal than any title this world can bestow. **"You are a chosen people, a royal priesthood, a holy nation, God's special possession,"** 1 Peter 2:9 says, **"that you may declare the praises of him who called you out of darkness into his wonderful light."**

You, friend, are a son or daughter of the King of the universe. You have a coveted reserved seat at God's right hand, next to his glorious throne, forever. And what do you need to do to earn that spot? Nothing. You don't have to be born in a palace or trace your family tree back to the Tudors. Through faith, Jesus earned that royal spot for you. You wear a crown that will never perish, spoil, or fade. Tell others! Declare God's praises! They can share in your royal inheritance also. No limits, no quotas.

Unlike Queen Elizabeth's golden crown, which will be incinerated on the day Jesus returns, your royal crown of life will last forever.

A shelter from the storm

Nathan Nass

A story is told of two painters who decided to have a contest: Who could draw a better picture of peace? The first man painted a beautiful mountain scene with a perfectly calm lake in the middle. Can you picture it? He didn't win. The second man painted a steep cliff with a violent waterfall. The sky was ominous. The wind blew across the canvas. Next to the waterfall stood a dead tree. A branch from the dead tree reached out in front of the thundering waterfall. There on that branch of that dead tree sat a little bird perfectly at peace in its little nest. The second painter won. True peace is finding shelter from the storm.

That's the peace that Jesus brings to those who trust in him. The prophet Isaiah wrote, **"You have been a refuge for the poor, a refuge for the needy in their distress, a shelter from the storm and a shade from the heat"** (Isaiah 25:4). True peace isn't having a trouble-free life. True peace is the strength to be at peace even in the middle of the storm, even in the middle of the heat. True peace is found in Jesus.

Jesus is your shelter from the storm. Your sins have been forgiven by Jesus' death on a cross. Jesus' presence means you're never alone. Jesus' promise of heaven robs even death of its power. In every trouble of life, Jesus is your shelter from the storm.

Behave like a creationist
Mike Novotny

If you want to avoid a physical, emotional, and spiritual crash, start at the beginning of the Bible. In the very first half of the very first verse of the very first book of the Bible, there is a blessing that will help you avoid burnout. Genesis 1:1 says, **"In the beginning God created."** Don't miss the implication of that statement.

Creators create the rules for their creation. Why do fish live in the water and die on the land? Because the Creator created them with gills. Why do eagles fly better than beagles? Because the Creator created them with wings instead of four legs. Fish and birds and dogs don't get to decide what they are or how their bodies work. Instead, they follow the rules that their Creator created them with.

That same principle applies to you. Thanks to the insights of biologists and nutritionists, we know more than ever about the rules that our Creator created for our bodies. Just as we know that we weren't made to fly, we also know that we weren't made for skimping on sleep, sitting all day, and eating whatever we want. No, we were made for work/exercise, a balance of the right foods, and significant amounts of rest.

One of the ways that expresses our belief in creation is to behave like a creationist. So the next time you go to the doctor, listen carefully. He or she just might be reminding you of something very spiritual, namely, the details of your Creator's greatest creation.

Born again
Liz Schroeder

I have given birth five times. While I expect neither applause nor gold stars for this feat, I will have you know that each time, the infant contributed NOTHING to the success of this venture. At no point did the doctor holler up the birth canal, "It's all you! You've got this, Baby Schroeder!" If they had, I might have "accidentally" kicked the physician in the face.

It's silly to think that a baby has a to-do list for being born, yet when it comes to being born again, the rule follower in our hearts craves a list.

When Jesus spoke with Nicodemus about being born again to enter the kingdom of God, Nicodemus was confused. As a Pharisee, Nicodemus knew rules and regulations better than anyone. His was the language of "Thou shalt" and "Thou shalt not." But being born again? For a baby, being born is a passive experience. Nicodemus must have wondered how he could put that on a list of rules.

If you are a box checker like Nicodemus (and me), may these words of Paul (a one-time rule follower) put our industrious hearts at rest: **"For it is by grace you have been saved, through faith—and this is not from yourselves, it is the gift of God—not by works, so that no one can boast"** (Ephesians 2:8,9).

The to-do list for your salvation was written by the Father. The Holy Spirit wrote his initials by every blank. The blood of Jesus crosses off every task.

Quit striving to earn the kingdom of God. It is yours.

Eliminate rather than resist
Matt Ewart

Some time ago, I was trying to reduce the amount of time I spent on my phone. But day after day, I found myself sucked into my screen far more than I intended.

A quick investigation revealed that the majority of my time was spent on one particular app. When I made this discovery, I knew that I could keep the app on my phone and try to resist it every day. Or I could just delete the app.

I deleted the app with this thought in mind: why resist in the future what I have the power to eliminate today?

This principle applies to the spiritual warfare that you go through. Each season of life presents its own temptations that try to steal you away from God. Each temptation is designed by the enemy to hit your weak points and challenge your faith. Why resist in the future what you have the power to eliminate today? Here's what it might look like:

Eliminate worry with worship.

Eliminate greed with generosity.

Eliminate apathy with prayer.

Eliminate selfishness with kindness.

When you identify a temptation that is difficult to resist, ask God to give you the strength to eliminate it.

"No temptation has overtaken you except what is common to mankind. And God is faithful; he will not let you be tempted beyond what you can bear. But when you are tempted, he will also provide a way out so that you can endure it" (1 Corinthians 10:13).

Doing right is worth the risk

Mike Novotny

Doing what is right can be risky. Just ask Dr. King, whose home was bombed by his racist neighbors. Or the apostle Paul, who was stoned for telling the nations about Jesus. Or Jesus, who had more enemies than friends despite being the Righteous One of heaven.

Confessing our most embarrassing sins is risky. While the right thing is to bring our darkness into the light, we tend to keep quiet about certain struggles. Confronting other people's sins is risky too. It is good and right to confront sin instead of enabling it, but we fear risking the relationship. Sharing our faith in Christ feels the same, a risk that we often aren't willing to take.

That's why we need to remember a classic verse from the book of Esther. When Esther was afraid to plead for the lives of her Jewish people, her cousin Mordecai urged her, **"And who knows but that you have come to your royal position for such a time as this?"** (Esther 4:14). Mordecai couldn't guarantee a perfect result, but he did believe that God put Esther in her position not to relax in the palace but to do what was righteous.

Our Father did the same for you. He gave you a church so you could be honest with your fellow believers. He gave you the chance to correct someone's wayward behavior. He gave you that neighbor to love and invite to learn of Jesus. I know it makes you nervous. But doing right is worth the risk!

What makes you so great?
Clark Schultz

Kevin Bacon was the star in the original *Footloose* movie. Remember the famous scene where he jumps around and dances in an old warehouse? About a decade ago, Kevin shared a conversation he had with his youngest son who had just seen the movie that had made his dad so famous. The boy asked Kevin about the warehouse scene and how he jumped on the roof and swung from the rafters. Kevin told his son that he didn't do that part. He told his son that a stuntman dressed like him and did the things he couldn't do that were too dangerous.

Next Kevin's son asked him how he spun around the gym bar and landed without falling. Kevin admitted that the stuntman did that too.

Finally, Kevin's son asked him what he actually did in the movie. Kevin replied sheepishly, "I got the glory."

Hmm. Someone else doing the work and giving the glory to someone else. That sounds familiar, doesn't it?

"I have been with you wherever you have gone, and I have cut off all your enemies from before you. Now I will make your name great, like the names of the greatest men on earth" (2 Samuel 7:9). In this verse, God is reminding King David where his greatness came from. Like David of the Bible, what makes you and me great is that Jesus took the punishment we deserved and gave us the glory! He did what we could not and gives us the fame.

Jesus alone makes us great!

Jesus took breaks
Mike Novotny

One of the reasons that Christian people so often burn out is because we believe that we are following the footsteps of Jesus. Jesus worked hard, didn't he? He sacrificed and served so that people could be healed and saved, correct? Shouldn't we do the same, putting everyone else's needs above our own?

Not exactly. Consider these curious verses from Luke chapter 5: **"Crowds of people came to hear him and to be healed of their sicknesses. But Jesus often withdrew to lonely places and prayed"** (verses 15,16). Jesus didn't serve people until every need was met. Instead, he worked and then he withdrew. He served and then he stepped away. He pushed hard and then he pushed pause. In fact, Luke notes that Jesus did that "often." That didn't make Jesus lazy or selfish. It made him a functional creationist who followed the rules that our Creator placed on the human body.

Some personality types, especially highly compassionate people and high-achieving people, struggle to slow down, step away, and say no to other people's requests. The sad result is that they quickly run out of energy and become rather unloving toward the people who know them the best. If that sounds like you (or someone you love), consider the perfect example of Jesus, the sinless Savior who "often withdrew to lonely places." Sometimes taking a day to enjoy your Father's presence and creation is the most Christ-like thing you can do.

Take a break. Be like Jesus.

Life lessons from *The Chosen*
Jan Gompper

My husband and I have been watching the faith-based TV series *The Chosen*. While biblical scholars may take issue with some of the story line and character embellishments, the series does a great job of fleshing out the humanity of Christ's "chosen" disciples.

We, of course, know the disciples weren't perfect, but the series makes their unique personality traits more vivid. The impetuous Peter is also the loving young husband who struggles with being away from his wife. Thomas is a perpetual questioner, which helps us understand why later he needed proof of Christ's resurrection. Judas is continually concerned with the finances of the ministry (**"Where your treasure is, there your heart will be"** [Matthew 6:21]). And Levi is an OCD-ish former tax collector, unsure of himself at every turn but drawn like a magnet to this "new rabbi."

The series also paints a beautiful picture of Jesus' interaction with his ragtag group of followers. He responds to their idiosyncrasies with gentleness, patience, sometimes humor—and always with love.

The portrayals in *The Chosen* remind us of how Jesus called ordinary, flawed people to follow him and be part of his ministry. He does the same today. *We* are now his "chosen," whom he still patiently, humorously, and unconditionally loves. And he now entrusts us (despite *our* flaws and foibles) to carry on his ministry. **"Being confident of this, that he who began a good work in you will carry it on to completion at the day of Christ Jesus"** (Philippians 1:6).

Five minutes later
Jon Enter

If you're old enough, you know exactly where you were when you heard that President Kennedy was assassinated or that Elvis Presley died. We only know of three people who never experienced death, and yet when someone famous dies, we are often shocked.

Which three people never died?

Don't read on until you've tried to answer . . . **"Enoch walked faithfully with God; then he was no more, because God took him away"** (Genesis 5:24). Melchizedek appeared before Abram in Genesis 14; then in Hebrews 7:3, he's described as **"without beginning of days or end of life."** Finally, **"Elijah went up to heaven in a whirlwind"** (2 Kings 2:11).

Besides these three men, everyone before us has passed away. But everyone on earth (past, present, future) has eternity waiting for them. How you live this life impacts the next. What is your focus? Money? Fame? Successful career? Beautiful home? Loving family? These things are blessings, but they distract us from the purpose of this life. Jesus directly revealed life's purpose: **"The one who believes in me will live, even though they die"** (John 11:25). This life is about believing in Jesus so you can live with Jesus in eternity's paradise.

Five minutes after Kennedy or Elvis or the next notable celebrity dies, it doesn't matter that they were famous. Five minutes after they die, it matters—eternally—if they had faith in Jesus.

Do you have faith in Christ? If the answer is yes, then anything else in this life is a blessing.

Faith over feelings
Matt Ewart

Have you ever wanted to have a deep faith in God but you just couldn't shake your feelings of doubt? Maybe you wanted to believe that God was with you, but you felt like nobody was there. Or maybe you wanted to believe he had a purpose for you, but you felt completely unworthy to have one.

It is great when your feelings line up with your faith, but sometimes the two can be in conflict.

One day a man who met Jesus was in the middle of that conflict. He thought Jesus' disciples could help his demon-possessed son, but they couldn't. He felt doubt swirl through his heart to the point where two things were true:

He believed Jesus could help him.

He felt uncertain if Jesus could help him.

Upon recognizing his inner conflict, there was only one thing this desperate dad could blurt out when Jesus arrived: **"I do believe; help me overcome my unbelief!"** (Mark 9:24).

There will be times in life when your feelings conflict with your faith. When that happens, remember which comes first. Let the certainty of your faith speak into the uncertainty of your feelings. Make your feelings subject to the faith that God has grown in you.

Whether you feel it or not, he loves you, is with you, has redeemed you, and has a purpose for you. Subject your feelings to the unchanging object of your faith.

Do you expect good leaders?
Linda Buxa

For the past handful of years, people from both political parties in the U.S. haven't exactly been thrilled with the president. It's as if we are surprised when leaders are selfish or arrogant or make decisions that don't benefit citizens.

The Egyptians (the ones who lived about 3,500 years ago) would probably laugh at us. They lived through nine devastating plagues that tanked their physical health and economy. But Pharaoh didn't back down. Even his officials begged, **"Let the people go, so that they may worship the LORD their God. Do you not yet realize that Egypt is ruined?"** (Exodus 10:7).

Apparently, Pharoah said, "Ruined-shmuined," because there was a tenth devastating plague. The firstborn son of every person and animal in Egypt would die. Even after Moses told him this would happen, Pharaoh—in a jaw-dropping display of arrogance—let his people suffer this pain.

For me, it's a reminder that people often live under self-centered rulers, because rulers are humans and humans are sinful. While we absolutely pray for our leaders because we know their authority has been established by God, we don't expect them to always act on our behalf.

Maybe that makes me a pessimist. But what it really does is make me even more thankful for a heavenly King who sacrificed his firstborn so that we would no longer be subjects but family: **"See what great love the Father has lavished on us, that we should be called children of God! And that is what we are!"** (1 John 3:1).

At wits' end
Andrea Delwiche

Psalm 107 tells four stories of God rescuing people from peril—peril of their own making or peril outside of their control. These stories paint vivid pictures that still apply today.

My favorite is the description of a sea voyage. The trip begins with great expectation, but a ferocious storm comes up: **"They mounted up to the heavens and went down to the depths; in their peril their courage melted away. They reeled and staggered . . . at their wits' end"** (verses 26,27).

Does being at "wits' end" seem relatable? Listen to what the Lord does for his seasick humans: **"He brought them out of their distress. He stilled the storm to a whisper; the waves of the sea were hushed. They were glad when it grew calm, and he guided them to their desired haven"** (verses 28-30).

While on earth, Jesus made time for disoriented women and men. He often helped them clarify their needs and desires by asking different variations on this question: "What is it you want me to do for you?"

Where are you feeling a need for God's Spirit to bring clarity? Jesus still has time to help you through confusion. Imagine Jesus asking you, "What is it you want me to do for you? Or what respite do you desire?" Take some time. What does the Holy Spirit allow to bubble up? Speak your request to Jesus. Come to him with it often. Let him guide you slowly but surely to your desired haven.

Peace be with you.

Balance in a burnout culture

Mike Novotny

Our modern, American, Christian culture sets you up to burn you out. First, a modern culture is disconnected from the natural rhythms that guided most humans for most of history. With our light bulbs and laptops, we can farm past sundown, work double shifts at the hospital, and answer work emails all night. Second, my American culture treasures growth, progress, and profit. Did you know that the average American employee outworks the average German employee by 435 hours per year? (I've never stereotyped the Germans as lazy people!) Finally, our Christian culture emphasizes church attendance, Bible reading, volunteering, evangelism, and good works for the kingdom. No wonder so many of God's kids are progressing from stressed to overwhelmed to flat-out burned out.

If that sounds like your life, it is time to read the *entire* Bible. There are certainly parts that push us to push, such as the scriptural value of hard work and sacrificial love (read 2 Corinthians 11). But there are other parts, equally biblical, that push us to rest. Think of **"be still"** from the Psalms (46:10) or God's insistence to **"remember the Sabbath day"** for his Old Testament people (Exodus 20:8) or Jesus' invitation to come to him and find **"rest for your souls"** (Matthew 11:29).

Good theology requires two truths. In our burnout culture, make sure to remember, believe, and apply both God's love for hard work and his gift of true rest. You are thoroughly biblical when you do.

AUGUST

The fear of the LORD is the beginning of wisdom,
and knowledge of the Holy One is understanding.

PROVERBS 9:10

Pace of change
Matt Ewart

There will be times in life when you want to change some things that will impact other people.

In my life, it usually has to do with changes to the way I do ministry. My church is used to doing things a certain way, but there are times when it is good for us to change.

Maybe in your life you want to change something that would impact the people you work with. Some changes require the approval and support of your family. Other changes could possibly impact your neighbors.

When you feel compelled to change something, it is important to be careful with the speed of change. Change too quickly and you'll lose important people. Change too slowly and there won't be any urgency behind it.

So at what pace should you pursue change? Take a cue from Ephesians 4:2: **"Be patient, bearing with one another in love."**

Putting it all together, you should change as fast as you can be faithful to your calling. Your calling includes your family, your personal health, your spiritual well-being, and the people who follow your lead. Change should not outpace grace.

What's incredible is how Jesus did this. He paused on a busy day to listen to the story of a woman who'd been healed. He slowed down to pray when crowds were acclaiming him. And he ultimately stopped, his body in a tomb for three days, because that is where he changed everything for you and me.

More blessing than you expected

Mike Novotny

In 2021, Florida businessman Bobby Read wanted to purchase some property next to the water tower in the town where he lived. He signed the papers, did the deal for $55,000, and then found out a shocking surprise— somehow, in a detail that neither Bobby nor the city realized—he had purchased the water tower too! He thought he was getting a little land, but he actually got a whole lot more! (Don't worry; he gave it back.)

That's like Jesus. Some think Jesus just gives us heaven. He lived for us and died to take away our sins so one day we might escape the pain of this life and be with God. And that's true! But there's so much more.

Because right now, Jesus gives us a water tower's worth of God's approval, more than enough to quench the thirst of our souls. We are weary and burned out because we want someone to think we're good, so Jesus made us good in the eyes of God. He gave us more approval than our souls can even hold, approval that will never end or run out. Because of Jesus, God will always be happy with his people. Always.

"Now to him who is able to do immeasurably more than all we ask or imagine, according to his power that is at work within us, to him be glory in the church and in Christ Jesus throughout all generations, for ever and ever! Amen" (Ephesians 3:20,21). Jesus gives you more than just heaven, immeasurably more. What a Savior!

Morning prayer and praise
Andrea Delwiche

"My heart, O God, is steadfast; I will sing and make music with all my soul. Awake, harp and lyre! I will awaken the dawn. I will praise you, Lord, among the nations; I will sing of you among the peoples" (Psalm 108:1-3).

As I mull over these words, a picture of this psalm writer's routine of early morning praise emerges. There are troubles to deal with, decisions to be made, but first, it's time to sit with the Lord in the early morning, waking with the daylight. And then, slowly prayer and praise rise from this sleepy person.

Imagine the many people through the centuries who have used the Psalms as prayer, sitting in the near dark as they begin their morning prayer practice: "My heart is steadfast, Lord."

These opening words are both prayer and reminder. "I am tired. I am worried, but I am here, Lord, trying to keep the eyes of my heart fixed on you, even as I struggle with sleepiness or doubts or worries."

Beginning the day by praising God focuses our attention. As we think of specific ways to give glory to God, we can begin to concentrate. It gives glory where glory is due. It sets our troubles in their proper framework—priming us to remember God's past goodness. Through remembrance, we can begin to trust that the One who was faithful in the past will meet us in our present need.

How could the world be changed by God's love if praise-filled prayer rose like chimney smoke from each of our homes each day?

Stay focused
Linda Buxa

While Jesus was busy going through towns and teaching people, some Pharisees gave him some bad news: he should leave because Herod wanted to kill him. Jesus replied, **"Go tell that fox, 'I will keep on driving out demons and healing people today and tomorrow, and on the third day I will reach my goal.' In any case, I must press on today and tomorrow and the next day—for surely no prophet can die outside Jerusalem!"** (Luke 13:32,33).

I know this was a serious conversation about a serious topic, but picturing it also makes me chuckle. My Jesus heard that a Jewish king wanted him dead, and he basically dismissed it: "Ah, I'll pass. I don't have time for that. I'm very busy traveling and healing."

Jesus knew for sure that ultimately he would go to Jerusalem and be killed. After all, he came to earth to die for us, and nothing was going to stop that goal. But he had work to do until then, and nothing was going to get in the way.

We know we will die too, at a time that only God knows. Until then, we have a purpose that requires our full focus: **"This is to my Father's glory, that you bear much fruit, showing yourselves to be my disciples"** (John 15:8).

Each day as we face distractions, temptations, and struggles, we remind ourselves that we must press on today and tomorrow and the next day—until God calls us home.

Stand your ground
Jan Gompper

When my oldest niece was about three years old, she had been naughty one morning during her preschool Sunday school class. When the teacher reprimanded her for her behavior, my niece stood her ground and said, "Don't you know Jesus died for our sins?!"

Her retort may have sounded a little flippant, but she clearly was not going to be weighed down by guilt for her wrongdoing.

Can you say the same? Are you hanging on to guilt over sins you've committed? Satan wants nothing more than to keep you wallowing there, because guilt leads to despair. Despair ultimately leads to an eternity with him.

But God promises, **"Those who belong to Christ Jesus are no longer under God's judgment. Because of what Christ Jesus has done, you are free"** (Romans 8:1,2 NIRV).

Satan does not give up easily, however. He may stir up memories of past sins in an effort to make you feel like God has not forgotten those sins either. But remember, Satan is **"the father of lies"** (John 8:44 NIRV).

Once you have acknowledged your sin and repented of it, you can forget about it—permanently—because God has: **"I will forgive their evil ways. I *will not remember their sins anymore"*** (Hebrews 8:12 NIRV).

So the next time Satan starts putting his guilt trip on you, stand your ground and say, "Don't you know Jesus died for my sins?!"

Just an average Christian
Nathan Nass

Maybe you don't feel very special. Average at best. Maybe you don't feel like you have any remarkable talents. No impressive qualities. You're just a regular human being. Maybe no miracles ever seem to be part of your life. Just day after day of the same thing over and over again.

I wonder if John the Baptist felt the same way. Do you know how the people of Israel described him? **"John never performed a sign . . ."** (John 10:41). So much for a great prophet, right? John the Baptist never did any miracles. Not a single one. Nothing fancy. Nothing special.

But do you know what Jesus said about John the Baptist? **"Truly I tell you, among those born of women there has not risen anyone greater than John the Baptist"** (Matthew 11:11). What? He didn't do any miracles. What made him so special? Here's the full description people had of John: **"Though John never performed a sign, all that John said about this man was true"** (John 10:41). John just pointed people to Jesus.

Maybe it's okay not to be very special, because Jesus is the One who's truly special. Maybe it's okay not to have remarkable talents, because Jesus is the One who forgives and loves and saves us. Maybe life is meant to be day after day of living out God's calling for you, while finding subtle ways to point people to Jesus. Jesus' grace makes just average Christians into the most special people around.

The surprising schedule of Jesus Christ
Mike Novotny

I reached out to a seminary professor to ask about Jesus' schedule. I had been pondering the issue of work and rest in the Bible and was curious about the calendar that God created for his people in the days of Moses.

The professor, with teaching experience in the Old Testament, replied, "An observant Jew in Jesus' day could have had off 52 Sabbaths, 1 day for Purim, 8 days for [Passover], 2 days for Pentecost, 2 days for Rosh Hashanah, 1 day for Yom Kippur, 9 days for [Feast of Tabernacles]. Jewish men were supposed to show up in Jerusalem for Passover, Pentecost, and Tabernacles, and it would have taken most of them some time to get there. Then, if you were a farmer, the land was supposed to lie fallow one year in seven. . . . Also, Jesus' time off was time *off*—not time to cram full of activities, digital distractions, and the NFL."

Interesting, isn't it? While God doesn't command us to follow the same calendar and festivals (Colossians 2:16), Jesus' schedule does make us think about what it means to be hardworking and faithful. If Jesus **"did not sin"** (Hebrews 4:15), then taking time away from work is not sinful. When Jesus and his stepdad, Joseph, left their tools in Nazareth and traveled to Jerusalem, they were being obedient to God, not lazy or rebellious against him.

Consider the schedule of Jesus and compare it to your own. And please remember—God isn't mad if you act like Jesus.

God's wrecking ball
Liz Schroeder

I am not the most mechanically inclined, but I love assembling furniture. Give me one of those sleek Scandinavian kits and an afternoon, and it is so satisfying to see the final product.

My aptitude is fertile ground for hubris, however. "I saw the floor model, so I don't need the instruction manual. I've got this!"

Inevitably, the front panels wind up facing the rear, and the cabinet doors are hung upside down. When I finally surrender and crack open the instructions, I have to demolish everything I have so carefully—but incorrectly—built.

This is what happened to the kings of Judah. They had cast aside God's instruction manual for years. By the time King Josiah found it, shrines, altars, and high places dedicated to false gods had been built all over the country. Josiah's demolition crew had their work cut out for them as they systematically desecrated all the sites for idol worship.

"Furthermore, Josiah got rid of the mediums and spiritists, the household gods, the idols and all the other detestable things seen in Judah and Jerusalem. This he did to fulfill the requirements of the law written in the book that Hilkiah the priest had discovered in the temple of the Lord" (2 Kings 23:24).

When we say we are broken before the Lord, this is what it means: we let God smash what our pride has built in order that he might construct a new life in us. Yes, it's painful, but the eternal product is more than satisfying— it's heavenly.

Bloom where you're planted

Katrina Harrmann

Last summer I was working outside when I noticed little green seedlings at the edge of my compost bin. On a whim, I left the tiny plants alone, since they didn't take up much space in my huge bin.

A few weeks later, some sizable plants had grown. Now I was curious what they *were*, so I left them alone again to see what what happen.

Soon, little vines had twisted into a lush green dome that completely covered my compost bin. They had even climbed halfway up a nearby telephone pole!

In July, we suffered one of the worst hailstorms in memory. My mystery plant took a beating (and many of my other garden plants were killed), but shockingly, my tough little "garbage" vine survived. It soon began producing multiple sizes and shapes of miniature, colorful gourds.

Sometimes we're put in weird places and expected to bloom. We might not feel like we can thrive where we're planted, but God always has a plan, and he'll never leave us.

Sometimes, like my mystery plant, we even find to our bafflement that we were made **"for such a time as this"** (Esther 4:14) and thrive despite our odd surroundings.

So the next time you feel like a fish out of water, think of the little gourd plant that grew beyond expectation and remember—God can do amazing things in your life, no matter where you are!

"The Lord is my helper; I will not be afraid. What can mere mortals do to me?" (Hebrews 13:6).

Finish the race
Jon Enter

Have you heard of a 0K (not OK, but zero kilometers)? One might be held at a minor league stadium. You walk the length of the first row of seats. There's a "hydration station" with microbrews in each section. When you cross the finish line (the end of the first row), you get a hot dog and a ticket to a baseball game. Want to join me?

In 2 Timothy, Paul wrote his last letter during his last days on earth. Looking over his years of serving Christ, Paul wrote, **"I have finished the race, I have kept the faith"** (4:7). Paul could've listed cities he visited as a missionary or the people he told about Christ. He didn't. Paul simply celebrated that he finished the race of faith.

In every 5K or marathon, only one runner wins. The race of faith is different. It doesn't matter if you sprint through life as a missionary to faraway places or slowly walk through life in faith. It matters that you finish. It doesn't matter if you get lost for a time or fall on your face. It matters if you finish. It doesn't even matter when you started. The thief on the cross next to Jesus received the same heaven as Paul. Five minutes after you die, it doesn't matter what you accomplished on earth; it matters if you had faith in Christ.

Too often we compare our Christian lives to others' lives. Some are sprinters. Let them sprint, and cheer them on. Simply be faithful. Keep moving forward in your faith. Keep trusting. God will lead you across the finish line!

Give your anger to God
Andrea Delwiche

"My God, don't turn a deaf ear to my hallelujah prayer. Liars are pouring out invective on me. . . . Give him a short life. . . . Make orphans of his children. . . . Turn his children into begging street urchins. . . . Since he loved cursing so much, let curses rain down. . . . Oh help me, GOD, my God, save me through your wonderful love; Then they'll know that your hand is in this, that you, GOD, have been at work" (Psalm 109, selected verses MSG).

These curses written by David don't seem to parallel Christ's words: **"Love your enemies and pray for those who persecute you"** (Matthew 5:44).

But psalms are not pious platitudes. They give us heart-words to use when our own words fail. They are honest even if not righteous. David calls on God and details his hurt and anger. He curses his enemies and appeals to God's justice. He pours out outrage on *God's* behalf. He places himself in God's hand.

Human anger does not surprise God. It's safe to give him our anger, even if it's vengeful. If we think we need to clean ourselves up to come to God, we are forgetting that God knows the contents of our hearts and has compassion and love for us.

Our Great Physician welcomes the opportunity to help us process and heal our pain. From the flames of anger, God picks the hot coals of the true hurts and longings. God gives forgiveness, justice, and serenity to those who stand before him with open hands and hearts.

Prayer over priorities
Matt Ewart

Right now, whether you wrote it down or not, you have a list of priorities for this next day. There are certain things that you will make sure to do. Where does prayer fit in with your priorities?

It's all too easy to neglect prayer as you address the other priorities in daily life. I often find myself replacing prayer time with busyness. (And skipping prayer often increases our busyness.) It is common for Christians to feel guilty about the way they practice (or don't practice) prayer.

But God doesn't want guilt to be your motivation to pray. He invites you to pray because of what prayer does for you. It helps you visualize the presence of a gracious God who so wanted to be in your life that his Son laid down his life for you.

In case you're looking for some encouragement, James shows a different way to think about prioritizing prayer: **"Is anyone among you in trouble? Let them pray. Is anyone happy? Let them sing songs of praise. Is anyone among you sick? Let them call the elders of the church to pray over them and anoint them with oil in the name of the Lord"** (James 5:13,14).

According to James, prayer isn't just another thing to do. Prayer is the means by which everything is done. Whether you are suffering, celebrating, or sick, any occasion is an occasion to pray.

Self-discipline training 101

Jan Gompper

Do you have a significant goal/dream you hope to accomplish in your life? I do. Yet days, weeks, and years have gone by, and I still haven't taken any meaningful steps toward accomplishing my goal. Part of my problem is that I often get distracted by or caught up in too many other things in my life that push my goal to the back burner. Other times, I suffer from a little voice in my head that says, "That's just a pipe dream. You'll never be able to really accomplish that."

Confession . . . my spiritual life is often hindered by these two obstacles as well. I tell myself over and over that I'm going to spend more time in God's Word each day. But many days I get distracted by or caught up in things that seem more important at the time, or, if I'm honest, by something that just seems more appealing. And sometimes Satan whispers in my ear, "You'll never be able to be the Christian you want to be."

Self-discipline is hard. It's even harder when we think we can achieve it on our own. But God promises, **"No discipline seems pleasant at the time, but painful. Later on, however, it produces a harvest of righteousness and peace for those who have been trained by it"** (Hebrews 12:11).

Practicing self-discipline trains us to be *more* self-disciplined. Best of all, we have an amazing coach: **"For the Spirit God gave us does not make us timid, but gives us power, love and self-discipline"** (2 Timothy 1:7).

Immortal until God's time
Nathan Nass

I get anxious about the future. Do you? I worry about all the things that could happen to me or my loved ones. Do you? There's so much we don't know. There's so much we don't control.

So I was encouraged by what an old pastor used to say: "I am immortal until my work is finished." Do you know what he meant? You cannot die until God's work for you is complete. I cannot die until God's purpose for my life has been fulfilled. You and I are immortal until God's time.

That isn't just an old pastor's saying. It's the truth from God's Word: **"All the days ordained for me were written in your book before one of them came to be"** (Psalm 139:16). Even before we were born, our loving God had already written down in his book how each of our days was going to go.

That doesn't mean life will be easy. That doesn't mean you'll live to a ripe, old age. Life might be hard. It might be shorter than you expect. You might face hunger or sickness or accident or war. But through it all, you can be confident of this: no one can change what God has ordained for you.

Even when that last day comes, you still won't have to worry. Because through Jesus, your last day is really just your first day of immortality in heaven. So live with confidence! You're immortal.

Do not be afraid of anything
David Scharf

Peace means there is no missing piece in life. Does that describe your life? Finish this sentence: "If I only had _____, then I'd have peace." Some never find it because they miss the point of this life.

Thrilled with their first successful flight in December 1903, the Wright brothers sent a telegram to their sister. "We have actually flown 120 feet. Will be home for Christmas," it read. Their sister took it to the local newspaper. "That's nice," said the editor. "The boys will be home for Christmas." You see the point? Don't miss the real news.

The angels announced it two thousand years ago: **"Do not be afraid. . . . Today in the town of David a Savior has been born to you. . . . Glory to God in the highest heaven, and on earth** *peace"* (Luke 2:10,11,14). The message didn't just say that a Savior had been born, but it included the most important words, *"to you."*

Only God could ever deliver a present to the entire world on one night. He delivered the missing piece, spelled p-e-a-c-e. Everything is the way it should be now. God doesn't provide the *how, why,* or *what.* God gives you better. He provides the *Who.* Jesus, the One wrapped in cloths at his birth, would also be wrapped in cloths at his death after he suffered the cross for us and was laid in a tomb. It is why he came. He came to give us the missing peace. So do not be afraid of anything!

Schedule with the gospel
Mike Novotny

One of the reasons that so many Christians are stressed, overwhelmed, and weary is because we pack our schedules with too many things. And one of the reasons that we pack our schedules with too many things is because we crave people's approval.

Isn't that true? We say yes to that invitation, that party, that opportunity, that ask, that sign-up sheet, that event, that promotion, that travel team, that tournament, etc. because we don't want to disappoint people. We want to be there for them, to help them out, and to get their approval. While not bad in itself, that attitude can lead us to overextending ourselves and ignoring the bodies that God has entrusted to us, especially their frequent need for sleep and rest.

But how do you cut back knowing that some will be disappointed in you? You schedule with the gospel. You remember that you have God's approval through the death and resurrection of his Son, a Father who takes **"great delight in you"** and **"will rejoice over you with singing"** (Zephaniah 3:17). Meditate on God's face shining upon you because of Christ. Let his approval fill up your heart and satisfy your soul.

That will enable you to schedule your own sanity, saying yes to the most important things and no to most other things. Not everyone will approve of your choices, but Jesus will give you all the heavenly approval you truly need.

Be an influencer
Ann Jahns

The other day I received an email from a local shoe store encouraging me to click on a link to see how social media "influencers" are wearing a particular pair of trendy boots. Let's just say as I am solidly into my 50s, these boots would look ridiculous on me. My husband would check for signs of a midlife crisis.

Who influences you? Celebrities or sports stars or pretty people on social media? In contrast, let's look at Jesus. The prophet Isaiah says, **"He had no beauty or majesty to attract us to him, nothing in his appearance that we should desire him"** (53:2). It sounds like Jesus was the kind of guy you could pass on the street without giving him a second glance. Can you imagine the architect and Lord of the universe looking like any other 30-something guy of the day but without a permanent roof over his head or a penny to his name?

But what an influence he had. The Son of God started a movement that began as a small spark in a corner of the world, and that spark has grown and spread into a roaring blaze across time and space. It is estimated that there are about two billion professing Christians among the more than seven billion people in our world. Talk about an eternal influence!

You can be an influencer too. You can influence your small corner of the world. You can faithfully and persistently share the message of the gospel in your home, workplace, and neighborhood, one relationship and conversation at a time.

The path to burnout
Mike Novotny

People burn out by following a predictable path. First, we compromise. We know enough about the human body to realize what we should do, but we cheat the system. "I know they say I should sleep for x hours, but I'm going to . . . I know my doctor says to slow down, but I've made it this far working this hard."

Second, we compensate. We weren't created for so little sleep, so we compensate with a pot of coffee or a six-pack of Diet Coke. We weren't created for so much work, so much stress, so little rest, so we unwind with a few beers or a couple of pills. We know we are always stressed, so we "fix it" by taking a vacation.

Third, we crash. We fall apart. We cry. We lose our drive, our desire, our smile. We grow numb, cynical, bitter, robotic, uninterested. We stop producing the fruit of patience, gentleness, and joy. We need serious help.

Do you see yourself somewhere on that path? It's not too late to remember that the Father created you, his Son saved you, and his Spirit lives within you. Notice to whom Jesus directs this invitation: **"Come to me, all you who are weary and burdened, and I will give you rest"** (Matthew 11:28). All who are weary can find rest in Jesus. No matter who you are or where you are or what pace you have pushed, that includes you. So come to Jesus and find rest for both body and soul.

Take your job seriously
Linda Buxa

Two thousand years ago, Peter, one of Jesus' apostles, was put in prison, and 16 guards were charged with keeping him there, some literally chained to him. Miraculously, an angel came and set Peter free in the middle of the night. **"In the morning, there was no small commotion among the soldiers as to what had become of Peter. After Herod had a thorough search made for him and did not find him, he cross-examined the guards and ordered that they be executed"** (Acts 12:18,19).

Yikes! If you lost a prisoner, you lost your life.

Well, it turns out that I am a guard—and the stakes are just as high. (If you believe in Jesus, you're a guard too.) Another apostle named Paul wrote to a young man named Timothy: **"What you heard from me, keep as the pattern of sound teaching, with faith and love in Christ Jesus. *Guard* the good deposit that was entrusted to you—*guard* it with the help of the Holy Spirit who lives in us"** (2 Timothy 1:13,14).

If you know the Bible (even a little bit) guard what you've been taught. If you believe that Jesus loves you so much that he came on a rescue mission to free you from Satan's prison, guard it. With the guidance of the Holy Spirit, stay chained to the Savior. Satan, with his sick sense of joy, would be despicably happy to rechain you to himself. And—yikes—if you lose your faith, you lose your eternal life.

So guard it!

Rest before work
Matt Ewart

"For in six days the Lᴏʀᴅ made the heavens and the earth, the sea, and all that is in them, but he rested on the seventh day" (Exodus 20:11).

On day six of creation, God created Adam and Eve. There was evening and there was morning, and then the seventh day came—the day that God set aside for rest.

As you put that together, think about this from Adam and Eve's perspective. Their first full day in this creation was spent resting. But resting from what?

Normally rest is something we do at the end of an activity. For me, the first thing that comes to mind is when I cut my lawn. It takes several hours to pick up after my dog, run the mower, trim along the fence, and put everything away. But when it is done, it feels great to rest and admire the job well done.

God offers you another kind of rest. Adam and Eve rested before they had done any work because they were able to admire God's good work. Their work would have a time and a place. But the most important thing on that seventh day was to adore God and admire his work.

Try that out this week. Don't save rest as the last thing you do. Begin with rest. Adore your Savior and admire his work of salvation. You already have his love and approval even before you've done a single thing.

Our Life Preserver
Clark Schultz

On a recent trip, I found myself laughing at the "joys" of flying. First there were the lines that forced people to zigzag through some elastic bands while hauling their carry-ons. And what is the definition of a carry-on? While placing my backpack under my seat, a lady jammed what looked like a small sofa into the overhead bin.

Then a curtain was drawn between the first-class passengers and the folks in back. Next the stewardess went over the flight safety instructions. She was telling us how to be safe, but around me folks were too busy sleeping and paying no attention to what she said.

Life is a series of zigzags, isn't it? You think you know where you are going, and then Bam!—bad health, death of a loved one, or a breakup turns you in the other direction. When these times occur, we often try to cram things into our overhead bins that aren't the right fit: pills, porn, or booze.

Sin separates us, like a curtain, from God, but just as the curtain in the temple was torn apart when Jesus died, now no curtain separates us from God. Christ gives us the safety manual—his life, death, and resurrection. Instead of being distracted by this life, we can focus and listen to his words and will for us. Emergency or not, we have a Life Preserver who is always with us. Jesus said, **"I am the way and the truth and the life. No one comes to the Father except through me"** (John 14:6).

No fear
Nathan Nass

I read a story about a man who lived through World War II in England. Every night air-raid sirens blared and enemy bombers dropped bombs. Every day news came of more casualties. There was so much death. So much uncertainty. So much fear.

So he found himself going back again and again to one verse from the Bible: **"They will have no fear of bad news; their hearts are steadfast, trusting in the Lord"** (Psalm 112:7). Even in the middle of that war, that man didn't need to be afraid because above all the chaos was "the Lord."

That didn't mean everything was going to go great. That didn't mean that death and heartache and pain wouldn't strike that man's family. But it meant that his loving, all-powerful God was in perfect control, even in the middle of all that carnage. His heart could be steadfast, trusting in the Lord.

Dear friend, you can live with that same attitude. The good news of the Bible is that Jesus is your Savior. He died to forgive every one of your sins. He has prepared a place for you to live forever in heaven through faith in him. He controls every moment of every day of your life.

That good news of Jesus means that no matter what carnage and chaos surrounds you, you don't have to be afraid of bad news. May your heart be steadfast, always trusting in the Lord.

Jesus will get you to the finish
Mike Novotny

Years ago I made the foolish decision to try to run a marathon way faster than I was trained to run. For the final ten miles of the race, I shuffled and groaned, unsure if I would make it to the finish.

When I came to a water stop in front of a local news station, a local weatherman named Bill spotted me. I must have looked like the walking dead because he grabbed a cup of water and walked toward me. Putting an arm around my shoulder, he handed me the drink and encouraged me not to give up but instead to keep running my race. Somehow I did. I made it to the finish line and got my fancy marathon medal.

Jesus is like that weatherman. You may have run a foolish race in your life, but Jesus is coming at you with compassion today. You may have done foolish things with your body, working too much or working out too little, but Jesus gave his body for your forgiveness. You may be burned out, but he is still offering you his blessing—his loving arm around your shoulder, his words of forgiveness for your tired soul, his Spirit to get you to the finish line. God is reaching out to his cramping, crashing kids with love, with grace, with forgiveness for every step where we shouldn't have sprinted.

Drink in these refreshing words from Jesus: **"Come to me, all you who are weary and burdened, and I will give you rest"** (Matthew 11:28).

Not just a pep talk
David Scharf

FDR famously said, "The only thing we have to fear is fear itself." Inspiring words! But they're just words, a pep talk. Is a pep talk the best someone can offer you to calm your fears today? God says, **"Do not fear, for I am with you. . . . I will strengthen you and help you; I will uphold you with my righteous right hand"** (Isaiah 41:10).

God promises to uphold you with his hand. That hand flung the stars into the sky and carved out the ocean beds. For love's sake, God let that hand become a human hand so that nails could be pounded into it and he could die on a cross for you. But the hand that upholds you also grabbed the doorway of his tomb as he stepped out of the grave. And that hand is still raised in blessing since he ascended into heaven.

Why does God say, "Do not fear"? Not because he has taken away every frightening thing but because he wishes to give you strength to bear whatever may come. The strength to say, "Your will be done" every day. The strength to call "good" whatever comes from his hand. The strength to know that God has the strength to do even more than we ask or imagine . . . and will. God doesn't say, "Don't be afraid; you can do it." Instead your God says, "Do not fear; I am with you." This is not just a pep talk.

Avocados aren't the answer
Nathan Nass

Avocados aren't the answer to sin. I never thought I'd have to say that. One of the "hit" commercials from a recent Super Bowl showed Adam and Eve in the Garden of Eden, right after Eve had eaten the forbidden fruit. The sky was dark. The world was falling apart. Until, thankfully, a squirrel showed up with an avocado. "Try this," he said. "They make everything better!" Thanks to avocados, the world became perfect again.

So I'm going to say it again: avocados aren't the answer to sin. Making jokes about sin isn't the answer to sin either. Nor is mocking the Bible. What a society we live in! We care more about creating funny commercials than about the wrath of God. If we think avocados can save the world, if we think the story of Adam and Eve is a stupid myth to laugh at, we'll be surprised one day when we face God. Sin is serious, and avocados aren't the answer to sin.

But God has provided the answer to sin: **"The blood of Jesus, his Son, purifies us from all sin"** (1 John 1:7). It took the life and death—the blood—of Jesus to pay for Adam's sin and Eve's sin and your sin and my sin. Through the cross of Jesus, you are forgiven! As our society jokes about sin, take your sin seriously. Repent of your sin each day. And remember this beautiful truth: "The blood of Jesus, his Son, purifies us from all sin."

Reckless love—Really?

Liz Schroeder

I was wrong.

Quite possibly, those are the three hardest words to say in the English language. Yet I couldn't be happier to say them.

For years, I have consoled myself and others with the incomplete theology that God doesn't waste anything. When a friend is suffering or a period of waiting feels interminable or the light at the end of the tunnel has burned out, I have assured them, "God doesn't waste a thing."

While I believe he does not waste a moment of his children's suffering, I do believe he "wastes" the most important thing of all: his grace.

Are you okay with the idea that God is wasteful? He lavishes his grace on a world that rejects him. Christ died for all sinners—not just for the ones who believe in him. A song with 166 million views on YouTube describes this kind of love as overwhelming, never ending, and reckless.

Today I praise God for his extravagant love that would pay for the sins of the entire world, even though many reject his payment. We don't deserve his reckless love.

I did not earn the right to be called his child: **"What great love the Father has lavished on us, that we should be called children of God! And that is what we are!"** (1 John 3:1).

God has *lavished* his love on the world: heaped, poured, covered, smothered, dripping down, and overflowing.

I was wrong. Isn't that great?

Run (don't sprint) your race

Mike Novotny

About a decade ago, I tried to qualify for the Boston Marathon. There was just one problem—I wasn't qualified to qualify for the Boston Marathon. I hadn't trained nearly enough, but for some odd reason, as I stood at the start line, I told myself, "I'm qualifying for Boston. Mike, just run!" So I found the pacesetter for my qualifying time, and when the gun fired, I ran with him for 16 miles! Not bad, huh?

Unless you remember that a marathon is 26.2 miles long! At mile 16, I crashed hard. I went from gazelle strides to a grandma after double hip surgery. For the next 10 miles, I stumbled and cramped and cried my way home. What happened? I wasn't honest about the way my body was created to work.

Are you? Psalm 139:13 reminds us that God **"knit me together in my mother's womb."** One of the specific ways that God knit you together, created and designed you, was for a sustainable pace, a balance of work and rest. He made your brain and your heart and your blood vessels capable of tremendous work, but not too much.

Some people walk through life lazy and irresponsible. Others sprint like I did during that foolish race, proudly assuming that they won't crash. A select few find a sustainable pace, pushing hard during unique seasons and taking guilt-free seasons of rest.

What kind of person are you? How might God be calling you to run (not walk, not sprint) the race of faith?

The blessing of routine
Katrina Harrmann

As a kid, I *loved* this time of year: BACK TO SCHOOL! By the end of August, I was always ready to leap into a new school year with a new teacher, brand-new books, and fresh supplies. By Labor Day, 12 weeks of sweltering summer had driven me to intense boredom, and I looked forward to seeing my friends again and getting back into old routines.

Routine is funny like that. When we're in the middle of it, we might roll our eyes and think it's anything but pleasant—such as getting up early every morning, showering, rushing through breakfast, and heading off to work. That's a routine many of us *think* we'd love to ditch. And yet, often when folks retire, they find to their enormous surprise that the "drudgery" of routine is what they miss most of all.

So the next time you think that something is just a boring routine, take a closer look. It might be a blessing you've taken for granted.

And the opportunity to start NEW routines is often a similar blessing. Even if you don't have kids heading back to school—consider picking up a new routine. Maybe read Scripture for 15 minutes every morning. Or enjoy some prayer time to start your day.

"Whatever you do, work at it with all your heart, as working for the Lord, not for human masters, since you know that you will receive an inheritance from the Lord as a reward. It is the Lord Christ you are serving" (Colossians 3:23,24).

Evangelism step 1: Pray

Mike Novotny

A few months ago, we sent out a survey to the members of our church about their spiritual habits. What did they rank as dead last on their lists? Evangelism. Compared to going to church or reading the Bible, sharing their faith was far, far behind.

You too? I think we fear talking about faith because we can't predict how people will react. Will they be interested or offended? Will they ask questions or think we're pushy? As the evangelistic efforts of Jesus and the first Christians prove, not everyone loves to hear the truth. So how do you overcome the fear of sharing your faith?

Paul has an idea: **"Devote yourselves to prayer, being watchful and thankful. And pray for us, too, that God may open a door for our message, so that we may proclaim the mystery of Christ, for which I am in chains. Pray that I may proclaim it clearly, as I should"** (Colossians 4:2-4). Did you catch the repetition? "Prayer . . . pray . . . pray." Sharing Jesus with them starts with talking to Jesus about them.

Maybe the door to talking about Jesus with your friend seems closed. It might be. If so, pray that God "may open a door for our message" so that your friend has an open mind about spiritual things. Write down a few names on a note card and stick it in your car cupholder, a reminder to pray for those who need the greatest news in the universe.

Evangelism isn't easy, so bring God into the process. Pray. And pray some more.

Evangelism step 2: Love
Mike Novotny

When you hear an unexpected knock on your door and peek out the window, is your attitude affected by whose face you see? For sure. You'll open the door with a smile if it's your best friend, but you'll crack open the door with a scowl if it's a stranger with a clipboard.

That's an important lesson about evangelism. The apostle Paul described conversations about Jesus as "open doors" (Colossians 4:3), a visual he reinforced a few verses later when he said, **"Be wise in the way you act toward outsiders; make the most of every opportunity"** (verse 5). When you are wise in the way you act toward non-Christian friends and leverage your opportunities to love and serve them, doors open that would otherwise be closed.

What would that look like for you? Maybe you'd ask how your neighbor was doing and really listen to his answer. Maybe you'd follow up with a text, "Thanks for being real about your struggles the other day. I was praying for your strength this morning." Maybe you'd notice someone going through a huge transition—the new kid at school, the new woman at work, the new widow, the new parents—and you'd let him sit with you at lunch or introduce her to your work friends or take her out for coffee or invite him to watch the game. When you're trying to love someone well, you'll see the opportunities. Make the most of them.

Who knows? God might open a door to share the best news of all.

Evangelism step 3: Say

Mike Novotny

If you've followed the apostle Paul's plan for evangelism, you've prayed that **"God may open a door for our message"** and tried to **"make the most of every opportunity"** to love your non-Christian friends (Colossians 4:3,5). But private prayers and acts of love cannot create Christian faith in a person's heart. Only the message can. No wonder Paul, in that same context, wrote, **"Pray that I may proclaim** [the message] **clearly"** (verse 4). Proclaim it. Share it. Say it.

But what will you say? There's no script, but the Holy Spirit will help you, so don't be scared. Maybe you "say" your story. "I haven't been a perfect person. Pretty far from perfect, to be honest. But Jesus says he forgives me, that he won't leave me. That's why I believe in him."

Maybe you "say" something about your church. "It's really helped me, and I'd love for you to join me. It's not as scary as you think. Can I pick you up some Sunday?"

Maybe you "say" an answer to their question. "Sounds like you're confused why God let that happen. I've felt that way too. We actually just talked about that at church, and I learned . . . Could I send you a link to that message?"

Don't let the devil deceive you. There is no one better equipped to share Jesus with your closest friends and family than you. They know you. They trust you. They are likely to listen to you. So pray first, love next, and say the name of the One who saved your soul!

SEPTEMBER

Finally, brothers and sisters, whatever is true,
whatever is noble, whatever is right, whatever is pure,
whatever is lovely, whatever is admirable—
if anything is excellent or praiseworthy—
think about such things.

PHILIPPIANS 4:8

No failed promises
David Scharf

God always keeps his promises. That's easy to say but sometimes hard for us to believe. God promised to lead the Israelites from Egypt into the Promised Land. But then Pharaoh trapped them against the Red Sea. It's much harder to believe God's promises when we see the Red Sea of challenges standing between the Promised Land and us.

God promises, **"Do not be afraid. . . . The LORD will fight for you; you need only be still"** (Exodus 14:13,14). Who fights for you? The Lord! The One who created the universe and sustains all things with his mighty hand, who destroyed the world with a flood, who sent ten miraculous plagues on Egypt to free his people, who sent his Son to save this world. That puts things in perspective. With that résumé, which promise is impossible for God to keep?

Are you worried about your forgiveness and your ability to forgive? You need only be still. Look at the cross and see the Lord fight to the death for you. Are you worried about things that could rob you of life: sickness and accidents? You need only be still. Look at the empty tomb, and see the Lord defeat death for you. Are you worried about having enough? You need only be still and see Jesus' ascended hands raised in blessing over you. In all those ways, you hear the gentle whisper of your Savior-God: "Do not be afraid. I will fight for you. You need only be still."

Show them grace
Matt Ewart

If you had one message to share with the youngest generation, what would you want to tell them?

There are the universal truths that are important to pass along, such as "don't worry so much about what other people think about you."

There are also some nuggets of wisdom that have been forged from your personal life experiences. There were things that you had to overcome the hard way, and it would be wonderful to help the younger generation avoid that.

But here's something to pause and consider. If all we can teach the next generation is what we got right, then they will have very little to learn. If all we can show the next generation is how to match our performance, then they will have very little to live up to.

There's a better target to aim for. The elderly apostle Paul said this to a young pastor named Timothy: **"But for that very reason I was shown mercy so that in me, the worst of sinners, Christ Jesus might display his immense patience as an example for those who would believe in him and receive eternal life"** (1 Timothy 1:16).

Paul had lived out plenty of things that Timothy could learn from, but the one thing Paul showed more than anything else was what grace looks like.

That is true of us too. If we can show future generations what it looks like to receive and give God's grace, they will have everything they need.

Your walking stick
Nathan Nass

Do you ever use a walking stick? I never did. My own two feet are good enough, right? Until I hiked in the Narrows. The Narrows is a rushing creek that flows through a narrow canyon in Zion National Park in Utah. You walk right in the middle of the creek, with water rushing by and lots of slippery rocks beneath the surface. Not only did I use that walking stick, but I leaned on it every step of the way.

I hope you have a walking stick for life, something to rely on in every situation. Know what it is? God's Word. A believer in God once prayed, **"Sustain me, my God, according to your promise, and I will live"** (Psalm 119:116). Each verse of the Bible is meant to sustain you as you walk through life.

When you're alone, lean on your walking stick: **"Surely I am with you always"** (Matthew 28:20). When you sin, lean on your walking stick: **"[God] is faithful and just and will forgive us our sins"** (1 John 1:9). When you're scared, lean on your walking stick: **"Call upon me in the day of trouble; I will deliver you"** (Psalm 50:15). When you face death, lean on your walking stick: **"I am the resurrection and the life. The one who believes in me will live, even though they die"** (John 11:25).

Life is slippery. Don't try to walk through life without the Word of God! Lean on your walking stick.

The B team
Ann Jahns

Were you ever on the B team? Unless you were a stellar athlete, you may have spent time on the bench, warm-up pants firmly on, waiting yet fearing for the coach to call your name.

Jesus' disciples may be the B-est B team in history. They were the unlikeliest bunch to be charged with the most important mission of all time: telling others about Jesus. They included lowly fishermen, a radical, a skeptic, a traitor, and even a despised tax collector.

In contrast, the A team of the day, the Pharisees, were bright and shiny, oozing with self-righteous biblical knowledge. Jesus reserved his harshest criticisms for them: **"You hypocrites! You clean the outside of the cup and dish, but inside they are full of greed and self-indulgence"** (Matthew 23:25). Their outsides looked pristine, but their hearts were black with sin. They desperately needed a Savior. They just wouldn't admit it.

Do you ever wonder why Jesus chose the B team over the A team as his messengers? Maybe because the B team lived and worked with people just like them: people who knew they were flawed and in need of a Savior. Perhaps their hurting hearts were healed by the gospel. Thanks to the B team, the message of Jesus spread like wildfire.

It's okay if you are on the B team. You don't need social standing or money to love and serve the people around you. You can simply share Jesus' message of salvation right where you have been placed.

Your screen and your soul
Mike Novotny

Technology is a tension, isn't it? Families feel this when they FaceTime siblings two states away . . . and when they sit in the same room with everyone in their own digital worlds. Friends feel this when their phones keep them together when they're apart . . . and keep them apart when they're together. Parents feel this when a tablet makes a long car ride a less than traumatic experience . . . and when that same tablet becomes their child's addiction. Christians feel this when their Bibles are closer than ever . . . but the fruit of patience and self-control seem much farther away.

In the upcoming devotions, I want to dig deep into the connection between your screens and your soul. My goal is to maximize the blessings, minimize the bad things, and help you create boundaries so that these screens are a net gain for your walk with God.

Paul, looking around at the culture of ancient Ephesus, encouraged the Christians there, **"Be very careful, then, how you live—not as unwise but as wise"** (Ephesians 5:15). I have a hunch he would say the same things as he observed our digital culture today. In an age where we "live" with screens on every side, may God give us wisdom to use technology always and only for his glory.

The blessing of technology
Mike Novotny

If you see modern technology as a bad thing and not a blessing, consider this—before there were screens, there were scrolls. And we know that early Christians leveraged the latest technology for spiritual good.

Like the book of Romans. Around A.D. 57, the apostle Paul was in the Greek city of Corinth, about 750 miles from Rome. He deeply wanted to go to Italy, but first he needed to deliver an offering for the poor in Jerusalem. In other words, Paul couldn't physically get to Rome. So what did he do? He leveraged the technology of his day—like papyrus scrolls, smooth Roman roads, and the common language of the people—and he wrote the Roman Christians a letter.

Romans is really good. For 16 chapters, Paul paints the big picture of the Christian faith. Sin, salvation, God, Jesus, what he did for us, what we do to say thank you to him, Baptism, conversion, salvation, election, sanctification, glorification. From 750 miles away, Paul wrote, **"No one will be declared righteous in God's sight by the works of the law"** and, **"For the wages of sin is death, but the gift of God is eternal life in Christ Jesus our Lord"** (Romans 3:20; 6:23).

In our day, technology is taking that same message farther and faster than ever before. So before we vent about the bad things or double down on our digital boundaries, let's thank the Creator of the people who created our screens, modern means to share the message of Jesus.

Thank God for technology

Mike Novotny

Have you ever pictured the reformer Martin Luther as the Elon Musk of ancient Germany, a man on the leading edge of technology? Around A.D. 1516, Luther was lecturing on Romans when he read, **"For in the gospel the righteousness of God is revealed—a righteousness that is by faith from first to last"** (Romans 1:17). *Righteousness.* That's how you get right with God. Luther noticed that the righteousness of God was "in the gospel," the good news about Jesus, and that it was "by faith from first to last." The whole thing was about trusting in Jesus, not in doing enough good things for Jesus.

Luther had to tell the world! So guess what he used? The internet of his day! Not long before Luther's birth, a fellow German had invented/brought the printing press to Europe, speeding up the publishing process exponentially. Martin Luther published. By 1519, he was the most published author in all of Europe, and his discovery about righteousness, about how you can only get right with God as his gift through faith in his Son, Jesus, spread like wildfire.

That fire is still spreading. In any given month, Time of Grace alone will connect real souls to a real Savior millions of times each month. Millions! And every soul has a story, just like yours. So join me in thanking God for screens!

Saving souls through screens
Mike Novotny

A few years ago, I was asked to consider becoming the next lead speaker for Time of Grace, a ministry that connects people to God through mass media. Before I made a decision, I asked a few people for advice. Should I spend a chunk of my limited time filming TV shows and recording online videos and writing books instead of spending all my time locally at my church? I got all kinds of feedback, but one comment stood out.

A fellow pastor shared, "I think you have to be sitting on a person's couch in their home to snatch them from the arms of the devil." I get why he said that. There is something about a physical, face-to-face relationship that is far better than a digital distance, as anyone who has had a long-distance relationship knows.

But, by God's grace, that pastor was wrong. So many of you whom I have never met have been blessed by God's Word through print, television, email, and Instagram. Souls have been saved, and lives have been changed (you emailed to tell us all about it!), as God flexes his divine power through all possible means.

Your stories remind me of Paul's words: **"I have become all things to all people so that by all possible means I might save some"** (1 Corinthians 9:22). There are so many ways and means to reach people with technology. That was true then. It's still true now.

How could you use your screens to help save people's souls?

Breaking the digital chains
Mike Novotny

If you had to give your relationship with your phone a letter grade, what grade would it be? That was the question I asked a counselor, a cop, a business COO, two teachers, and a few others. And most everyone responded with expressions of regret, sighs of embarrassment, or low-level shame. Based on our self-given grades, my friends and I are not the valedictorians of the digital age.

How about you? Do you struggle with your devices? Despite their blessings, screens can be a bad thing. Here's a key question to ask yourself: Are screens separating you from your family? After spending all day at school with your friends, do you come home to your family and still focus digitally on your friends? Or after eight hours at work, do you come home to your family and still focus digitally on more work? Do screens get in the way of serious conversation and connection? Does your phone own you?

In 1 Corinthians 6:12, Paul wrote, **"I have the right to do anything . . . but I will not be mastered by anything."** You have every right to buy a phone, a tablet, and a smart TV, but wisdom asks, "Does your phone control your behavior? Do you find it hard to break those digital chains?"

If so, start to pray for eyes to see the depth of your problem, for grace to deal with your guilt, and for spiritual power to set wise boundaries. Your Father would love to help set you free!

Face-to-face with friends
Mike Novotny

Imagine trying to have a conversation with a friend while surrounded by a crowd of people who are tapping you on the shoulder and whispering *pssst* in your ear. Distracted? Now imagine that your friend is surrounded by a similar crowd. Sound like a great conversation?

Yet this is precisely what happens when we try to talk without turning off our phones. Any person, app, or email that buzzes, dings, or rings is distracting for both of us. Ever been there? Ever seen a group of kids at a coffee shop with the soft glow of distraction on their faces? Or a staff trying to discuss an issue while half the room is checking texts and returning emails? I know it's the new normal, but there is something not okay about our pseudo-conversations.

There's a curious verse in 3 John that says, **"I have much to write to you, but I do not want to do so with pen and ink. I hope to see you soon, and we will talk face to face"** (1:13). Pen and ink were the latest tech of John's day. But John knew that true joy, complete joy, required something better. He needed to be face-to-face with his friends. It would take more time to visit them, but that time would produce a greater joy. Anything less would be something worse for him and for his friends.

What would it take to talk without tech? to silence the interruptions and truly connect face-to-face so that your joy might be complete? Consider your answer and take action today.

Setting boundaries
Mike Novotny

My greatest fear for Christians in our digital age is not online bullying or mature websites. It's the impact that all this scrolling has on our soul's ability to stare at Jesus.

When you see something new, interesting, arousing, shocking, or dramatic, your brain releases the feel-good chemical called dopamine. However, just like with any other high, the happy feeling wears off, and you need more stimulation to feel the same way. You need faster, funnier, better, new, and now. Soon real life will be boring by comparison, and that boredom will feel unbearable. You'll reach for your phone at stoplights, in store aisles, anytime, all the time. Why? Because you have trained your brain to need it.

So guess what happens when you go to church? You can turn off your phone, but can you calm your brain? Can you focus on your faith and fix your thoughts on Jesus without your brain going wild?

Hebrews 3:1 says, **"Fix your thoughts on Jesus."** Don't scroll through your Jesus with a quick like and a share; stop and stare. Contemplate the compassion that took him to a cross. Meditate on the mercy that held him there. Fix your mind on the forgiveness you have because of God's Son.

That is what your phone will rarely allow you to do. So before your screens sabotage your soul, cry out to God for grace, wisdom, self-control, and the strength to set the boundaries you need to protect your brain. Your ability to think about Jesus depends on it.

Lose the messiah complex
Mike Novotny

You will never be able to set wise boundaries with technology until you reject your messiah complex. Ever heard that term? A messiah complex believes that the people in your life *need* you. They can't live without you. If you aren't like God—omnipresent, always available, 24/7 there to help them—their universe will fall apart.

If you don't have your phone on all the time, if you don't sleep next to it and eat next to it and work next to it and worship with it, something tragic will happen. Your mom will have a stroke, and you won't be there to save her. Your son will be caught in the cold, and you will be responsible for his chilly death. A friend will need you, and your voicemail won't be able to help her. How else do you explain the dings, rings, beeps, buzzes in church, in meetings, at movies, at dinner, everywhere? For some reason, we think we have to be as available as God.

Isaiah reminds us, **"I am the Lord, and there is no other; apart from me there is no God"** (Isaiah 45:5). It's good to be a good friend, a good kid, or a good parent. It's bad to think that you have to be like God. Let him be the all-powerful, ever-present, there-in-your-time-of-need Savior.

That will allow you to put down your phone, recharge your soul, and find the rest you need to truly serve the people you love.

The allure of screens
Mike Novotny

The book of Proverbs, written around three thousand years ago, doesn't say much about tablets and TikTok, but it can teach us wisdom with technology. In Proverbs 5, a loving father is trying to protect his sons from a local woman who doesn't care much about marriage vows. She, apparently, is very attractive and, apparently, very aggressive with guys no matter their relationship status. Thus the father pleads, **"Now then, my sons, listen to me; do not turn aside from what I say. Keep to a path far from her, do not go near the door of her house"** (verses 7,8). In other words, "Boys, don't get too close, or you'll go too far."

What is true for some sexually is true for most digitally. When we get too close, we go too far. When our devices are always with us, always able to get our attention, we end up scrolling and scrolling (and scrolling and scrolling), wasting our limited time and ignoring the people who need our full attention. Depending on your personal relationship with screens, you may need to "not go near" their alluring presence.

What does that mean? Ask a few friends or Google it (irony noted) for some ideas about wise boundaries. This may seem like an unrelated step to your walk with God, but keeping your screens on a digital leash will allow you to love people better and focus on the Word longer. Few things matter more than that.

Jesus deleted your sins
Mike Novotny

Food and phones have something in common. Most of us feel bad about our relationship with both of them. We struggle to enjoy them without being consumed by them. Maybe your screen time is proof that you, like many Christians, struggle to scroll in moderation.

That's why I want to comfort your heart with our flesh-and-blood Jesus. Two thousand years ago, when Jesus saw a world broken with sin, he didn't use some convenient, created invention to fix the problem. He could have scribbled on a scroll and sent it down from heaven. But he didn't. Instead he came in flesh and blood. **"The Word became flesh and made his dwelling among us. We have seen his glory, the glory of the one and only Son, who came from the Father, full of grace and truth"** (John 1:14).

Jesus gave humanity his full attention. That's where he saw the depth of our need and his opportunity to save . . . when your friend felt ignored because you got lost on your phone . . . when your spouse wanted to talk but you were playing some trivial game . . . when you sinned on your screen. Jesus highlighted every one of your sins and dragged them to the eternal trash can.

Your sins are gone, digital and otherwise. The files are deleted. So go today in peace. Because Jesus is full of grace.

God's arms are open wide
Ann Jahns

He made the long journey home, the apology repeating in his head: "Dad, I'm sorry. Dad, forgive me."

In his youthful arrogance, he thought he knew what he wanted. And it wasn't his father's rules. So he begged for his inheritance early, and his father reluctantly gave him his wish. The son practically ran to the farthest city.

And there he did it all. But the money ran out, and so did his friends. Suddenly his home, where he had been loved, didn't look so bad. Broken and starving, he started home, terrified. Had the locks been changed? Were the gates tightly shut?

But someone was waiting for him. Night after night. Watching. Hoping. Finally, face-to-face, father and son fell into each other's arms, weeping. **"I have sinned against heaven and against you,"** the son whispered. **"I am no longer worthy to be called your son"** (Luke 15:21). But the reply was drenched in grace: **"Let's have a feast and celebrate,"** his dad cried, **"for this son of mine was dead and is alive again; he was lost and is found"** (verses 23,24).

We may never have blown our inheritance and fled from home, but we've all attempted life apart from God, our sin erecting a barrier to his love. But because of Jesus' redeeming work, God throws his arms wide. All is forgiven. We are his.

Are you living apart from your Father? No matter what you've done, the doors are unlocked and the gates are open. God's full and free forgiveness is waiting for you.

Delighting in God's goodness
Andrea Delwiche

Imagine today is your day to praise the Lord in front of the family of believers. Someone hands you a microphone, and as the houselights go down and the spotlight glows, you begin to attest to all that God has done for you. What do you say? How do you thank God aloud in conversation?

"Praise the LORD. I will extol the LORD with all my heart in the council of the upright and in the assembly. Great are the works of the LORD; they are pondered by all who delight in them. Glorious and majestic are his deeds, and his righteousness endures forever" (Psalm 111:1-3).

The psalmist says that God's great works are pondered by "all who delight in them." To delight in something means that the something "gives great pleasure." What has God done in your life that gives you great pleasure or that you delight in?

If we sit for a minute and ponder (in silence with our phones far away from us), what will we come up with? There will probably be a mix: some very public examples and some very personal joys. Some days and seasons it will be hard to remember the great things God has done, and perhaps it's in those times we most need the Holy Spirit's help. Remembering God's past goodness in sending his Son renews our confidence in God.

May God walk with you as you spend this time with him. May your pondering bring great blessing to you and to anyone with whom you share it.

Filled with peace and joy
Jon Enter

What's crushing down on you?

Years ago, a nuclear-powered submarine, USS *Thresher*, disappeared in the ocean depths. A small valve had frozen up from condensation, causing the sub to dive too deep. Everyone inside perished. Because of new technology, another submarine went into the area where the *Thresher* disappeared. This new sub was thick-plated, thick-glassed, highly pressurized and, therefore, capable of going into deep water. When the *Thresher* was found, it was discovered that the sub had imploded; this hunk of steel had been crushed like a piece of paper. Yet around the collapsed sub swam tiny sea creatures. They had big eyes, their skin was thin, and they swam joyfully in the same environment that crushed metal. How?

The natural pressure inside these deep-sea creatures was opposite and equal to the pressure pressing on them. God designed them for it.

God did not design humans to be within the pressure of a sinful world. That's why we are overwhelmed, crushed, and imploding. King David, who was crushed by his sin and overwhelmed by his surroundings, gave this encouragement: **"You make known to me the path of life; you will fill me with joy in your presence"** (Psalm 16:11). The only way to avoid being crushed by this sinful world is to be filled up with Christ.

What is crushing down on you? Wait patiently for the Lord. Wait for his providence and protection. Wait for him to show you what he is planning for your life. Follow his path, and you'll find peace and joy in his presence.

Your worth is found in Jesus
Clark Schultz

In 2023 the cost for a 30-second Super Bowl commercial was between 6 and 7 million dollars. Yikes! That's a lot of Cool Ranch Doritos (best chip ever)!

Perhaps you have made this statement: "If I just had more money, I could (insert temporary happiness here)." What would it take to make you happy and content? To be upfront, money is not evil. The LOVE of money is the major issue. But you can't take money or possessions with you after you die.

Someone should have told the Pharisees of Jesus' time that. **"The Pharisees, who loved money, heard all this and were sneering at Jesus"** (Luke 16:14). What follows this passage is the story of the rich man and poor Lazarus.

Maybe each day you have to make a choice between paying for diapers or paying the utility bill, or maybe you are well off. Money will get you nice things, and there's nothing wrong with that. But if that becomes your sole purpose in life, you will miss the big picture. Your worth is not found in the bank or in your wallet or even in your Paypal app. Your worth is found in Jesus!

If your diet allows, grab a bag of Doritos and ponder this quote from the reformer Martin Luther for 30 seconds or more: *"God doesn't love us because of our worth; we are of worth because God loves us."* Now that is priceless!

Never alone
David Scharf

Feeling alone is scary. When the Old Testament prophet Elisha and his servant were surrounded by an enemy army, the servant cried out, **"Oh no, my lord! What shall we do?"** (2 Kings 6:15). Have you ever found yourself in a situation where it seemed like you were all alone? Maybe not surrounded by an army, but there likely have been situations where you felt the loneliness of Elisha's servant and cried, "What do I do?"

"Don't be afraid," Elisha said. **"'Those who are with us are more than those who are with them.' Elisha prayed, 'Open his eyes, Lord'"** (2 Kings 6:16,17). The Lord opened the servant's eyes to see the hills full of horses and chariots of fiery angels surrounding the city! What about our lonely battles? Lord, open our eyes!

Jesus told his disciple Peter, **"Do you think I cannot call on my Father, and he will at once put at my disposal more than twelve legions of angels?"** (Matthew 26:53). Imagine. There were 72,000 mighty spirits chomping at the bit to intervene in Jesus' defense. But the legions were idle. You can almost picture them at the cross, straining to come to Jesus' aid, but the Father's hand held them back.

Why? Why did the Father do that? He did it so that his care for you would never be held back. He did it so you would never be alone. No matter the battle, those who are with you are more than those who are with them.

The deceitfulness of wealth
Matt Ewart

Jesus chose an interesting word to describe wealth: *deceitful*. (See Matthew 13:22.) If something is deceitful, it promises one thing while delivering something else. Here are three deceitful things that wealth whispers in our ears:

"I will give you security." A common worry is that we won't have enough. Wealth makes a promise that it will always take care of us. That's deceitful because wealth accumulated over many decades can be wiped out in a single moment.

"I will give you happiness." Advertisements and commercials lure us into the idea that the more we can buy, the happier we will be. That is deceitful because the more we focus on material things, the less room we have for the relationships that really matter.

"I am proof that you matter." A big temptation is to look at our net worth and equate that with our personal worth. Wealth tells us that the more of it we get, the more important or valuable we are. That is deceitful because sometimes the accumulation of wealth comes at the cost of more important things.

The best way to see the true nature of wealth is to see the true nature of Jesus. Jesus gives you true security that lasts for eternity. He gives you joy even in the midst of poverty. He determined your value when he paid for your life with his own blood.

Whatever wealth is whispering in your ear today, remember how Jesus offers so much more.

Little tin cup
Katrina Harrmann

One item in my yard holds great value. I bought it for $1. It's a little tin cup that I hang on a hook from our old pine tree. In the summer, when I'm gardening and overheated, I take joy from filling that cup directly from the hose and enjoying a long cold drink of water. Yes, there is the slight tang of garden dirt and tin, but that's the best part.

You see, when I was little, my great grandparents (who came over from Germany) had a little tin cup just like it tied to the water spigot outside their farmhouse. And whenever I wanted a drink . . . oh, the taste of those memories!

I love history. Anything old with a story gives me a thrill. As you can probably imagine, I love antiquing . . . seeing the odd assortment of items that used to constitute a home and life for people who lived a long time before me.

I feel like there's a lot to learn in this space.

God talks many times in the Bible about giving consideration to people and events that happened long ago. The Bible books of Chronicles and Kings are stuffed full of stories of various leaders, good and bad. And the word *remember* in Greek or Hebrew is in the Bible over *250 times.*

Remembering is important. This goes for the big stuff and the little stuff. So take some time today to remember. And thank God for all that came before.

"Remember the former things, those of long ago" (Isaiah 46:9).

The wisdom of margin
Mike Novotny

You can learn a lot from a piece of notebook paper. Just think of those little red lines near the left-hand side, the ones that create a margin. Why leave that space blank? Why not fill up a page from edge to edge?

Because margin leaves you room to add things you didn't think of just yet. Or to edit or offer improvements to make your first draft better. Plus, the sight of a jam-packed page is visually stressful and unnerving. Seeing one makes you think, "This person needs help!"

How much margin is there in your life? If last week was a piece of paper, how much blank space was there? For too many of us, there is very little margin. No space to slow down, no time to be interrupted by someone's urgent need, no chance for God to edit our packed plans. We aren't just busy. We are busy, busy, busy. And that makes me think, "We need help."

Solomon wants to help. He wisely reminds us, **"There is a time for everything, and a season for every activity under the heavens"** (Ecclesiastes 3:1). There is a time to work like crazy (semester exams, a newborn baby, Holy Week for those in ministry), and there is a time to go in late, leave early, and enjoy a blank day on the family calendar.

If you are overwhelmed with work these days, let your next piece of paper preach at you. Writing works best when there's blank space. Life does too.

Lukewarm
Jon Enter

When was the last time you read Revelation? It's a fascinating book full of prophecy and the providence of God's grace. The first three chapters contain seven letters written to seven pastors of seven Christian churches in modern-day Turkey. The last church, Laodicea, received zero praise from God: **"Because you are lukewarm— neither hot nor cold—I am about to spit you out of my mouth"** (Revelation 3:16).

These words were very personal to the Laodiceans because they couldn't find any drinking water. Hierapolis was known for its medicinal hot springs. Colossae was known for its snow-cold water. Hot and cold water. Laodicea had none. They spent major money building aqueducts from Hierapolis to Laodicea to have fresh water, but it arrived a nasty lukewarm temperature. It wasn't refreshing to drink; they wanted to spit it out of their mouths.

God felt the same about the Laodiceans' lukewarm spiritual laziness. They were so busy enjoying God's blessings that they forgot about God. What's causing you to be spiritually lukewarm? What blessing is distracting you from faithfully focusing on Christ? Sports. Cabin. Children. Career. Restfully sleeping in.

The Laodiceans broke the First Commandment. They placed things before Christ. So do we.

The amazing truth is that Jesus didn't condemn them; he called out to them. He wanted their hearts. He wants yours. He loves you. He calls out to you to reprioritize your life. What needs to be less so that Christ becomes more?

The cure
Clark Schultz

Chicken soup is the only cure for the common cold. You should rub honey on a beesting. My grandma said the best way to cure hiccups is to stand on one foot and drink a glass of water upside down.

Do these home remedies work? Not all the time. What about sin? What's your remedy to get rid of your past, present, and future missteps? Ignore them? Bury them in an addiction? Point out others who are worse than you?

What about when problems come your way, whom do you rely on? You may battle illness. You might have problems in your home or even in your school with friends or classes. When all these things weigh you down, what do you do?

The only cure is Jesus Christ. **"God is our refuge and strength, an ever-present help in trouble"** (Psalm 46:1). Jesus is the Lord over all sins and troubles.

The devil might tempt you to think you have to solve or come up with a cure on your own. You might become too proud to take it to God, or you might be tempted to think he doesn't care. But your comfort lies in the fact that God is always available and always willing to give you the strength you need to overcome obstacles and to accomplish great things for him. Pray to him for help!

Jesus is the cure for all sin and trouble because he is the Lord.

You call that prayer?
Matt Ewart

We worry out loud and call it prayer.

We get bossy with God and call it prayer.

We complain about our circumstances and call it prayer.

We ask for a shortcut to avoid work and call it prayer.

If God were to grade the quality of your prayers, what kind of grade would he give you? He does not just grade based on the words you say but based on the thoughts and motives that are behind your words.

Our prayers can reveal worry.

Our prayers can reveal idolatry.

Our prayers can reveal lack of trust.

Our prayers can reveal laziness.

It is impossible for you to pray perfectly. But whatever you do, don't let that stop you from praying.

God hears your prayers as perfect for Jesus' sake. By faith in Jesus, your prayers not only reach heaven. They are pleasing to God in heaven. And he answers.

Jesus already handled the sinfulness that can come out during your prayer time. He took it away and replaced it with his righteousness. Jesus became the perfect prayer and the perfect answer to every prayer. So even on the days when you're afraid you're getting it wrong, lift up your prayer to God. He hears and answers for Jesus' sake.

"Hear my prayer, Lord; listen to my cry for mercy. When I am in distress, I call to you, because you answer me" (Psalm 86:6,7).

You might be plagued
Linda Buxa

I've been hearing the story of the ten plagues in Egypt since I was little. Maybe you've seen it portrayed in the classic (but now kitschy) Ten Commandment movie featuring Charlton Heston.

Because Pharaoh wouldn't let God's people go, God turned Egypt's rivers, streams, ponds, and house water to blood. Then frogs infested the land (even bedrooms!). After that, gnats swarmed people and animals.

With the fourth plague, God changed things: **"On that day I will deal differently with the land of Goshen, where my people live; no swarms of flies will be there, so that you will know that I, the LORD, am in this land. I will make a distinction between my people and your people"** (Exodus 8:22,23).

Oh! It took me 51 years to realize that in addition to backbreaking work as slaves, God's people suffered through the first three plagues. In the middle of those plagues, they didn't know God would allow their suffering to end, that he had a plan for how to use their struggles.

We can relate. Sometimes it's tempting to think that because we love Jesus we shouldn't be plagued by suffering. But we will. It's not easy in the middle of hard times to confidently believe that God will use suffering for our good and his glory. But he will. We just don't know how or when. So we keep working and living, knowing that there is a day coming when we will be set free and God yet again "will make a distinction between my people and your people."

Paving the way

Jan Gompper

A longtime work friend of my husband's recently visited us. He's a Christian who is zealous about proclaiming the gospel to "save people from going to hell." As he shared his passion for evangelism, our eyes began to glaze over from the wall of words he uttered.

Sometimes Christians can be so on fire to share the gospel with anyone within earshot that they speak on and on, reciting every Bible passage they've learned about sin, repentance, and salvation. They think they can "talk" the person into believing.

Most people who don't know Christ aren't won over by wordiness. But they may be drawn to someone who takes a sincere interest in them by asking questions and listening.

Asking questions was one of Jesus' greatest teaching tools. He didn't tell everyone the answers; he led his listeners to conclusions by asking them questions. (See Matthew 16:26 and 22:20,21.) Questioning is a powerful teaching method because it stimulates critical thinking. Good questions make an audience want to find answers.

Another of Jesus' greatest teaching tools was modeling. He practiced what he preached. He didn't just tell us to pray; he frequently withdrew to pray (Luke 5:16). He didn't merely talk about loving sinners; he had dinner with them (Matthew 9:10-12). When people see faith in Christ *modeled*, they are often curious to know what we have that they do not.

Our ears and our lives can pave the way to eventually opening our mouths with the good news of Jesus.

Connecting with God's roles
Katrina Harrmann

Do you have different friends who excel at different tasks? Perhaps you have a friend who's good at listening. Maybe another is better at being your exercise buddy. And still another might be the best at giving you good advice.

The same is true for God.

One day he may be our Counselor, another time our Healer, still another our Warrior or Father or Friend. All these are different roles that he fulfills for us.

And it's okay to approach God specifically in one of his roles. When you're sick, you visit a doctor. When you need to talk, you see a counselor.

So if you're ever unsure how to pray or feel like words are failing you, it helps to ask yourself this: Which aspect of God do I need to connect with today? Do I need a healer? a friend? a father? a warrior? He's good at all of it.

And it makes sense to approach God, asking for what we know he's good at doing. He has so many different roles for *just this purpose*. No matter what we are going through in our lives, we can be confident that there is a role or title that he carries that will qualify him to help us.

"For to us a child is born, to us a son is given, and the government will be on his shoulders. And he will be called Wonderful Counselor, Mighty God, Everlasting Father, Prince of Peace" (Isaiah 9:6).

When one and done doesn't cut it
Liz Schroeder

I'm not telling Time of Grace how to spend its budget, but couldn't Pastor Mike just write the definitive devotion on grace and call it good? One and done.

"My grace is sufficient for you" (2 Corinthians 12:9), but hearing about it one time is insufficient. That's because grace is like a diamond. With its many facets, perfectly proportioned, its polish and symmetry are breathtaking. Viewing it from one angle doesn't cut it.

When people ask to see our daughter's engagement ring, she holds out her hand and tilts it ever so slightly so the light can hit all the different reflection points. Friends ooh and ahh, commenting that her fiancé did such a good job designing the ring.

That's why there are so many words written about grace. When the light catches it in a different way, it's like we are seeing it for the first time. We wonder how we could've settled for a narrow understanding of God's love, and we marvel at how he designed his plan of salvation.

I need more devotions because I need to know that the gospel still applies to me today after what I did last night. I need to see God's love for me reflected in his Word the same way a teen searches his dad's face for approval. I need more grace every day.

"But grow in the grace and knowledge of our Lord and Savior Jesus Christ. To him be glory both now and forever! Amen" (2 Peter 3:18).

Awe at God's wonders
Nathan Nass

I recently visited Las Vegas for the first time. Have you been there? It's pretty cool. I was passing through on a road trip, so I only had an hour to walk around the strip. That was plenty of time to see extravagant hotels, tall skyscrapers, huge TV screens, bright lights, fountains, and lots of people.

The next day, I hiked in Zion National Park in Utah. It was the opposite. No buildings. No lights. No screens. Hardly any people. Know what I realized? God's creation is way more awesome than our creations. What God does is so much greater than even the greatest things we humans accomplish. Vegas lights have nothing on God's mountains.

Do you stand in awe at God's wonders? King David did: **"You answer us with awesome and righteous deeds, God our Savior, the hope of all the ends of the earth and of the farthest seas, who formed the mountains by your power. . . . The whole earth is filled with awe at your wonders"** (Psalm 65:5,6,8).

We get so excited about what we build, but what God built is way better. We are so proud of what we accomplish, but what God has done is so much greater. Think about it: God came to save us, to die on a cross for you and for me.

Find some time today to put away all the screens. Take your eyes off what we humans do. Stand in awe at God's wonders.

OCTOBER

The LORD is a refuge for the oppressed, a
stronghold in times of trouble. Those who know your
name trust in you, for you, LORD, have never
forsaken those who seek you.

PSALM 9:9,10

Disciplined
Matt Ewart

Sometimes I wish I were more disciplined. I wish it were easier to automate good habits. I wish temptations weren't so tempting. I wish I had some inner superman strength that allowed me to crush goals without effort.

But instead of superman strength, I find weakness. Temptations will always be tempting. The easier path will always be, well, easier. It takes a lot of time and energy and grace to develop the kinds of habits that lead to a disciplined life.

If you are working to be a more disciplined person, there's one thing to be careful about: Make sure you do not view discipline as a way to get closer to God. Avoid the motivation that comes from "God will be happy with me if I do this" or, "God will be pleased with me if I do that." No amount of discipline can increase God's favor toward you.

The best form of discipline flows out of the favor God already has toward you. You used to be a slave to sin, helpless and powerless because of the death that loomed over you. But Jesus took death's power away, forgiving every sin and sticking your sinful nature into his tomb. His resurrection gave you a new birth into a living hope.

Remember that the power of your discipline comes from the Spirit of God. He is working in your heart to transform your life with grace.

"We . . . have fled to take hold of the hope set before us" (Hebrews 6:18).

Letting go
Katrina Harrmann

I'm never sure if it's easier to "let go" quickly or over a long time. I've lost loved ones very unexpectedly. Other times the loss was drawn out over years.

Letting go is never easy. Some say the season of fall is all about learning what it means to let go, year after year. And I suppose this is true. We learn that pain is usually only for a season . . . that life goes on and that we will eventually have a NEW season of hope and joy.

How did our Lord and Savior deal with letting go?

Well, he wept over Lazarus. And in the days before Jesus died, he spent time in intense prayer and with his loved ones—talking with them and spending time in fellowship.

But even though he was God, I'm gonna guess that letting go wasn't *easy* for him. And, therefore, he knows that letting go is not easy for us. He's been there.

Connecting with a God who understands just what you're going through can get you through a season of letting go. Whether it's a relationship, a job, the loss of health, or the death of a loved one, you can always lean on the Lord in prayer. He had to let go sometimes when he lived on earth. But he'll *never* let go of YOU.

"For I am the Lord your God who takes hold of your right hand and says to you, Do not fear; I will help you" (Isaiah 41:13).

When Friends Cheat
Mike Novotny

One of the hardest times to be a good friend is when your friend cheats (or is cheated on). When adultery happens by or to someone you love, it's hard to know what to do. What do you do when she is furious or numb or done, obsessed with what must be wrong with her or unwilling to admit that anything is wrong with her? What do you say when he is so ashamed or not ashamed enough, when he is sick with guilt or when he's sick of talking about the same things over and over and over? What do you do when friends and family are picking sides, pointing fingers, sharing gossip, or stepping back altogether? Statistically, sooner or later, adultery will happen in your family, your church, or among your friends. So what does being a Christian look like in those moments?

Here's a simple answer to that very complex question. When friends cheat, give them grace and truth. Give *them*. Both of them. Him and her. The betrayer and the betrayed. Grace *and* truth. *And*. Not one or the other but both. That's how you take God's side and help them rebuild, to the best of your ability, a happy, holy home. Jesus was described as a Savior who came from the Father **"full of grace and truth"** (John 1:14).

What does that look like in real life? Let's answer that essential question in the upcoming devotions.

Grace shows up
Mike Novotny

What do you do if your friend was cheated on? How do you show grace and truth as they try to put together the pieces after adultery?

You show grace when you show up and share Jesus. Sound easy? It's not. Many experts suggest it takes up to two years for unfaithful couples to start to heal. And that means it's a marathon you are suddenly running without much training. This chapter of your friendship might feel pretty one-sided, like you're listening and listening and giving and giving and not getting a lot in return. Most friendships are fueled by fun experiences, but dealing with adultery isn't fun. Which is why most friends fade away. But grace shows up. **"Better a neighbor nearby than a relative far away"** (Proverbs 27:10). Draw near, especially the first year, and give them the Jesus they need to experience unfailing love and move forward with hope.

You give truth when you remind them of the work. No, the adultery wasn't their fault. Sin is never explained away or excused. Yet there is work to do for those who have been sinned against. A woman I know told me that after her husband's affair, she needed to hear God's law even more than she needed the comfort of God's gospel. Her heart wanted to excuse her own hatred, bitterness, and unforgiving attitude, so she needed reminders of the calling God had upon her life.

Helping friends survive and, hopefully, thrive after an affair is hard but holy work. Embrace it, and ask God's blessing upon it.

Show up and show Jesus
Mike Novotny

What do you do if your friend cheated on their spouse? How do you show grace and truth as they try to put together the pieces after adultery? (No, you aren't reading the same devotion as yesterday!)

You show grace when you show up and share Jesus. Sound easy? It isn't. Adultery is so painful and brutal that many people keep their distance. But showing up is what Jesus did: **"Now the tax collectors and sinners were all gathering around to hear Jesus. But the Pharisees and the teachers of the law muttered, 'This man welcomes sinners and eats with them'"** (Luke 15:1,2). Your presence will be a gift only surpassed by your reminders of Jesus' love for the worst sinners.

You give truth when you remind them of the work. Like telling them to own this sin (instead of excusing it on their spouse's behavior) and accept that the consequences are their fault. Or maybe their work is doing something nice, no matter what their spouse is doing for them. Suggest putting a note in their spouse's lunch with five things they respect about him or her. Have them find a babysitter, take a walk, and agree to talk about something besides the affair. Help your friend set a short-term goal for their work, and hold them to it. Applaud them if they make it. Forgive them if they fail. They'll need the encouragement.

Helping friends survive and, hopefully, thrive after an affair is hard but holy work. Embrace it, and ask God's blessing upon it.

Life as sure as death
Nathan Nass

Death is certain. It's unavoidable. That's something just about all people can agree on. You can take all the vitamins you want. You can exercise like crazy, but you're still going to die. As the old saying goes, "The only certain things in life are death and taxes."

Actually, there is one more thing that is as certain as death itself. Know what it is? Eternal life. Listen to the Bible's promise: **"Christ has indeed been raised from the dead, the firstfruits of those who have fallen asleep. For since death came through a man, the resurrection of the dead comes also through a man. For as in Adam all die, so in Christ all will be made alive"** (1 Corinthians 15:20-22).

Do you hear God's promise? Just as all will die, it is absolutely certain that all will be made alive. Just as Adam brought death into the world through his sin in the Garden of Eden, it is absolutely certain that Jesus brought eternal life into the world through his resurrection. Life is as sure as death!

The only question is where you're going to spend eternity. There are only two options: heaven or hell. Today's the day to take your faith seriously. Today's the day to treasure God's Word. Today's the day to love the Lord with all your heart. Because life is as sure as death and eternal life in heaven is only yours through faith in Jesus Christ.

Perfect days
Linda Buxa

You have 15 perfect days a year according to a survey of two thousand American adults commissioned by the U.S. Highbush Blueberry Council. The council also discovered that the average person's "perfect day" is sunny and 74 degrees, with time spent outside, time spent with family and friends, and time spent watching TV.

In addition to the perfect days, people also believed they had 204 good days. What made them good? Finding money in their pockets, sleeping in without waking up to an alarm, lying in bed listening to the rain, receiving a small act of kindness, and performing a small act of kindness for someone else.

This is good news for people who believe in Jesus because it means we have a chance to make people's days not just good but great and perfect, all by following the new command Jesus gives us: **"Love one another. As I have loved you, so you must love one another. By this everyone will know that you are my disciples, if you love one another"** (John 13:34,35).

By consistently loving other people, we not only bless their days, but we improve our own days too. Then when they ask why we're being so kind, we have the perfect opportunity to talk about what Jesus has done for us—and how, thanks to him, there's a place called heaven, where every single day will be perfect.

On-again, off-again
Andrea Delwiche

"So [God] saved them from the hand of the foe and redeemed them from the power of the enemy. And the waters covered their adversaries; not one of them was left. Then they believed his words; they sang his praise. But they soon forgot his works; they did not wait for his counsel" (Psalm 106:10-13 ESV).

Do these words, written to describe the children of Israel and their on-again, off-again relationship with the Lord, remind you of anyone?

I know they could describe my own relationship with the Lord. You too?

Now this isn't self-flagellation for the sake of wallowing in my failings. Rather, it's an honest examination of my patterns of living so I do a better job of honoring God who *does* rescue me daily. It also helps me turn toward living more in line with God's good counsel and his desires for me.

Perfection will not come in this lifetime. But by the power of the Holy Spirit, you and I are able to see where we have failed in the past, admit our failings, learn from them, and move forward with new insights. God continues to work powerfully for us because he loves us unwaveringly. He gives us good counsel to guide us in his ways of peace.

Maybe the Lord is showing you a place in your life where you have forgotten his work or ignored his advice? What rises to the surface when you consider this question? Grounded in his forgiving love, move into another new beginning.

Our obstacle race is won!

Jan Gompper

Do you remember Jack Paar? He was an American talk show host, author, comedian, and film actor. He was also the second host of the *Tonight Show* from 1957 to 1962.

Jack Paar once mused that his life was like an obstacle race, and he was the main obstacle.

Do you ever feel like you're the main obstacle in your life's race? Sometimes I do. Even at the age of 64 (and counting), I still trip over myself, repeating past mistakes and committing the same sins I sought forgiveness for the day before.

The apostle Paul also knew what it was like to be his main obstacle: **"I want to do what is good, but I don't. I don't want to do what is wrong, but I do it anyway. I have discovered this principle of life—that when I want to do what is right, I inevitably do what is wrong. Oh, what a miserable person I am!"** (Romans 7:19,21,24 NLT).

I don't know if Jack Paar had help in overcoming his main obstacle, but Paul did, and so do we: **"Who will free [us] from this life that is dominated by sin and death?** . . . [God] **sent his own Son in a body like the bodies we sinners have. And in that body God declared an end to sin's control over us by giving his Son as a sacrifice for our sins"** (Romans 7:24; 8:3 NLT).

Our sins will continue to trip us up, but thanks to Jesus, our obstacle race is already won!

Jesus is worth it
Mike Novotny

I once witnessed a reluctant two-year-old who did not want to go up for the pastor's children's sermon. I could hear him rejecting his parents' urging to join his siblings. But things changed when the pastor said, "Kids, today you're going to get candy." I tell you under oath that toddler legs have never moved that fast! That kid hurled his little body into the group like a major leaguer diving into second base.

Maybe that sounds like your story. You might have thought that God and Jesus and the Bible and religion weren't worth your time, that Christianity was unnecessary and/or undesirable. Maybe that's why you stayed away for so many years. But then you heard a clear explanation of what God wanted to give you, an eternity way sweeter than a handful of candy. God wanted to be with you in a place where the relief and the rejoicing never end. Despite your reluctance and rejection, he wanted you still!

When the Holy Spirit opens your heart to see the glorious gift of God, you run to Jesus like the little kid I saw that day. You want his grace. You'll do anything to be close to his love.

That's what happened to Paul. After his change of heart, he wrote, **"What is more, I consider everything a loss because of the surpassing worth of knowing Christ Jesus my Lord, for whose sake I have lost all things. I consider them garbage, that I may gain Christ"** (Philippians 3:8). No matter what he costs you, Jesus is worth it.

If you're a Christian, you're creative!
Liz Schroeder

When a creative person dares to present an outside-the-box idea, there always seems to be a hater lurking in the shadows: "Looks like *someone* has too much time on their hands!" The dissenter then explains why the group should side with the safer option and take the road well-traveled.

I wonder if that happened to God after he created the platypus and narwhal. I bet some fallen angel in the peanut gallery muttered, "Looks like *Someone* has too much time on his hands. One type of fish is plenty!"

What's a better response? After contemplating the ingenuity of the Creator, the psalmist was inspired to write a love poem: **"How many are your works, Lord! In wisdom you made them all; the earth is full of your creatures"** (Psalm 104:24).

How many are the Lord's works? Try counting them. Go outside and make a mental list of all the things you could never make in a million years. Then praise God for what he made in six days. Imitate the Creator. Honor him with your originality. Glorify him with your resourcefulness, and put the spotlight on him with your innovation.

The term *Christian creative* should not be an oxymoron ("jumbo shrimp") but a redundancy ("true facts"). As human beings created in the image of God, creativity can be commonplace. In the boardroom, the classroom, and the kitchen, let creativity flourish! Think outside the confines of the concrete, take the road less traveled, and fan that creative spark. It was woven into your fiber by the Creator.

Burning comes before light
Nathan Nass

Before there's light, something has to burn. Have you noticed that? For a candle to give light, the wick has to burn and wax has to melt. For the lights to come on in your house, somewhere something is burning—coal, gas, solar rays—to create that light. For your campfire to light up the night, wood is burned to ashes. Before there's light, something has to burn.

Could the fires you're passing through today actually produce something brighter than you can ever imagine? Could the struggles you face today be leading toward something better than you can picture at the moment?

Here's God's answer: Yes! **"For our light and momentary troubles are achieving for us an eternal glory that far outweighs them all"** (2 Corinthians 4:17). I can't promise how your life on earth is going to go, but you can trust in God's promise for how it all turns out: eternal glory in heaven through Jesus.

Burning comes before light! The troubles you face today are nothing compared with the eternal glory that's waiting for you in heaven. The struggles that burden your soul are part of God's plan to refine your faith for what he has planned next for you.

For Jesus, it was first the cross and then the crown. Should it be any different for you and me? Don't lose heart. The fires you see today are leading to eternal glory. Burning comes before light!

4 steps to more church joy

Mike Novotny

Spiritual growth happens in a fairly predictable way: read, teach, ask, explain. First, someone reads the Bible. Second, someone does their best to teach the Bible. Third, listeners admit what they don't understand about the Bible. Finally, someone explains the Bible so listeners can understand.

That's what happened in Nehemiah 8 at a church service to celebrate the rebuilding of Jerusalem. First, "[Ezra the priest] **read** [the Law] **aloud from daybreak till noon.**" Second, "**the Levites . . . instructed the people in the Law.**" Third, "**all the people had been weeping as they listened to the words of the Law,**" an emotional admission that they didn't truly grasp God's forgiveness for their sins. Finally, "**the Levites calmed all the people, saying, 'Be still, for this is a holy day'**" (selected verses).

The result? "**Then all the people went away to eat and drink, to send portions of food and to celebrate with great joy, because they now understood the words that had been made known to them**" (verse 12). There is "great joy" for those who understand the Word of God.

This means that key habits for your spiritual growth include turning your ear to someone who teaches the Bible and admitting it when you fail to get it. The people of Israel wept due to their ignorance. You might need to ask a longtime Christian an honest question or email your pastor if the sermon went over your head.

Those can be embarrassing moments, but they are what God will use to send you home to celebrate with great joy.

My best friend in the morning
Karen Spiegelberg

I saw a commercial for a coffee creamer recently. The actor in the ad said, "This is my best friend in the morning!" As Christians, we can chuckle knowing that Jesus is our best friend first thing when we arise.

But do we really embrace Jesus as such? I can't raise my hand in acknowledgement of that. I'm guilty of putting many things in front of him each morning. Checking texts, emails, social media, the weather, whatever it is!

In this devotion I'm calling myself out to be better at sitting at the feet of my Lord and Savior to continue to gain his wisdom for my life. I'm asking you to come along with me in a commitment to do the same. Soaking up the pages of Scripture has the power to change our lives. Hebrews 4:12 says, **"For the word of God is alive and active. Sharper than any double-edged sword, it penetrates even to dividing soul and spirit, joints and marrow; it judges the thoughts and attitudes of the heart."** And John 8:31,32 says, **"If you hold to my teaching, you are really my disciples. Then you will know the truth, and the truth will set you free."**

Taking time to be in God's Word and apply it to our lives gives us the power to mature in Christ and glorify God in our daily walks.

Pour me a cup of coffee but hold the creamer. I'm going to spend some time with my *true* best friend this morning!

No bones means . . . he lives!
David Scharf

Neil Armstrong was the first to ever walk on the moon. Shortly after, he went on a tour of the Holy Land. When Armstrong made it to the steps of the temple, he sat down and wept. He said later that he had walked in many different places, but being in the place where his Savior walked was the most meaningful.

But of all the places we know with certainty that Jesus walked, we do not know where he was laid to rest. Search as you might, you will find no grave site containing the bones of Jesus on which the epitaph reads: "Jesus of Nazareth, the Crucified." The apostle Paul said, **"If Christ has not been raised, your faith is futile; you are still in your sins"** (1 Corinthians 15:17). He went on to say, **"But Christ has indeed been raised from the dead"** (1 Corinthians 15:20). No one knows where Jesus' grave is because in all the supposed sites where people think he may have been laid, there are no bones to prove it.

What does that mean for you? I'll let Jesus tell you that. Jesus said, **"Because I live, you also will live"** (John 14:19). Jesus' empty grave means yours will be too. And when he returns to take you to heaven, your gravestone will read, "He is not here; he is risen."

Where are you?
Katrina Harrmann

What is one of the most common questions we throw at God when things aren't going according to plan? When we're having a bad day, or when someone gets sick or an unthinkable tragedy has occurred?

Where are you?

We throw up our hands in frustration and bellow it at the sky . . . often in rage and frustration. This very question has caused so many people to abandon their faith and wander away from God.

Where are you, God?

But it's important to note that this question goes both ways. Incidentally, it was the first recorded question that God asked of mankind as he walked in the Garden of Eden in the cool of the day.

"Where are you?" (Genesis 3:9).

The Hebrew word that is used here is *Ayekah*. Many interpret this word not in a directional sense (Adam and Eve weren't *that* good at hide-and-seek after all) but rather in a spiritual sense: "Where is your heart? Where are your priorities? Where is our relationship?"

God asks this of us constantly . . . if we would but open our ears and hear him. So the next time you're feeling adrift, consider where your spirit is at in relation to God. Imagine him asking you, "*Ayekah?* Where are you today? Where are you in relation to my heart? Are you and I aligned? Are you listening to me?"

Take time daily to align your inner compass to God's voice, and whatever comes next will be bearable.

I don't want to, but I have to

Mike Novotny

Imagine you and I are at the best dinner party ever. Smoked brisket, mango salsa, fresh mozzarella, and not one but two chocolate chip cheesecakes! Even better than the food are the easy-to-talk-to and supremely likable people. In the middle of the best party ever, I duck downstairs to grab you your favorite drink, which is where I smell something off. Gas! As I hear another roar of laughter from above, I smell the gas leak below. So what should I do? I don't want to crash the party, but I have to.

Our faith is like that too. **"Dear friends, although I was very eager to write to you about the salvation we share, I felt compelled to write and urge you to contend for the faith that was once for all entrusted to God's holy people"** (Jude 1:3). Jude had to write an intense letter of correction even if he would have preferred a tender letter about salvation.

Don't run away from "have to" moments in your faith. A friend might text you something hard. A pastor might need to say something harsh. A parent might insist on having a heart-to-heart. Fools run from such moments and become more foolish. But wise Christians are willing to be corrected, which makes them wiser. Those "have to but don't want to" conversations are what God will use to make you more like Jesus.

Will you have ears to hear it?

It's all about love
Andrea Delwiche

For much of my life, *delight* was not the word that came to mind when I thought about God's commands. Even though I may have been told otherwise, God's commands seemed like a list of opportunities for me to disappoint people or like a checklist of strictures that God consulted when he looked me over.

"Blessed are those who fear the Lord, who find great delight in his commands" (Psalm 112:1). Why would I delight in God's commands?

Here's a realization that changed things for me. Each of God's commands has to do with love. God's love for us, our love for God, our love for neighbor, and love for ourselves as creatures loved by God. It's true. Find a list of the Ten Commandments in Exodus 20 and look them over. Can you see God's fingerprints of love? Take some time with the Sermon on the Mount, Jesus' teaching on loving God, others, and self in Matthew 5-7. Do you see an opportunity to delight in God's commands by following Jesus' teaching on love?

What about Jesus' words: **"A new command I give you: Love one another. As I have loved you, so you must love one another"** (John 13:34)? When I remember to love others, regardless of whether I find their opinions and behavior palatable, life opens into a blossom of blessing for them and for me. Anger and fear dissipate. Jesus knows what he's talking about!

Lord God, let us see your rules for living well as a chance for delight and an opportunity to love. Amen.

Jesus is our best investment
Mike Novotny

A few months back, I wandered into a local collector's shop and struck up a conversation with "Rick," the owner who soon shared his life story with me, one that included years of substance abuse as well as a serious sports cards collection. At one point, he mentioned a few rare baseball cards he had owned that were valued at thousands of dollars each. "Whoa!" I reacted. "Do you still have them?"

Rick shook his head in regret. "No, I think I traded them for a cheeseburger when I was high."

Poor Rick, right? He got caught up in the moment and traded something he craved for something that was worth so much more, a foolish exchange similar to Esau who swapped his birthright for a bowl of soup (Genesis 25:33).

Every time I hear of someone walking away from church because they don't want to be judged for their lifestyle, their sexual choices, their divorce, etc., I think of Rick and Esau. There is no doubt that following Jesus can be painful, especially when you're "hungry" for what sin can temporarily satisfy.

But please remember that Jesus is a better treasure, a long-term investment who will provide for your eternal future. This is why Peter confessed, **"Lord, to whom shall we go? You have the words of eternal life"** (John 6:68). I won't lie and promise you that Christianity is easy, but I will tell you the truth: only Christ leads to eternal life.

Love means . . .
Jan Gompper

When the movie *Love Story* hit the big screen in 1970, a line from the movie became a popular slogan: *"Love means never having to say you're sorry."* It could be found on posters, refrigerator magnets, coffee cups, etc.

The implication was that if you love someone, they will automatically know you're sorry. No words necessary. I wonder how many marriages ended in divorce because of following that pithy piece of advice?

Love, in fact, *always* means saying you're sorry. Sometimes, however, even the words *"I'm sorry"* ring hollow because too often they're followed with a three-letter apology killer—*but*. "I'm sorry, *but* you started it." "I'm sorry, *but* you just don't understand."

A sincere apology replaces the word *but* with two different words: *forgive me.* Asking for forgiveness demonstrates that we accept full responsibility for the sin we've committed and the hurt we've caused, without excuse or blame.

Conditional apologies don't cut it with God either. God sees expressions of regret such as: "I'm sorry, Lord, *but* . . . it's my parents' fault . . . you made me this way . . . the woman you gave me made me eat the fruit . . ." as hollow and unreliable.

Thankfully, God offers us a *but* we *can* rely on: **"But if we confess our sins to him, he is faithful and just to forgive us our sins and to cleanse us from all unrighteousness"** (1 John 1:9 NLT).

Love means *always* having to say, "Forgive me."

Ignorant Christians
Mike Novotny

About every four weeks, I feel fairly ignorant. That's because the barbershop where I, an ethnically white man, get my hair cut is not a predominately white place. The owners are Black, the barbers are mostly Black, and most of the clientele is Black. Thus, with every single fade, I am faced with my own ignorance. There are words I don't know, cultural references I don't get, and expressions that are unknown to me. That gap between their knowledge and mine means I can either smile and nod like I get it or swallow hard and admit I don't.

Have you ever felt that way around other Christians? Maybe they take notes in church, soaking in the sermon, but you don't really understand what is being taught. Or they have 16 things to say at Bible study, but you are still trying to figure out what verse 1 means. Sooner or later, you'll be next to Christians who know more than you, which means you'll face the same pressure that I do at the barbershop.

This wisdom applies in such moments: **"Humble yourselves before the Lord, and he will lift you up"** (James 4:10). People who fake it and act more intelligent than they are rarely rise up to new levels of faith. But those who are humble enough to admit their ignorance are lifted up and learn more about Jesus.

No one wants to feel like the only one in the room who doesn't get it. But honesty is always the best policy, especially when it helps you learn more about grace.

Two valleys tell one story
Daron Lindemann

Two valleys surround Jerusalem, just as Jesus surrounds us.

The Kidron Valley runs between Jerusalem's eastern edge and the Mount of Olives. In Bible times, a dry streambed called a *wadi* flowed through it.

During King Hezekiah's reign, priests removed pagan objects from the temple and carried them off to be dumped into the valley.

In the other valley, a worse dumping ground took place. Before Jesus' time and before the Israelites lived in Jerusalem, pagan religions sacrificed babies to their idol god, Molech. Sadly, some of the Israelite leaders copied this practice. The place they committed this sin was in the Hinnom Valley (2 Chronicles 28:1-3; 33:6). During Jesus' time, the Hinnom Valley became a stinky garbage dump full of dead animal carcasses and household waste.

When Jesus came, he walked in both of these valleys. **"Jesus left with his disciples and crossed the Kidron Valley. On the other side there was a garden, and he and his disciples went into it"** (John 18:1).

That night, Jesus was arrested and began his ultimate suffering and death as the promised sacrifice for the sins of the world. He experienced **"being condemned to hell"** (Matthew 23:33), hell described with a Greek word for "Hinnom."

Valleys always serve the loving purposes of our God (see Psalm 23:4). They are never too low for him and never too dark for him. They are never too foul and never too foreboding. Jesus can cross them. Still today.

Miserable wrestling match
Matt Ewart

I was on the wrestling team in high school. I had great coaches who cared for me and amazing teammates who felt like family. The one thing I didn't like was making sure I stayed at a certain weight.

One year as we were getting ready for our first wrestling meet, I was worried that I would be overweight. I didn't eat much in the days leading up to it.

The day of the meet came. I stepped on to the scale. I was so underweight that I was close to hitting the next weight class down. So for the next several meets, my goal was to hit that lower weight class. It was a miserable goal for a high school student going through a growth spurt.

Maybe you've had some miserable goals in your life too. You might not know what it's like to make weight for high school wrestling, but everyone knows the misery of trying to be someone you're not.

You see the way someone else lives, and you try to meet their lifestyle. You notice the way someone else dresses, and you try to meet their fashion. You look at the skills of others, and you try to match what they do.

It's exhausting trying to be someone you're not. It's like a miserable wrestling match against reality. Remember that God made you unique. Who you are is found in Jesus, so be faithful to his calling.

"For physical training is of some value, but godliness has value for all things" (1 Timothy 4:8).

Seek God continually

Andrea Delwiche

The opening words of Psalm 105 read to me like a letter from an enthusiastic and wise elder:

"Oh give thanks to the LORD; call upon his name; make known his deeds among the peoples! Sing to him, sing praises to him; tell of all his wondrous works! Glory in his holy name; let the hearts of those who seek the LORD rejoice! Seek the LORD and his strength; seek his presence continually! Remember the wondrous works that he has done, his miracles, and the judgments he uttered" (verses 1–5 ESV).

This verse stands out particularly to me: "Seek the Lord and his strength; seek his presence continually!" What an extraordinary piece of advice! Seek both the Lord and his strength—*continually.*

This might sound intimidating or tedious, but it's also freeing. I'm glad this elder in the faith tells me this is the important way to spend my life; it's not wasting time. When I sit quietly or walk attentively, listening or talking to God, I'm following God's will for me.

This call to seek God's presence reminds me a bit of the sparrows that fly down into the grass in my backyard to hunt tiny flowers and grass seeds painstakingly. Perhaps it's a time-consuming process, but they seem glad to be doing it. I hear all sorts of chirrups and twittering as they search out what they need. There is no guilt or anxiety or grumpiness in their actions. It's simply part of their day. They seek and God provides.

May you and I seek God each and every day . . . continually.

Why I love imperfect worship
Daron Lindemann

When I gather with others and we worship together, it is not heaven because . . .

I'm here, and I'm imperfect. We all have sin living inside us. The relationship between two selfish people in worship might be broken, and neither is excited about reconciling. The kingdom of darkness lurks in the shadows watching . . . waiting . . . working.

After our worship team has struggled with imperfect audio or ushers or attendance for a worship service, we joke that we "almost had a perfect Sunday." We all nod and say, "Maybe next Sunday." Then we laugh.

It's not going to happen. Worship won't be perfect this side of heaven. Which is why I love it. Worship here lifts our spirits to our perfect Savior, Jesus Christ, who is in heaven, far above us and this imperfect world.

Worship inspires our faith to rise above the imperfections of this world. We claim the new mercies and strength of Jesus we need to live in this world.

"Who shall separate us from the love of Christ? Shall trouble or hardship or persecution or famine or nakedness or danger or sword? No, in all these things we are more than conquerors through him who loved us" (Romans 8:35,37).

Those things won't be in heaven, but they are here now. Worshiping Jesus now, we rejoice in his inseparable love and in our invincible life of victory over all the imperfections.

Praise God! There won't be anything like it in heaven. See you in church!

God can use YOU
Linda Buxa

"Have Aaron your brother brought to you from among the Israelites, along with his sons Nadab and Abihu, Eleazar and Ithamar, so they may serve me as priests. Make sacred garments for your brother Aaron to give him dignity and honor" (Exodus 28:1,2).

What a vote of confidence for Aaron! I mean, when Moses was called to lead the Israelites out of slavery in Egypt, Aaron was Moses' right hand and spokesman. Here he got another honor as the first high priest in the history of God's chosen people.

You know what's really astonishing to me? Later in Exodus, Aaron gives in to the will of the people. They lose patience with Moses taking so long on the mountain getting the Ten Commandments, and they demand a god! So Aaron builds them an idol—a calf made out of their gold.

But it wasn't astonishing to God. Even though he knew Aaron would do this, he still commanded that Aaron receive garments of honor. Because of God's love, because of his grace.

It's the same for us. We've been called to serve God and the people around us with the gifts he's given us, and God knows we will sometimes fall short. Yet he still gives us this vote of confidence, this high honor of doing his work. And now, because of his love, because of his grace, **"I delight greatly in the Lord; my soul rejoices in my God. For he has clothed me with garments of salvation and arrayed me in a robe of his righteousness"** (Isaiah 61:10).

The offending of the five thousand
Mike Novotny

You may have heard of the feeding of the five thousand, but what about the offending of the five thousand that followed Jesus' miraculous meal?

Jesus preached, **"I am the bread of life. Whoever comes to me will never go hungry, and whoever believes in me will never be thirsty. For I have come down from heaven not to do my will but to do the will of him who sent me."** But the stuffed crowds were offended. **"At this the Jews there began to grumble about him because he said, 'I am the bread that came down from heaven'"** (John 6:35,38,41).

What offended 99 percent of the five thousand? Jesus' claim to be "from heaven." If Jesus had been their earthly equal, they might have loved him, but when he claimed to be their heavenly superior, they turned on him.

That's a very human reaction. Think of how angry we get with referees, coaches, teachers, pastors, presidents, parents, and governments who flex their authority and tell us to do something we prefer not to. No wonder some of the five thousand walked away.

But don't miss what the authoritative Jesus is offering you—life. You'll never be hungry for love or thirsty for acceptance if you come to the bread who came down from heaven. Yes, he is holier than you. Yes, he always gets the last word. Yes, he will call you to change your sinful ways. But Jesus, along with his heavenly authority, wants to satisfy your soul.

Let your sinful nature be offended. Jesus is always worth it.

More than enough
Nathan Nass

You can never have enough money. Have you learned that yet? It's a hard truth for us to grasp. We always feel like we almost have enough. We just need that one more thing. One more project to complete. One more check . . .

Here's what wise King Solomon learned: **"Whoever loves money never has enough; whoever loves wealth is never satisfied with their income. This too is meaningless"** (Ecclesiastes 5:10). Isn't that the truth? When you love money, you never have enough. When you love stuff, you never have enough.

The more you have, the more you want. The more you want, the less content you are.

Stop! There's another way to live. **"When God gives someone wealth and possessions, and the ability to enjoy them, to accept their lot and be happy in their toil—this is a gift of God"** (Ecclesiastes 5:19). What a difference! To recognize that everything comes from God, to accept what God has given you, and to be happy with the work you have to do, this is a gift of God.

Here's the truth: God has given you and me more than enough. He's given us Jesus, who died to forgive us and rose to give us eternal life. He's given us life today and strength to serve him in whatever he's called us to do. He's given us food and clothes and so much more. You can never have enough money. But when you have Jesus, you have more than enough.

Join in God's work
Andrea Delwiche

"**Who is like the** LORD **our God?**" *Hmm.* My heart gets stuck on that question from Psalm 113:5. It's worth thinking about. Who has done what God has done in creating and sustaining our galaxy and world? Who besides our God has enacted and carried out a plan like he did, intimately joining each of us to himself through Jesus?

That alone is worth sitting and meditating upon.

And then I turn to the rest of the psalm: "**He raises the poor from the dust and lifts the needy from the ash heap**" (verse 7). This is *another* great work of God—his care for everyone, regardless of how they feel about him.

More and more I see that while we are certainly not God, as Christ's followers we *must* participate in the work of God: helping the poor and needy.

Yes, *must.* God is emphatic about this throughout Scripture. Consider the words of the prophet Micah: "**And what does the** LORD *require* **of you? To act justly and to love mercy and to walk humbly with your God**" (6:8). Jesus himself said, "**'Love the Lord your God'** . . . **and 'Love your neighbor as yourself.' There is no commandment greater than these**" (Mark 12:30,31).

Who is like our God? No one. Praise him! And yet joined with God and each other in praise, we get to join this incredible God in the fields where he works.

Punctuation matters
Liz Schroeder

We're not going to get into an argument about grammar, OK? But please understand that one person's heart may swell at a well-placed *whom* while another may dangle participles with abandon. Rest assured, God loves you whether you're a spelling bee champ or if your phone's autocorrect function has given up on you.

But I invite you to get nerdy with me for a second. Read the following words of Jesus carefully: **"The Son of Man is going to be betrayed into the hands of men. They will kill him, and after three days he will rise"** (Mark 9:31).

Now go back and put your finger on the comma. When sin came into the world, death came with it. Death was followed by a period. It was The End. The comma, however, changed everything.

The comma meant that although Jesus would be abandoned, crucified, and left to die, it would not be the end. Jesus would use his dying breath to proclaim, "It is finished," and then he would rise three days later.

The comma changes everything for you too. Your grandma whose memory has been ravaged by old age? Not the end. Your dad's cancer treatment, which the doctor moved from palliative to hospice care, does not mean the end. The infant whose still body you held in your arms for way too short a time—it's not the end. And whether you live another 40 years or 40 minutes, you have an eternity with your Savior to look forward to. (And that's worth ending a sentence with a preposition.)

Simple gestures
Katrina Harrmann

When I was in grades 7-12, I trick-or-treated every year on Halloween with a group of friends in the same neighborhood. At the house of an elderly couple, we learned it was the man's birthday. Our group of six sang a rousing rendition of "Happy Birthday," which delighted the older gentleman.

As it was so dark, we never remembered *exactly* where this house was, but every year we happened across it and sang happy birthday to the same elderly man.

During our senior year, we sadly told the man and his wife that this would be our last year because we were all headed off to college next fall. He looked stricken. But we sang one last time and then waved our goodbyes.

About an hour later, we were still trick-or-treating when a car pulled up. Out popped the same little old man, his arms full of homegrown flowers. He had gone into his yard in the dark and cut blooms for us—to thank us. He handed them to us with tears in his eyes.

I never saw him again after that night.

It was such a simple thing. But it made an impact. Simple gestures very often do. You might think you can't do anything to make a difference in someone's life. But you can. Just a word, a kind thought, a simple hello can often mean all the difference in the world to someone.

"Love each other as I have loved you" (John 15:12).

NOVEMBER

Do not be anxious about anything, but in every situation, by prayer and petition, with thanksgiving, present your requests to God.

Philippians 4:6

Jesus is the LIGHT of the world
Mike Novotny

You can learn a lot about Jesus from thinking about what light is like. In one of his most famous self-defining statements, Jesus declared, **"I am the light of the world. Whoever follows me will never walk in darkness, but will have the light of life"** (John 8:12). Recently, I had the chance to read all 398 Bible passages that use the words *light, dark,* and *darkness,* and I realized that Jesus was packing five key biblical truths into this verse, which fit into the acronym LIGHT.

L stands for *life*. Plants live in the light, and souls live in the light of Jesus. *I* stands for *illumination,* the light that allows you to see the truth of your surroundings, an apt description of those who see the world through the light of Jesus' words. *G* stands for *growth*. Just like trees grow in the sunlight, your faith grows in the light of Jesus' love. *H* stands for *harsh,* because light hurts the eyes of those who are used to the dark. *T* stands for *safeTy* (okay, I know that's cheating), because it's dangerous to walk around in the dark and much safer to live life in the light.

I don't expect to win any awards for best acronym of the year, but I do hope, in the devotions to come, to help you understand and enjoy the Jesus who claimed to be your Light and, even more, the Light of the world.

L stands for *life*

Mike Novotny

Do you remember from back in science class how plants stay alive? They live, in part, because of photosynthesis, the process by which they soak in the light that gives life to their cells. In fact, if my research is accurate, the few plants that seem to live in total darkness actually feed off of other plants that have previously been in the light! In summary, light = life.

This is part of what Jesus meant when he claimed, **"I am the light of the world. Whoever follows me will never walk in darkness, but will have the light of life"** (John 8:12). Just as plants need the sun, people need the Son. The light of Jesus' forgiving love is what gives life to the cells of our souls. Without Jesus, we would shrivel and die spiritually, but with Jesus, we have life.

The devil would love to convince us that we are still in the dark, that we are going to die and not be holy enough to rub shoulders with angels. But that great deceiver has failed to mention that every follower of Jesus will *never* walk in darkness but instead have the light of life.

Friend, don't let the devil lie to you today. Because of Jesus, you are already in the light and, because of his constant rays of love, you always will be. You will have the light of life! You, because of Jesus, are **"the light of the world"** (Matthew 5:14).

I stands for *illumination*

Mike Novotny

A few years ago, my wife and I almost became prey to two giant predators in northern Thailand. We were at a hotel complex that included a zoo (key detail!) and decided to squeeze in a morning run. The first problem was that it was so dark that we could barely see the sidewalk in front of us. The second problem was that we got lost in the twists and turns of the hotel complex. The last problem was that we ran into the glowing eyes of two giant beasts that towered above my 6'2" frame!

Turns out that they were just bushes! The hotel had a topiary garden where they trimmed bushes into the shapes of giant animals. Once the sun rose, we realized that we had come face-to-face with two towering leafy rabbits! Ha!

It's hard to see in the dark, but the truth is pretty obvious in the light. That's part of what Jesus meant when he claimed, **"I am the light of the world"** (John 8:12). Jesus' words illuminate the truth and enlighten our minds. While scholars stumble in the dark, trying to figure out where life came from, how life ends, and what happens after death, followers of Jesus see the simple answers.

We are created by God the Father. We are saved by the blood of Jesus. We are led by the truth of the Spirit. We are awaiting the glorious judgment. What a blessing to see the truth as we walk in the light of our Lord!

G stands for *growth*
Mike Novotny

Plants don't just live because of light; light also makes them grow. Soaking in the rays of the sun causes cells to swell and then divide, which makes a plant bigger and stronger and, eventually, fruitful. Nature preaches to us that light is essential for growth.

That's part of what Jesus meant when he said, **"I am the light of the world"** (John 8:12). Soaking in the truths of his Word causes our faith to grow and, eventually, for the fruit of the Spirit to show up in our lives. Do you want more peace as you read the war-filled headlines? More joy as you deal with a throbbing back? More love for your crotchety neighbor? More self-control against your tendency to worry about all the terrible things that might happen to you? The best way to grow is to bask in the light of Jesus.

If you're reading these words, I'll assume that you already have a regular connection to Jesus' teaching. If so, let me encourage you today not to just read but to meditate on the biblical quotes you find in these devotions (you'll always find at least one!). Turn your thoughts toward every word and phrase like a flower angling toward the brightest rays of the sun.

Light makes plants grow. Jesus does the same for you.

H stands for *harsh*
Mike Novotny

Light can be harsh. Have your parents ever busted into your room to wake you for school and flipped on the lights? Harsh. Has anyone ever shined a flashlight in your face while sitting around a campfire? Harsh. Have you stepped out into a bright day without sunglasses? Harsh.

If Jesus is the Light of the world, that means he can be harsh. **"This is the verdict: Light has come into the world, but people loved darkness instead of light because their deeds were evil. Everyone who does evil hates the light, and will not come into the light for fear that their deeds will be exposed"** (John 3:19,20). Why didn't everyone love Jesus? Because he was the Light who exposed the sins of men, which feels harsh to hearts that want what they want.

Jesus' light might feel harsh to you too. If you want to live your truth, follow your heart, claim autonomy and authority over your body, and think that going to church means you don't have to change, you will want to hide from Jesus' light. Because Jesus points his Word like a helicopter spotlight on your heart and says, "That's wrong. That has to change."

Jesus, like light, is a complex reality. While he can feel harsh at first, his light is the source of life, illumination, and growth. So don't run back to the dark. Eventually, life is much better in the light.

T stands for *safeTy*

Mike Novotny

Okay, I know I am cheating with my acronym, but Jesus wants you to know that the dark is dangerous while the light offers safeTy. Think of waking up in a dark hotel room and stubbing your toe on an unseen dresser. Or the threats that lurk down a dark alley if you're walking home alone at night. You can breathe easier and stay safer if you're in the light.

It's the same with Jesus. He claimed, **"I am the light of the world. Whoever follows me will never walk in darkness"** (John 8:12). You are *never* in danger of being alone, never in danger of being unloved, never in danger of not having God's ear or being on God's heart, never in danger of missing heaven, never in danger of ending up in hell, never in danger of having to pay off your own spiritual debt, and never in danger of seeing a disappointed look on the face of God. Never! Why? Because Jesus is the Light of the world.

Fear is rooted in the gloomy thought that our sin has put us in danger with God, which is why Jesus dissipates our fear with the bright promises of his love. Thank God that Jesus is the Light of the world, a world that includes you.

We *did* start the fire!
Karen Spiegelberg

I'm going to go out on a limb and guess that anyone reading this has heard the famous Billy Joel song "We Didn't Start the Fire." The lyrics are a rapid-fire succession of mostly historically tragic events. It refers to the thought that history has been ongoing and is not the fault of those currently living in this world. The refrain explains that we didn't start the fire of problems in the world. They've been burning since the beginning. While pondering those words, a thought popped into my head. Wait a minute; we *did* start the fire! When sin entered the world through Adam, we were collectively responsible.

Romans 5:12,13 informs us, **"Therefore, just as sin entered the world through one man, and death through sin, and in this way death came to all people, because all sinned—To be sure, sin was in the world before the law was given."** But the apostle Paul does not stop there and leave us hopeless. In verse 17 he says, **"For if, by the trespass of the one man, death reigned through that one man, how much more will those who receive God's abundant provision of grace and of the gift of righteousness reign in life through the one man, Jesus Christ!"** Beautiful, beautiful.

I encourage you to read Romans 5:12-21. It is a wonderful reminder that there was death through Adam (and us) but life through Christ. We *did* start the fire, but God's gift of our Savior extinguished it eternally.

Our Redeemer lives
Nathan Nass

What do you say when everything goes wrong? when life falls apart? when it feels like you can't go on? What do you cry out in the darkness of life when it seems like the sun is never going to rise again?

Job was in the middle of one of those dreadful moments. Suddenly, inexplicably, he had lost everything. His possessions. His servants. Every single one of his ten beloved children. His health. It was gone. Everything was going wrong. It seemed like it would never be okay. Can you relate?

Here's what Job shouted when everything went wrong: **"I know that my redeemer lives, and that in the end he will stand on the earth. And after my skin has been destroyed, yet in my flesh I will see God; I myself will see him with my own eyes—I, and not another. How my heart yearns within me!"** (Job 19:25-27).

What a defiant cry in the face of sin, death, and the devil: My Redeemer lives! Job's faith in his Savior gave him courage, strength, and hope even as his flesh was being eaten away. No earthly struggle can possibly undo the victory that Jesus won through his life, death, and resurrection for us.

May God's Holy Spirit allow you and me to have that same courage, strength, and hope, even when everything goes wrong. Our Redeemer lives! In darkness, there is light. In death, there is hope. Our Redeemer lives!

God with us

Mike Novotny

Last summer my family saw the war tent of General George Washington. We sat in an intimate theatre in Philadelphia's Museum of the American Revolution where the pre-reveal hype, in my opinion, was a bit much. We were told that the tent would move us to tears and be "an unforgettable experience." I leaned over and made some crack to my family about the marketing hype.

But then it happened. The lights dimmed, and the video started, explaining how Washington, the commander of the Revolutionary Army, didn't keep his distance from suffering. Instead of staying home in Mount Vernon, he dwelt with the soldiers, setting up this very tent right next to his men. He endured the pain of sweltering summers and the chill of bitter-cold winters. Even though he was their lord, he lived their pain so he could lead them to victory. (I couldn't help but think of Jesus. Jesus should have kept his distance from all this, from us, from me, but he didn't.)

So when the curtains lifted and the music swelled to reveal the tent that had survived 250 years, I ate my words. I fought back the tears. I didn't, couldn't, forget what I experienced.

Who has the power to avoid pain but chooses it anyway? Who gives up their rights for others? George did. Jesus did first. **"The Word became flesh and made his dwelling among us. We have seen his glory, the glory of the one and only Son, who came from the Father, full of grace and truth"** (John 1:14).

Be the tree!
David Scharf

Have you ever thought, "When I read the Word, I don't feel like I get anything out of it"? You want immediate gratification because you want a good return on investment. God says you do, but you won't always see the return immediately.

Chinese bamboo spends four years without showing a sign of growth above the soil, nothing you can see anyway. During that time, it's putting down deep roots. In the fifth year, the growth above the soil is explosive. In 30 days, it can grow 90 feet! The first four years were not worthless but were preparation for future explosive growth! That's what it's like when you read God's Word. You don't always see it, but the growth is happening.

Psalm 1 says, **"Blessed is the one . . . whose delight is in the law of the Lord, and who meditates on his law day and night"** (verses 1,2). *Meditate* means "to turn it over in your mind over and over." The word has the idea of "murmur" behind it. God wants you to get lost in his Word and to delight in it. What will happen when you do?

Psalm 1 continues, **"That person is like a tree planted by streams of water, which yields its fruit in season and whose leaf does not wither—whatever they do prospers"** (verse 3). Like a strong tree that can weather storms, the one in the Word will have endurance to meet life's challenges. Be the tree!

Jesus' mission for us
Daron Lindemann

Sometimes my own man-pride watches a YouTube video about how to fix a leak and then struts confidently through the Home Depot plumbing aisle. But honestly, I see four different options for O-rings, get confused, and silently hope an associate comes with gentle, knowledgeable mercy that says, "Can I help you?"

Oh, the wave of relief, even rescue, when that happens. "I'm gonna make it. I'm not lost."

One more thing I've noticed about Home Depot. In October the Christmas decorations appear. In late February the spring planting and gardening supplies show up.

Home Depot is on their mission. They connect people to life's needs. Plumbing. Christmas. Gardens.

If Home Depot has their act together for earthbound projects related to plumbing or gardening or decorating that will eventually be lost, left, or destroyed, shouldn't Christians gathered in churches have our act together even more?

Our mission can make all the difference. Listen to Jesus' promises and also his purpose, or mission, for us in what is often called the Great Commission.

"All authority in heaven and on earth has been given to me. Therefore go and make disciples of all nations, baptizing them in the name of the Father and of the Son and of the Holy Spirit, and teaching them to obey everything I have commanded you. And surely I am with you always, to the very end of the age" (Matthew 28:18-20).

Follow this mission and fewer people will get lost.

Love each other!
Katrina Harrmann

When my sister and I were little and we'd argue, my parents would make us hold hands and say to each other, "My sister is my friend." Ohhhh, how we HATED doing that! There were times when we were so angry that we couldn't even look each other in the eye, and we gritted our teeth and fairly GROWLED the words to each other—resentfully.

But do you know what generally happened by the time we'd finish speaking? We'd roll our eyes at the ridiculousness of the situation and often dissolve into reluctant smiles or giggles.

The fight was forgotten.

Forced love and tenderness . . . maybe it IS effective! I'm laughing as I write those words and yet . . . *AND YET!* When I think about it, God never *suggests* that *maybe* we should love each other. He doesn't say we should love each other *only* when we're "feeling" it.

It's a command! A call to action! And some days, we really DO have to choose to love *despite* . . . right?

When my own kiddos were small, I found myself employing the same technique. I added a line so they would say, "My sister/brother is my friend! *I LOVE my sister/brother!*"

It *always* worked. It diffused the situation and reminded them how much more important it is to love. It is in fact of the *upmost* importance.

After all, John 15:11 says, **"I have told you this so that my joy may be in you and that your joy may be complete."**

You *will* go home again
Jan Gompper

Have you ever gone to a class reunion or back to visit a former place of employment? Neither is quite the same, is it? Old classmates seem like strangers. Your old company has survived without you, and previous colleagues aren't overly interested in reliving "the good old days." In other words, "You can't go home again."

Author Thomas Wolfe initially coined this phrase in his novel of the same name. *You Can't Go Home Again* was published in 1940, just two years after his death from tuberculosis at age 37.

Jesus also knew what it was like not to be able to go home again. The very people whom he had grown up with in Nazareth rejected him when he returned to minister to them. Because of their lack of faith, Jesus warned, **"A prophet is honored everywhere except in his own hometown and among his relatives and his own family"** (Mark 6:4 NLT).

Nazareth was not Jesus' final destination, however. Though he would have to endure continued rejection, suffering, and an agonizing death, Jesus would eventually return to his *real* home with his Father in heaven.

The apostle Paul reminds us that Jesus' real home is ours also: **"But we are citizens of heaven, where the Lord Jesus Christ lives"** (Philippians 3:20 NLT).

Earlier in his life, Wolfe published his most acclaimed novel, *Look Homeward, Angel*. It seems he too knew that his earthly life was not his final destination. He *would* go home again.

And so will we.

Remember and fight
Liz Schroeder

When you're under spiritual attack and can't get out from under the weight of discouragement, read Nehemiah 4-6. It's a slow burn of good overcoming evil with an unlikely backdrop: a construction site.

The people of Judah were rebuilding the wall around Jerusalem under the leadership of Nehemiah, who, as the king of Persia's royal sommelier, had received favor and resources. This was the Lord's work they were carrying out, and it attracted the attention of naysayers, fearmongers, and enemies who used intimidation and violence to stop the work on the wall.

God's chosen people responded with spiritual and physical defenses for this physical and spiritual attack. They prayed AND posted a guard. They held a plumb line in one hand AND a spear in the other. They remembered the Lord AND they fought.

"Don't be afraid of them. *Remember the Lord*, **who is great and awesome,** *and fight* **for your families, your sons and your daughters, your wives and your homes"** (Nehemiah 4:14).

These masons turned soldiers practiced constant vigilance. Nehemiah and his men had their weapons in hand all the time, even if it was just to get a drink of water.

When you are doing the Lord's work—when you are raising kids to follow Jesus, when you are witnessing in the workplace, when you are making music for the worship of God—you will face attacks from the enemy who wants to see you fail. Practice constant vigilance.

Remember your great and awesome Lord, *and fight.*

God plans ahead of time
Linda Buxa

In my 20s, I took a short-term job in addition to my full-time work. I was looking forward to the extra money. However, for the next four months, I ended up with unexpected expenses that were about equal to the amount I made. That's when it dawned on me that God provided ahead of time.

God did that for the Israelites too. A few months after he freed them from Egypt, God gave instructions to build a tent-church. That's when Moses told the people God's command: **"From what you have, take an offering for the LORD. Everyone who is willing is to bring to the LORD an offering of gold, silver and bronze"** (Exodus 35:5).

These people had been slaves. How did they have gold and silver? This is where God provided ahead of time. When Moses was going to tell Pharaoh about a tenth plague, God told Moses to give the Israelites a message too: **"'Tell the people that men and women alike are to ask their neighbors for articles of silver and gold.' (The LORD made the Egyptians favorably disposed toward the people, and Moses himself was highly regarded in Egypt by Pharaoh's officials and by the people.)"** (Exodus 11:2,3).

Oh . . . that's where the people got gold and silver! God knew there would be a tabernacle. He knew he would ask for an offering, so he led the Egyptians to give their gold and silver away—ahead of time.

He did it for me. He did it for the Israelites. He does it for you too.

Sing with your heart (and your head)
Mike Novotny

I love worship music. But I also find worship music incredibly dangerous.

Why? Because there's something powerful about the harmonies and rhythms of music that can make you fall in love with a song even if you don't know what it means. Ask a teenager what his favorite song is. Then ask him what that song is about. I bet he hesitates as he tries to figure out why he loves the song so much. Music can bypass your head and still stir your heart.

But when it comes to Christian worship, God wants to move your heart by instructing your head. In his discussion on speaking in tongues, the apostle Paul said, **"Since you are eager for gifts of the Spirit, try to excel in those that build up the church. I thank God that I speak in tongues more than all of you. But in the church I would rather speak five intelligible words to instruct others than ten thousand words in a tongue"** (1 Corinthians 14:12,18,19).

Paul preferred one measure of a song ("five words") you understand to four entire songs ("ten thousand words") you don't. What builds up the church of Jesus is the message of Jesus, not the temporary emotional impact of a well-written melody. Skip the message, and the melody might deceive you into assuming you are worshiping. Focus on the message, and the melody will help you worship God.

So let the music move your heart as the message moves your mind. That kind of worship will bless you long after the last note.

God's intentions, not mine
Karen Spiegelberg

It can be discouraging to be a Christian in today's social and political culture. We are pressured not to express our faith or God's biblical views on important issues.

As a member of my city's common council, I'm often interviewed for the newspaper. I constantly want to sprinkle my faith into my comments. Nothing scripturally heavy, just genuine ways to share God's plan or his blessings. Then the newspaper comes out. My comments are quoted but *rarely* are my references to God's Word or my faith. I often think, "What's the point?" Then I do a quick hand smack to my forehead as I tell myself that it's not about me or my intentions!

Isaiah 55:10,11 says: **"As the rain and the snow come down from heaven, and do not return to it without watering the earth and making it bud and flourish . . . so is my word that goes out from my mouth: It will not return to me empty, but will accomplish what I desire and achieve the purpose for which I sent it."**

God compares his Word to the rain and snow because, like them, it always fulfills his purposes. I need to remember that at the times my faith-filled comments are not used in the paper. Maybe God used those words to share with the interviewer, not the reader? It is important for us to be reminded that God's Word may not do what we expect it to, but it will accomplish what he intended it to!

We need a doctor
Nathan Nass

"Why do churches talk about sin? Wouldn't it be better to focus on God's love?" Have you ever wondered that? If you have, you're not alone. In our culture, sin isn't mentioned as much as it used to be. Why talk about the bad stuff? Let's just focus on love!

Except, think of this: Why do doctors talk about cancer? Why do doctors point out high cholesterol or heart blockages? To save us! Why don't doctors tell us, "Everything's great! Don't worry about anything!"? Because we need to know the truth. We can't be healed unless we realize that we are sick.

Here's what our Doctor says: **"It is not the healthy who need a doctor, but the sick. . . . I have not come to call the righteous, but sinners"** (Matthew 9:12,13). Like any good doctor, Jesus is honest with his patients. He tells us the truth about ourselves: We are sick with sin. We can't heal ourselves. We desperately need a cure.

Thankfully, like any good doctor, Jesus doesn't shy away from sick people. He came to save us! "I have not come to call the righteous, but sinners." What a promise! We can't truly understand God's love until we understand what we're really like. We can't truly understand Jesus' sacrifice on the cross unless we understand what we needed to be saved from.

This is why churches talk about sin—so that you and I can find healing and salvation in our Doctor—Jesus!

Leave me alone! (No, don't)
Karen Spiegelberg

Recently I took time off from work and personal obligations for a weekend away. I needed some quiet time to relax. During my stay, my three daughters called many and various times. They weren't trying to ruin my alone time; they just love chatting and know that I'm always accessible. But at one point, my brain screamed inside, "Leave me alone!" Then the thought of them actually doing so crossed my mind, and I whispered to myself, "No, don't." I love when they want to come to me for guidance or just to chat.

So does God, our heavenly parent.

Prayer. It's our personal relationship and chat time with God. He wants us to come to him anytime. He knows the desires and troubles of our hearts before we even ask, but he loves and wants to hear from us— whether asking for guidance or in thanksgiving. It draws us closer to him. King David had so much to say about prayer in his psalms. One of my favorites is Psalm 4:1: **"Answer me when I call to you, my righteous God. Give me relief from my distress; be merciful on me and hear my prayer."** And Psalm 145:18 reminds us, **"The Lord is near to all who call on him."**

God is our ever-present help. He doesn't take time off to relax. He's there 24/7, 365/to eternity. He would never say, "Leave me alone!" He says, **"Come to me, all you who are weary and burdened, and I will give you rest"** (Matthew 11:28).

God's test
Daron Lindemann

Kids test their parents all the time.

How many times can they say, "Mom, Mom, MOM!" until she answers? How long can they play a video game before Mom says, "Turn it off!"

Kids are always testing their parents. They're very good at it, and most of the time parents don't like it. Actually, most people don't like being tested whatever the circumstances.

But we're not the only ones being tested.

God actually invites and expects us to test him. Specifically, to test his ability and willingness to do what he says. Will he keep his Word? Will his promises come true for us?

"'Test me in this,' says the Lord Almighty" (Malachi 3:10). Wow! What does that say about God's confidence level? about yours?

Take more God-honoring risks in your praying and living. The reason you're holding back is not God but you. God can do the impossible. God makes incredible promises. God calls you his child. And God says, "C'mon, just try me."

The reformer Martin Luther talked about rubbing God's ears with his own promises. Like kids pestering their dad: "You said we could have ice cream!" That's not disrespect. It's calling on Dad to be true to himself and his Word.

Can you give more generously? Can you initiate that difficult conversation? Can you be a better parent? Can you survive therapy? Can you complain less and compliment more? With God's help, yes. He is faithful. God can do it. He will pass the test. Every time. Now, ask!

Good friends
Matt Ewart

"There is a friend who sticks closer than a brother" (Proverbs 18:24).

There will be all sorts of people who are part of your life, but it is important to be intentional with what role they play.

The "bad" friends are often obvious. These types of people might be fun to hang out with, but they take your life in a direction you don't want to go. They emulate qualities that you do not want to have for yourself. Maybe the only reason you still call them friends is because it would be too awkward to do anything else, so you keep them at arm's length.

Then there are "general" friends. You might cheer for the same team or be involved in the same hobby. But if it weren't for that team or that hobby, you wouldn't be together. It's good to have plenty of people in your life who are general friends, but there's something even better.

The best friends are the ones who are not just fun to be with. They are the kind of people you'd like to become. They don't just join you on your journey occasionally because they are headed for the same destination. These friendships will continue to grow when what you have now is gone.

And as you are intentional with what role various people play in your life, don't forget your greatest Friend, Jesus. He changed your destination from death to life, and he walks with you closer than anyone else can.

A case of the grumbles
Katrina Harrmann

Why are we so good at grumbling?

Whenever I ask my kids to load the dishwasher, I usually get at least ten minutes of grumbling. Then, when they finally do it, it only takes half that amount of time to finish.

The same holds true for fun stuff. "Let's have a game night!" Grumble, grumble! But within minutes, we are having fun, with everyone begging for one more round.

Humanity as a whole has grumbling down to an art form.

Remember the Israelites wandering around in the desert? They grumbled about everything! No food, too much manna, bad leadership, lack of Google maps! Moses must have been *so tired* of hearing them grumble!

Aren't we guilty of this too? We grumble about gas prices and politics and the guy next to us in traffic. We grumble when the game we wanted to watch isn't on TV or when someone eats the leftovers we wanted.

But what if we looked at all the PLENTY behind those grumbling moments? We are able to put gas in our cars! We are blessed to even have cars! We have televisions to watch sports and leftovers in a world where so many go without!

Wow. That kinda puts it in perspective. The next time you feel a grumble coming on, remember what you've been BLESSED with. And keep one step ahead of the grumbles!

"Every good and perfect gift is from above, coming down from the Father of the heavenly lights" (James 1:17).

The Lord is your shade
Nathan Nass

It's really nice to be in the shade. I learned that this past summer. Here in Oklahoma, the highs were over 100 degrees for weeks. The heat index was around 110 degrees each day. Sound bad? It was hot! Unless you were in the shade. It was almost unbearable to work or play out in the sun. But to sit in the shade? It was actually nice! The temperature was the same, but shade made all the difference in the world.

That helped me appreciate one of the Bible's beautiful descriptions of God: **"The Lord watches over you—the Lord is your shade at your right hand; the sun will not harm you by day, nor the moon by night"** (Psalm 121:5,6). What's God like? He's our shade. Over 100-degree temperatures are bad, but here's what's worse: The weight of guilt and regret. The pain of disappointment and hurt. The daily jabs of other people's anger and spite. Sin beating down on us. Day after day. That's unbearable!

So come into the shade! "The Lord is your shade." He took your sin and nailed it to his cross. He takes your regret and drowns it in his promises of his control over your life. He fills the holes left by disappointment and insult with his love. Do you know how Jesus' forgiveness and love make you feel? Cool. Refreshed. Restored. It's hot out in the sun. So come into the shade. "The Lord is your shade."

Jesus' most offensive metaphor?
Mike Novotny

Jesus' words don't get much more offensive than this: **"I am the living bread that came down from heaven. Whoever eats this bread will live forever"** (John 6:51).

Think of bread (a.k.a. food) for a second. Your body, despite its wonderful complexity, is absolutely dependent on outside nutrition. It is completely incapable of self-generating the calories it needs to function. In other words, unless something comes from the outside to save it, your body will quickly die and end up in the ground.

Jesus is saying that he is to your soul what bread is to your body. Your soul, despite its immense value, is absolutely dependent on outside salvation. You are completely incapable of self-generating the goodness and holiness that you need to be with God. In other words, unless Someone comes from the outside to save you, your soul will quickly die and end up in hell.

Offended? I suppose if you think that you're a good person who doesn't need saving, you would be. But acknowledging the reality of your body's need for bread is simply wise. Acknowledging your soul's need for Jesus is the same.

Sinners who flatter themselves walk away from the Bread of Life, forfeiting the only One who can save their souls. But sinners who are honest about their desperate condition feast on the promises of Jesus, grateful that he came down from heaven to offer beggars like us this "living bread."

Character traits of good leaders
Jan Gompper

Most leadership training seminars will tell you that four of the most important character traits of good leaders include: integrity, accountability, empathy, and humility. These traits should be especially evident in leaders who also wear the badge of Christianity.

Sadly, too often we tune into news stories of religious, social, and political leaders embroiled in controversy. How the person in question reacts often reveals volumes as to whether they possess the aforementioned traits.

King David certainly would have appeared on the nightly news had such existed in his day. His ego and sexual appetite led him to commit adultery. Compounding his sin, when he found out Bathsheba was pregnant with his child, he arranged to have her husband killed.

David thought he could get away with his actions until the Lord sent his investigative reporter, the prophet Nathan, to the scene. How did David respond? Did he try to excuse or justify his actions? No. **"Then David said to Nathan, 'I have sinned against the Lord'"** (2 Samuel 12:13).

A leader of integrity, accountability, empathy, and humility won't play the denial or blame game. He/she will admit past sins, repent, and ask for forgiveness.

As we consider whom to elect for leadership positions in our churches, communities, or government, we would be wise to do our own investigating into the past actions and *reactions* of the leaders we support to see if they truly possess the character traits of a "good" leader.

Help wanted!
Nathan Nass

"Help wanted." Those words are printed on signs all over the place, at least in the city where I live. My sixth grader recently asked, "Why does every single restaurant need workers?" It's not just restaurants. It seems like just about every company, every school, every agency needs workers. Help wanted!

Did you know that God has a "help wanted" sign posted? God is looking for more workers too! God could just zap people with faith in Jesus, but he doesn't work that way. He creates faith in people's hearts through hearing God's Word and being baptized. How do we hear the Word? When other people share it with us. Listen to what Jesus said, **"The harvest is plentiful but the workers are few. Ask the Lord of the harvest, therefore, to send out workers into his harvest field"** (Matthew 9:37,38).

The workers in God's kingdom are few! Just about every Christian denomination needs more men to train to be pastors. Just about every Christian school system needs more men and women to train to be Christian teachers. Could you consider that? Is there someone you could encourage to think about full-time ministry in God's church? God wants more people sharing his Word.

There is such a need, isn't there? A need for God's forgiveness. A need for encouragement from Jesus' love and promises. A need for God's Word to change hearts and lives. God's "help wanted" sign is up! Let's pray for more workers in God's harvest field.

Spared from evil
Liz Schroeder

"Good thing you got out when you did!"

These are the words I imagine saying to Aunt Annette when I meet her in heaven. My aunt went home to be with her Savior when she was just eight years old. The year was 1973, and I wasn't born yet. Annette got out before the bloody reign of Pol Pot in Cambodia, mass suicide in Jonestown, and the Iranian hostage crisis. She didn't have to watch the evening news and see the funerals of U.S. Marines who lost their lives in a terrorist attack in Beirut or witness the slaughter of thousands at Tiananmen Square.

And just like Billy Joel's "We Didn't Start the Fire," this list is hardly exhaustive and barely gets us out of the 1980s.

When Annette was born with Down Syndrome, her life expectancy was not great. Today a person with this condition is expected to celebrate their 60th birthday. In the 1960s, however, you were blessed to get ten candles on the cake. If she had been born in a later decade, we might still have her with us. But I wouldn't wish that on her.

Annette's short life brings to mind the first two verses of Isaiah 57: **"No one understands that the righteous are taken away to be spared from evil. Those who walk uprightly enter into peace; they find rest as they lie in death."**

I am happy for Annette that she got out when she did and was spared from evil. And I can't wait to hug her in heaven.

The *way* and the *where*
Mike Novotny

The other day in a sermon-inspired experiment, I asked Siri, "Give me the directions." Can you guess what she said back? Without missing a beat, my phone replied, "Where are you going?" Good logic, Siri. You can't know the *way* unless you know the *where*.

This reminds me of Jesus' conversation with his disciple Thomas: **"'You know the way to the place where I am going.' Thomas said to him, 'Lord, we don't know where you are going, so how can we know the way?' Jesus answered, 'I am the way and the truth and the life. No one comes to the Father except through me'"** (John 14:4-6). Good logic, Thomas. You can't figure out the directions unless you know the destination. So Jesus told him in the simplest terms: "My Father's house is the where, and I am the way. If heaven is your destination, then point your faith in my direction."

Don't you love the simplicity of it all? There's no mystery here, no wondering if you're doing enough or improving enough or are enough. No needing to doubt that your lifelong battle with sin will dead-end before arriving at God's address. Jesus makes the simple and breathtaking offer that he is all you need to get into the arms of God. Our Father in heaven is the where. His Son, Jesus, is the way!

What flourishing looks like
Andrea Delwiche

"May the LORD cause you to flourish, both you and your children. May you be blessed by the LORD, the Maker of heaven and earth" (Psalm 115:14,15).

What does it look like to flourish? A flourishing lemon tree has glossy green leaves and is covered with yellowing lemons at the appropriate time of year. A flourishing burr oak can grow to 100 or even 150 feet. In the fall the surrounding ground is littered with large acorns. Flourishing brilliant green moss doesn't grow much above the soil surface but makes a cool carpet beneath our feet.

Depending on the plant, signs of flourishing can look very different. Human flourishing is also very specific to each of us.

We have a lifetime to flourish by making use of the gifts God has planted in us. What is life-giving for you? What are you capable of that is life-giving for others?

We flourish as we listen to the Holy Spirit and work with the Spirit to cultivate our gifts. Sometimes we presume to know how God is working in someone else's life. Flourishing doesn't necessarily produce the fruits of earthly success: money, power, or prestige. How often have I tried to force someone else's flourishing to resemble my own ideas of what it means to succeed? Flourishing is about connection to God and community, blessing both God and others.

Consider asking the Holy Spirit to help you understand flourishing as God sees it. Would your daily walk look different if you followed God's definition?

Music's message matters more
Mike Novotny

There is an argument that every teenager has with their parents sooner or later. It's when a parent asks, "What is this song about?" And the teenager says, "I don't know. I just like it." And the parent raises an eyebrow, "Is that swearing?! What is this music teaching you?" And the teenager says, "I don't know! I just like it, okay?"

Paying more attention to the sound than the substance of a song is a dangerous habit for teens and adults alike. Because good music without a good message can move you, but it can't do much good for you. It's a distraction instead of a solution.

Maybe that's why the songs in the Bible, especially the Psalms, have short references to the tunes but full descriptions of the texts. Like when the singer-songwriter David wrote, **"Great is the Lord and most worthy of praise; his greatness no one can fathom. One generation commends your works to another; they tell of your mighty acts. They speak of the glorious splendor of your majesty—and I will meditate on your wonderful works"** (Psalm 145:3-5).

Catch that? David longed to meditate not on the beat but on the blessed works of the Lord. As we prepare our hearts for the holiday season, let's do the same, giving our attention to the message we find within the nostalgic music. If and when we do, we will find a peace that endures long past the last measure.

DECEMBER

Rejoice greatly, Daughter Zion! Shout, Daughter
Jerusalem! See, your king comes to you, righteous
and victorious, lowly and riding on a donkey,
on a colt, the foal of a donkey.

Zechariah 9:9

"Away" in a manger
Mike Novotny

If there's one lyric that grabs my attention at Christmas, it's the "away" in "Away in a Manger." *"Away in a manger, no crib for a bed/the little Lord Jesus laid down his sweet head."* Away implies distance, like when a friend lives far away or she goes away to an out-of-state college. There in Bethlehem's manger, Jesus was away from his happy home in heaven. Jesus stepped away from the praise of angels and spent his first postpartum night in a feeding trough covered in barnyard drool. That's how far away from home the Lord Jesus was.

I once ran up Mount Arbel, a national park near the Sea of Galilee in Israel. The views were breathtaking, but the trail up the mountain was nasty. Herds of cows roamed the hills, and those beasts did their business right on the path. As I was dodging the brown puddles of bovine waste, it hit me—Jesus walked here. His feet traveled these same Galilean hills, but in open-toed sandals!

What a reminder of the Lord's willingness to give so that you and I could get! Jesus came down to this dirty, broken world and walked with us despite all the messiness of this life and the misery of the cross. He did that for you and me so that we could get "away" from our sin and shame and end up with him in the happiness of heaven.

"'The virgin will conceive and give birth to a son, and they will call him Immanuel' (which means 'God with us')" (Matthew 1:23).

Putting first things first
David Scharf

The church father Augustine talked about priorities when he called God the "highest good." We cannot properly love God's gifts if we put those gifts above him. They become idols. So what has priority in your life?

Jesus said, **"But seek first his kingdom and his righteousness, and all these things will be given to you as well"** (Matthew 6:33). The way to seek his righteousness is to see his love for you in worship through the Word, Baptism, and the Lord's Supper. Is God being redundant? No. Jesus knows your heart. He knows how easily you can doubt his love. You hear the pastor say, "Your sins are forgiven." Does Jesus mean you? Absolutely! But it's so easy to think, "He wouldn't say that if he knew what I've done." Then Jesus takes you back to the font and says, "Here I made you my child. I love you. I forgive you." Does Jesus mean it? Absolutely! But you might think, "Yeah, but that was long ago. I have walked away from you, Jesus." Finally, Jesus brings you to the Lord's Supper and says, "Take and eat. Take and drink. My body and my blood for your forgiveness." And your heart has no escape. Jesus means you!

That love helps you and me put all the other things in our lives in the right place. Let's reevaluate our priorities in life and seek first the kingdom of the One who sought us first.

Let's go fishing
Nathan Nass

God wants you to go fishing. Did you know that? Listen to what he says: **"Cast your cares on the Lord and he will sustain you; he will never let the righteous be shaken"** (Psalm 55:22).

Cast. That sounds a lot like fishing, doesn't it? "Cast your cares on the Lord." Just like you might cast your hook and bobber as far as you can into a lake or river when you go fishing, cast your cares on the Lord. Throw them on God! He can handle them. He will sustain you. He will never let the righteous be shaken.

But when you're fishing, you don't just cast one time, right? The hook and bobber eventually get reeled in right back to you. So what do you need to do? Cast them out again. Over and over and over again.

Isn't this a Christian's life? You cast your cares on Jesus and trust in his grace. You feel peace and confidence in your heart. But, little by little, those cares come back and fill your heart again. So what do you need to do? Cast your cares right back on Jesus. Again and again. God's forgiveness never ends. His love never fades. His grace never runs out.

So let's go fishing. Oh, worried heart, "cast your cares on the Lord." Then, tomorrow, "cast your cares on the Lord." Then, the next day, "cast your cares on the Lord." He will sustain you!

Better than a five-star hotel
Mike Novotny

What's the best room you've ever stayed in? I've never spent a night in a five-star hotel, but I have been in a few gorgeous rooms, the ones where the mattresses are softer than mine at home and the bathrooms are bigger than my bedroom!

Living in luxury makes me excited for our eternity. Jesus promised us, **"My Father's house has many rooms; if that were not so, would I have told you that I am going there to prepare a place for you? And if I go and prepare a place for you, I will come back and take you to be with me that you also may be where I am"** (John 14:2,3).

Heaven is not like buying a sprawling house in the good part of town or getting a hotel room on game day weekend. It's not reserved for the richest and most successful people in town. There's room, Jesus says, for you. What Jesus said to Peter, who was hours from denying him, he says to sinners like us, who have denied Jesus in different ways. Despite our major spiritual flaws, there is still room for us in heaven. Jesus went to prepare our places, and he will come back to take us there. He promised, and Jesus never fails on his promises.

I know life can be hard, but your reservation has been made. Jesus can't wait to show you your room!

Worthy of whatever
Mike Novotny

Phil Wickham's modern rendition of "Away in a Manger" ends with some stirring lyrics about worshiping Jesus for all the days of his life as God, Savior, and King.

That's a big thing to sing about, because to worship Jesus means to say to Jesus, "You are worthy of whatever. Whatever you say, Jesus. Whatever you want, Jesus." That's worship.

Jesus, you want me to go to church? I don't have much time, but you're worth it. You want me to be generous with my money? I don't have a ton of money, but you're worth it. You want me to love that guy from work? forgive that person from my family? resist the urge to say something snarky about my least favorite politician? That feels impossible, but I'm going to try, because you're worth it. You say that sex is only for marriage? that marriage is one man and one woman? that I should love her, respect him, no matter what? Um, I'm going to need some help with that one, but I want to, because you're worth it. You're worthy. If you left your home and ended up away in a dirty manger to save me and make me clean, you are worth it.

Jesus is your God, Savior, King, and Friend. Consider what he sacrificed despite all your sins. Then you too will sing, along with all of heaven: **"Worthy is the Lamb, who was slain"** (Revelation 5:12). He's worthy of whatever he wants.

People of peace and rest
Andrea Delwiche

Consider this line from Psalm 116:7: **"Return to your rest, my soul, for the Lᴏʀᴅ has been good to you."**

What does it look like when our souls are at rest? Do Christians and non-Christians alike consider followers of Jesus to be people whose souls are at peace, whose mindsets are restful? Do you think of yourself this way?

Jesus was a restful person and sought to help his followers grow in restfulness. He encouraged them to look to God and avoid worry. He taught them to take their troubles to their heavenly Father. He offered to walk with them and share their burdens. He modeled restfulness by often retreating to quiet places to pray. Before he left this earth, he specifically told his followers, **"My peace I give you"** (John 14:27).

Jesus was, and is, a green oasis, a spring of water in a dry and thirsty desert. Now it's our turn to become people of refreshment and rest for the tired, thirsty, irritable world.

We have been bequeathed this peace that passes understanding. But like any spiritual gift, we can grow and cultivate it so that this peace of Christ blossoms in our own souls and extends its refreshment to the world. It's worth reading through Scripture with this quest in mind.

What would it look like for Christians to be known as restful, Spirit-led, welcoming people? What burdens could be laid down? How would it change you and me to live with a picture of ourselves as havens of rest?

Keep the stem
Matt Ewart

"Remain in me, as I also remain in you" (John 15:4).

I like blueberries. I have them just about every day. But there's one thing about them that I never liked.

In every package there's always a few of them with a little piece of the stem still attached. It's not a big stem or anything. Just a tiny mini-twig that's barely noticeable. But once you do notice them, you can't stop looking for them and picking them out.

One day I noticed something unexpected. A carton of blueberries was lost in the back of our fridge for at least a month. When I finally found it and opened it up, the blueberries were all shriveled up. All, that is, except for the ones with stems in them. Somehow the stems allowed them to stay fresh longer. So even though the stems seem like an inconvenience, they don't bother me so much now.

Many people in the world won't like you because of your faith. It might make you stick out as different and unappealing. And because of that, there might be times when you hide your faith or even detach yourself from it.

But take a lesson from the blueberry. Just like a blueberry shrivels without its stem, so also you become empty without Jesus. So stick with it. Even though it's so easy to go along with the crowd, keep the stem.

The ripple effect

Daron Lindemann

Joyce Kwan is a sustainability and community leader who believes in the ripple effect. She raised funds in a Polar Plunge and was team captain for a Tower Climb. She heads to the beach with gloves and garbage bags too. Each time, she's not just raising money or serving the community. She's also inspiring others.

That's the ripple effect. One person makes a difference. Then others make a difference. Like throwing a rock into a pond.

But sometimes we don't want to get into the water. Without an initial splash—big or small—there are no ripples.

We need the rippling waves of God's forgiveness and mercy, new life from the Holy Spirit, and strength and truth from Jesus to carry us farther away from our small selves into his bigger opportunities and purposes for us.

With one command, Jesus healed ten men of incurable leprosy. For one man, Jesus broke the evil hold of two thousand demons: **"So the man went away and began to tell in the Decapolis how much Jesus had done for him. And all the people were amazed"** (Mark 5:20). With one drop of water at your baptism, Jesus empowered every single drop of his blood to wash your many sins away.

One splash—no matter how big or small—creates ripples in an entire pond, an entire family or church, an entire team, a community, and even the world.

Dear Jesus, Master of the ripple effect, carry me away from my small thinking out into your ocean of opportunities for me. Amen.

The person teaching you
Matt Ewart

"The Spirit clearly says that in later times some will abandon the faith and follow deceiving spirits and things taught by demons" (1 Timothy 4:1).

The letters contained in the New Testament are filled with warnings about false teachers who lead people away from God. The demonic forces driving these false teachings want nothing more than to drive people away from God's grace. So these teachings should be obvious, right?

Not always.

False teachers can be extremely helpful people. They have practical wisdom when it comes to how to navigate relationships, how to make financial plans, and how to figure out your purpose in life. So how do you know a false teacher when you see one?

Don't just consider what you are being taught. Consider where you are being led.

For example, if you listen to a financial podcast that helps you be a great steward of your finances, that's awesome. But if the podcast is leading you to approach finances from a place of worry and fear, that's not where God wants you to be.

Or if you find a book that helps you make sense of your personality type, that's a good thing. But if it leads you to a place where your identity is not defined by God's grace, that's not where God wants you to be.

Have some of these voices slipped into your life? Watch out for them, and don't let anything compete with the beautiful gospel of grace.

Hark! (a.k.a. Hey!)
Mike Novotny

Way back in 1739, Charles Wesley wrote a Christmas song soaked with Scripture. If "Away in a Manger" is like Cool Whip on a Christmas torte, Wesley's "Hark! The Herald Angels Sing" is like a simmering soup with 32 ingredients. Just consider the first quarter of the first verse: *"Hark! The herald angels sing/'Glory to the newborn King.'"*

Hark! is an old-school word that means "Hey!" or "Don't miss this!" *Herald* (not Harold!) means "messenger." These angels were messengers who showed up and sang, "Hey! You! Pay attention!"

Why? Because there was a newborn King. How can a newborn be a king? If you're the king and queen's latest kid, you're the newborn prince. So how could Jesus be the newborn King? Answer—Only if Jesus is God. Then he would be King and Lord from day one. The angels were singing, "Hey! That baby in the manger looks like just another kid, but he's not. He's more. He's the newborn King! He's Christ the Lord!"

This might seem basic if you've been a believer for a long time, but the baby Jesus is God. The little guy in Mary's arms, wrapped in swaddling clothes, is the same Lord that angels bow down and worship. God should not be in such lowly places, but our God chose to dwell with us, to be among us, to become Immanuel, which means "God with us."

Hark! Hey! Don't miss this! **"A Savior has been born to you; he is the Messiah, the Lord"** (Luke 2:11).

You flicker. Jesus doesn't.
Daron Lindemann

I had this desk lamp that flickered. It would suddenly turn off. I'd ignore it and keep working. Then it would turn back on.

Do you ever feel that way about you and God?

One day you are dialed in, trusting him above your feelings and living victoriously. The next day you lose your cool or bury yourself in blankets of despair or complain about all your problems.

Sometimes God is so near, and other times it seems like he's busy on the other side of the galaxy.

On. Off. On. Off. On. Off. You try to ignore it and keep living. But it's just not right. Maybe you're doing something wrong. Maybe God isn't as good as he promises.

"In [Jesus] was life, and that life was the light of all mankind. The light shines in the darkness, and the darkness has not overcome it" (John 1:4,5).

Maybe you're just not seeing God's light. You might be looking for Jesus in the sky, but he's in the manger. You might be expecting the Father to change your circumstances, but he wants to change you.

"God with us" (Immanuel) is always here. You don't need to go through life waiting for God to show up, as if a desk lamp has suddenly gone out and you hope it comes back on soon. Jesus Christ is here.

Dear God, open my eyes of faith to see your light. As Christ's light lives in me, reflect him through me to others. Amen.

Don't say too much
David Scharf

It is tempting to say that we know why God allows what he does in our lives.

A farmer's horse ran away. The neighbors said, "Oh, what a terrible thing that your horse ran away."

The farmer said, "You say too much. We don't know what is good or bad in the things that happen. You should only say that I lost my horse."

The next day the horse came back leading 11 horses right into the corral, and the neighbors said, "Farmer, now we know what you mean; how good it is your horse ran away."

And the farmer said, "You say too much. You should only say that I have 12 horses now."

The next day the farmer's son broke his leg breaking those horses, and the neighbors said, "We finally understand! Those horses are bad."

The farmer said, "Always you say too much! You should only say that my son has broken his leg."

Soon after the country went to war and all the young men had to go fight except those with broken legs. Seeing the neighbors coming, the farmer said, "Ah—don't say too much."

God says, **"My ways [are] higher than your ways and my thoughts than your thoughts"** (Isaiah 55:9). Don't say too much. Only say, "God sent his Son for me." Only say, "I know God's plan for me eternally." Only say, "God is good and loves me no matter what I see in my life."

Don't make a mountain out of a snowball

Katrina Harrmann

One winter I called my son to complain about our 12 inches of snow. We'd had so much of it that winter, and I was sick of it. My son attends college in the upper peninsula of Michigan. He listened to me and then calmly announced: "Mom, we've had 81 inches of snow in the last two weeks, and it's 4 feet deep right now. They had to bring in bulldozers to clear the roads!"

Oof. Perspective, right?

There's a famous cartoon of a man getting hit with a pebble in the head and throwing a gale-force tantrum because he feels life is so unfair. And in the background, we see Jesus holding back an avalanche, protecting him, even though he doesn't notice.

This is not to suggest that God CAN'T hold back the pebbles too. The point is—*perspective.*

It's important to keep perspective. Yes, we may be going through storms, but we really have no idea of the storms others are facing. Or the storms that God has held at bay before they reached our doorsteps.

We also can't understand God's bigger picture. We don't see the whole puzzle like he does. We can't understand his motives or his plans. So instead of being impatient with God or grumbling, let's spend more time on our knees in prayer, trusting our heavenly Father who always, *ALWAYS* wants the best for us—even if we can't understand.

"'For my thoughts are not your thoughts, neither are your ways my ways,' declares the LORD**"** (Isaiah 55:8).

Reexamining "Doubting Thomas"
Jan Gompper

Have you ever thought the disciple Thomas got a bad rap? Because he wanted proof of Jesus' resurrection, he was dubbed a nickname that has lived on in perpetuity—Doubting Thomas.

True, Thomas had doubts about what he heard from the other disciples about Jesus' resurrection. He had heard Jesus say he would rise from the dead, and he had seen Jesus raise others. Still, this wasn't a common occurrence. He wanted to know for himself that Jesus had truly risen.

I'm guessing many of us have struggled with spiritually related doubts at one time or another: How can God love someone like *me*? Is there *really* a heaven? What if I'm not a good enough Christian to get there? In his book *Wishful Thinking,* Presbyterian theologian Frederick Buechner wrote, "If you don't have any doubts, you are either kidding yourself or asleep. Doubts are the ants in the pants of faith. They keep it awake and moving."*

Thomas' doubt didn't cause him to blow off the claims of the other disciples and walk away. Rather, it led him to *seek* the truth from the very source—Jesus.

Because of sin, humankind will always be plagued with spiritual doubts. Let's face it, the story of a **"God** [who] **so loved the world that he gave his one and only Son** [to die in our place]**, that whoever believes in him shall not perish but have eternal life"** (John 3:16) defies human logic.

When spiritual doubts arise for you, be like Thomas and seek Jesus!

* Frederick Buechner, *Wishful Thinking: A Seeker's ABC* (San Francisco: Harper One, 1993).

Are you good?

Mike Novotny

Back in 2013, Oprah gave a commencement speech at Harvard where she revealed a question that she had been asked by President Bush, President Obama, national heroes, local housewives, and countless others in her epic career of interviews. Once the camera was off and the interview over, almost everyone would ask Oprah, "Was that okay?" Even Beyoncé asked it after confidently blasting her latest hit to adoring fans! Because deep down, no matter how good you are and how much good you do, you want to know if you are good enough.

That's true with God too. You can try so hard to be a good person, but you'll still wonder, "Am I good enough? We good, God?" Or maybe you know you've messed up a million times and assume you know the depressing answer to that very question. "We're not good, are we, God?"

But listen to the lyrics of a classic Christmas carol—*"Hark! the herald angels sing/'Glory to the newborn King/ peace on earth, and mercy mild/God and sinners reconciled!'"* Reconciled. That's a fancy way of saying that God is saying to you, "We're okay! We're good!" Jesus came with mercy and a message of peace so that God and you could be good.

The whole world is aching to be enough. Through faith in Jesus, you are enough for God. You're good! **"The Lord make his face shine on you . . . and give you peace"** (Numbers 6:25,26).

Seeing Jesus
Linda Buxa

It was the day Jesus rose from the dead, and two disciples were heading from Jerusalem to their homes in Emmaus. All of a sudden, there was another guy walking with them. (Hint: It was Jesus.)

They were bummed because they thought Jesus was THE GUY who was going to fix things politically and religiously—but then he was killed on a cross. Yet their friends said some women found the tomb empty on that Sunday morning.

Jesus started explaining how this fulfilled the Scriptures they had learned as children. Like the women who found the tomb empty, these two men didn't *see* Jesus either. It wasn't until they were eating, when Jesus took bread, gave thanks, and broke it. Then their eyes were opened.

All of a sudden, he disappeared. But **"they asked each other, 'Were not our hearts burning within us while he talked with us on the road and opened the Scriptures to us?'"** (Luke 24:32).

Living two thousand years later, there are times I wish I could see Jesus—in person—too. But like the disciples who didn't "see" him, my heart burns within me as other people share the reason for the hope they have, as pastors preach on Sundays, as friends share their insights.

We don't have to see him with our eyes to know that he fulfilled the Scriptures, which allows us to see him with our hearts and minds. And that gives us all the hope we need to wait until he calls us home and we see him face-to-face.

Unmasked expectations
Liz Schroeder

One of the most startling occurrences during the COVID pandemic was meeting people with their masks on and then seeing them later with their masks off. I don't know what I was expecting, but it was always different from the picture I had in my mind.

For those of us who have had the veil of unbelief lifted from our faces, the reveal is just as startling. **"And we all, who with unveiled faces contemplate the Lord's glory, are being transformed into his image with ever-increasing glory, which comes from the Lord, who is the Spirit"** (2 Corinthians 3:18). The world expects us to look one way, but when we profess Christ as our Lord and Savior, we begin to look like him.

So if you get comments from people like, "You just have a different energy" or, "You're always so happy," use that opportunity. Use that as an opening to tell others what Jesus has done for you. Don't leave them wondering if you've found the secret pill or hack to being happy. Don't gatekeep the reason for your joy. Be ready to give an answer for the hope you have (see 1 Peter 3:15).

And if you get comments like, "Why so glum, chum?" and, "Why so sad, Chad?" or non-rhyming questions like, "What is WITH you today?"—you might want to take that to heart. Indeed, why are you downcast? You have seen the glory of God! That question is a chance to reframe your melancholy: "I'm sorry. You just caught me feeling homesick for heaven."

Angels watching over me
David Scharf

Open up the Bible, and you will see the blessing of angels in the lives of God's people. An angel wiped out 185,000 Assyrian soldiers threatening Jerusalem in a single night! Angels with flaming swords surrounded an Aramean army and saved the prophet Elisha and his servant! Do you have an angel story?

I remember seeing a deer come out of a ditch while I was driving, giving me no time to react. I was about to obliterate that deer and vice versa! Then I saw the most amazing thing. The deer tripped. He was held up for a fraction of a second, and he crossed the road right behind my car. I didn't see an angel with a flaming sword, but I wonder if an angel stuck out a wing and gave him a little trip!

Who knows how many times God protects you through his angels without you even knowing it. And the greatest way that angels have served us was when they didn't act. When our Father in heaven refused to let them intervene when Roman soldiers were putting Jesus to death on a cross. That inaction saved our lives, not temporally but eternally.

Even if you can't think of a time when you may have been blessed by angels, rest assured that you have angel stories. After all, God promises, **"For he will command his angels concerning you to guard you in all your ways"** (Psalm 91:11)

He can do anything
Andrea Delwiche

As Christians raised in a culture where we tend to believe only what we see, the miracles of Scripture may run past us, like the current of a fast-moving river. We may not consider or dive into what those miracles tell us about the God we worship.

Psalm 114 recalls how God worked wonders with the physical qualities of the earth itself to keep safe and care for the Israelites. By God's guidance, the Red Sea parted, the sun stood still during battle, and quail and manna settled on the ground. By God's guidance, much-needed water flowed from solid rock.

And then the psalmist turns us to see these events as a witness to God's capability and character: **"Tremble, earth, at the presence of the Lord . . . who turned the rock into a pool, the hard rock into springs of water"** (verses 7,8).

Imagine being in the disbelieving, thirsty crowd as water gushed from that hard rock. What emotions and thoughts would go through your head to see a pool of water where dry ground had been only minutes before?

Witnesses of miracles, in faith-filled moments, remember that anything is possible with God. They are in awe of God but also trust him. What is an example of God's strength and majesty in Scripture or in your own experience that convinces you of God's ability to work wonders for you?

Take some time to sit and pay attention. Then walk forward on your adventure with the One who can do anything.

God + man = Jesus
(and really good news!)
Mike Novotny

Ready for a mental workout? Then read the lyrics of this classic Christmas carol—*"Christ, by highest heaven adored/Christ, the everlasting Lord/late in time behold him come/offspring of a virgin's womb/veiled in flesh the Godhead see/hail the incarnate Deity/pleased with us in flesh to dwell/Jesus, our Immanuel."* Could you explain that to a kindergartner? Let's try.

Jesus is God. He's "by highest heaven adored." He's "the everlasting Lord." See Jesus, and you see "the Godhead," a fancy name for God. He's "Deity." He's "Immanuel," a Hebrew name that means "God with us." That's five different ways of saying the same thing—Jesus is God.

And human. When the time had fully come, Jesus was the "offspring of a virgin's womb," a baby. He was "veiled in flesh," meaning you could see that Jesus was God through the "veil" of his human body. Christ was "the incarnate Deity." *Carn-* means "flesh or meat," like a carnivore eats meat, so "the incarnate Deity" is God in human flesh. It pleased Jesus to become "flesh to dwell," to be Immanuel, God with us. That's four different ways of saying one thing—Jesus is man.

Or, as Paul put it in Philippians: **"Christ Jesus . . . being in very nature God . . . being made in human likeness"** (2:5-7). God should have run away from you, with all your baggage and drama and sin, but instead he ran toward you by taking on human flesh.

What great lyrics! What an even greater Lord!

The Lord delights in you
Nathan Nass

I love watching my kids. It's not always easy being a parent, but my kids bring me so much joy. I love watching their sports games, hearing their naïve questions, and seeing them interact with each other. It really is a delight to be a dad.

Do you know who feels that way about you? The Lord! **"The LORD takes delight in his people; he crowns the humble with victory"** (Psalm 149:4). Isn't that amazing to hear? The Lord delights in you. In you! No matter who you are, God delights in you like I find great delight in my kids.

But . . . I'm sure there's a "but" on your mind. "But I . . ." "But how come . . ." "But why . . ." We sure don't deserve God's love. Doesn't he know all the bad things we've done? We don't always feel God's delight. Why does he let so many struggles come? Every day life tries to convince us that God doesn't love us.

So hold on to these beautiful words from the Psalms. God's delight in you isn't dependent on the great things you do. It depends on God's grace—his undeserved love for you that never fails. He crowns the *humble*. And God's delight doesn't depend on everything going great in your life today. You might have to wait a while to see the final victory.

Live today wrapped up in the grace of God. The Lord delights in you!

God works for good
David Scharf

"We know that in all things God works for the good of those who love him, who have been called according to his purpose" (Romans 8:28). We can't always see the good that God has in mind.

My sister Erika was killed by a drunk driver. I was angry. I was angry at the man who drove drunk with 9 other DUIs. I was probably even angry at God for allowing it to happen. *"But we know . . ."* I won't claim to know all that God accomplished. But there were blessings I could see. I took comfort in this: **"No one understands that the righteous are taken away to be spared from evil. Those who walk uprightly enter into peace; they find rest as they lie in death"** (Isaiah 57:1,2).

Who knows? Perhaps God was sparing my sister from something awful or from something that would have robbed her of faith. If that's the case, then I will be eternally grateful. *Good.* Her death drew me closer to my Savior. *Good.* Her death gave our family a chance to live our faith, impacting who knows how many lives. *Good.* I was able to witness my dad read a letter at the sentencing and do what most would consider unthinkable: he forgave the driver. He pointed him to Jesus' cross for his forgiveness. That man may never have heard that before. *Good.* I know Erika died in the faith, and I will see her again in heaven. *Good.*

Got room for Jesus?
Mike Novotny

In his classic Christmas carol "Joy to the World," Isaac Watts encouraged, *"Let every heart prepare him room."* Jesus, the Lord and King, wants room in your heart. But I should warn you—Jesus is a big King. He's not a little 8-pound, 6-ounce baby who waits in the corner to be your on-call counselor when you're in a crisis. He's not a Google God you reach out to only when you need something. No, he's the Lord of the world, the King of the earth, the Boss of the universe. The Boss of you.

Is there room in your heart for a Jesus like that? Are you willing to tell "my truth" to pack her bags and evict any personal beliefs that don't line up with the Word of the Lord? As the biblical proverb says, will you **"trust in the Lord with all your heart and lean not on your own understanding; in all your ways submit to him"** (Proverbs 3:5,6)? Honestly, most people won't and don't. Their hearts cling to the final vote, and submitting to anyone, even Jesus, is unthinkable.

But you don't have to be like most people. You can trust that the Lord who lived for you loves you, that you don't have to doubt the only One who died for you. Trust Jesus. Change your mind, and agree with him in everything. Let your heart prepare him room.

Christmas "feast"
Katrina Harrmann

There's a tradition in my family that I love.

When my parents were young church workers, fresh out of college, they didn't make a lot of money. This was in the 70s, and one Christmas, with less than $20 to spend on the holiday meal, my dad went to the store and came home with bread, pickles, cheese, and sausage. We made a little appetizer "feast" and opened our presents on Christmas Eve with this simple meal. And we never felt like we were lacking.

Today, we still have our Christmas Eve feast, but oh how the table groans under the weight of all the amazing food! But always—*always*—I remember how it started and remember to be grateful for every little blessing in my life.

Our good Father provides for us. He gives us every good thing we need to sustain us.

So this Christmas season, as you're enjoying a turkey or the various yummy baked goodies that parade out of the kitchen oven, remember from whose good and gracious hands these blessings flow. And take a moment to be aware and thankful.

"Therefore I tell you, do not worry about your life, what you will eat or drink; or about your body, what you will wear. Is not life more than food, and the body more than clothes? Look at the birds of the air; they do not sow or reap or store away in barns, and yet your heavenly Father feeds them. Are you not much more valuable than they?" (Matthew 6:25,26).

Saved
Mike Novotny

In late 2022, a sunken boat left three Louisiana boaters stranded 25 miles off the coast. By tying their ice chests together, they were able to stay afloat for 28 hours, but soon the sharks came. One opened its jaws and ripped into the front of one man's life vest until he jammed his thumbs into the predator's eyes, buying the desperate men a bit more time. One of the boaters took a terrifying risk, left the ice chests, and swam for miles in the shark-infested waters, hoping for a cell phone signal to call for help. Against all odds, he found one. A helicopter arrived before the four blacktip sharks struck again. In that moment, those desperate men "got saved."

That's a vivid picture of our spiritual story. After Adam and Eve crashed humanity into the iceberg of sin, we were all left floating in the deep waters of death. The demons were circling, hungry for our souls, waiting for our last breaths so they could claim more sinners forever.

Until our Savior saved us. Like a helicopter from heaven, Jesus flew down to rescue us from danger. No wonder the angels said his coming was **"good news that will cause great joy"** (Luke 2:10). Imagine for a moment if Jesus hadn't been born. Now imagine for a million moments the fact that he was. A Savior has been born for you! That's why you, through faith in him, are saved.

When you slip, Jesus saves
Mike Novotny

Everyone was feeling the tension during a crucial moment of filming the 2000 movie *Reindeer Games*. Light was fading fast, and the director was ready to snap. The actors and crew had one last chance at filming a scene. The scene involved a few actors scaling a snow-covered ladder, including Danny Trejo and his coactor/friend Donal Logue. But just moments before "action," Donal slipped. He lost his balance and his grip on the ladder, a fall that would have ruined the shot, ended the day, and damaged his career.

But Danny Trejo saved him. In the nanosecond of that moment, Trejo reached out one arm, snatched Donal by the scruff of his coat, and held all 200 pounds of him in midair! With one arm! Before the director noticed Donal's fall, Trejo gently set his friend back on the ladder and whispered, "I told you I had your back."

Isn't that just like you and Jesus? When you slip and sin and are helplessly falling from God, Jesus reaches out with his mighty right hand. The only Savior who has the power to rescue you also has the love to want to, even if your sin was more intentional than Donal's slip.

Christmas is a stunning message. It teaches us that the God of power came down to express his love. The Lord of all creation came down to save you. **"I bring you good news that will cause great joy for all the people. Today in the town of David a Savior has been born to you"** (Luke 2:10,11).

Jesus is willing
David Scharf

A man with leprosy approached Jesus with a beautiful prayer: **"If you are willing, you can make me clean"** (Mark 1:40). Jesus was filled with compassion and then did the unthinkable! He touched the man, a leper! But can you imagine what that touch must have meant to the man? Everything. Then Jesus spoke words that were equally beautiful in their simplicity: **"I am willing. . . . Be clean!"** (Mark 1:41). Immediately the man was healed. A simple prayer. A powerful answer.

Have you ever felt like an outcast? Sometimes it's your fault. Sometimes it's not. Maybe your family doesn't understand you or your coworkers look down on you or the kids at school make fun of you. You can simply pray, "Help!" Listen to Jesus' answer to your prayer, *"I am willing. Be clean!"*

Jesus was willing to reach out and touch you too. Jesus' compassion drove him to you. Why leave the pleasures of heaven for the slime pit of earth? Why would he trade his holiness by touching you and taking all your sin on himself on a cross? He did it because he loves you! No matter what may be happening in your life, always run to the cross to hear Jesus speak these beautiful words to you: "I am willing. Be clean!" And every time you realize that you are not following God's will for your life, know that forgiveness is there for every sinner. No need to hope, "If you are willing." Jesus is willing.

Truth in an elevator
Katrina Harrmann

Many years ago, my pastor was giving a sermon and told an interesting story about his trip to a shopping mall during Christmastime.

This particular mall was in a major city and was jam-packed with shoppers during December. You can imagine the craziness! At one point, a large group of people was cramming into a huge elevator.

As the doors slid closed, someone grumbled nastily, "I'd like to kill whoever is responsible for this holiday."

In the quiet, a voice from the back said sadly, "Don't worry. We did."

Silence. No one laughed or rolled their eyes. No one made a joke. Everyone simply held still as the elevator finished its silent glide to the ground floor.

WOW. What a powerful moment! What perspective!

It's easy to let the craziness and "circus" of secular holidays overwhelm us and affect our love and joy at Christmastime. Often, we lose sight entirely of what we're REALLY celebrating!

So take some time to remember, and keep your perspective in check. Whenever possible, try to focus on the real meaning of Christmas and how thankful we are that God sent his Son in human flesh to take our sins upon himself. All the crowded shopping malls in the world can't dim that joy. It helps to remind ourselves the TRUE reason for our Christmas hope and happiness!

"I have come that they may have life, and have it to the full" (John 10:10).

The other Noah
Daron Lindemann

Noah is described as a righteous man. God chose him to build an ark (Genesis 6). Noah and God wanted other people in it too. "Repent! There is room. Come aboard."

Noah's cries became desperate as the floodwaters rose. The skeptics who had laughed at Noah cried in regret because the ark was shut tight. Noah's heart grieved, "It's too late."

Centuries later, Jesus walked the same earth. People who repopulated it were skeptics again. They laughed at Jesus' claims to be the Son of God and the Savior of sinners. They killed him.

Jesus was a righteous man. God the Father chose him to build the kingdom. He wants other people in it too. "Repent! There is room. Come aboard!"

Like Noah was lifted up (above destruction and drowning) by beams of wood in the ark, Jesus was lifted up by beams of wood, **"the righteous for the unrighteous"** (1 Peter 3:18). Except Jesus wasn't spared.

Jesus was sacrificed into the angry waters of God's justice for sin. He died, rose to life, and then descended into hell and preached to the same people who had rejected Noah. His heart grieved, "It's too late."

The thing is, billions are still alive. It's not too late for any of us. "Repent! There is room." It's not too late for a wicked world or unbelieving friend.

The wooden beams holding up the righteous man can now save the unrighteous ones. The other Noah saves. "Come aboard!"

Is God stingy?

Linda Buxa

I know the Lord is not slow in keeping his promises, but I am impatient when he doesn't answer my prayers the way I think he ought to. When life is going well, the thought creeps in that I'm due for something bad to happen, as if I've used up my quota of blessings for the month. When I've done the same boneheaded sin for the 147th time, I might act as if it's time to do some extra good works for the extra forgiveness he gave me—as if I ran his forgiveness bucket dry and need to pay him back. It's almost like I think he's stingy. It's as if I've never heard him say, **"How much more will your Father in heaven give good gifts to those who ask him!"** (Matthew 7:11).

Imagine how different my life would look if I lived in quiet confidence every single day that **"my God will meet all [my] needs according to the riches of his glory in Christ Jesus"** (Philippians 4:19). Imagine if I trusted that I am already blessed in the heavenly realms with every spiritual blessing. Imagine if I lived a life of joy, knowing that my cup overflows because my Father is not stingy but is actually the giver of every good and perfect gift.

"Now to him who is able to do immeasurably more than all we ask or imagine, according to his power that is at work within us, to him be glory in the church and in Christ Jesus throughout all generations, for ever and ever! Amen" (Ephesians 3:20,21).

Why so few Christians?
Mike Novotny

When I was kid, about nine in ten Americans claimed to be Christian. Now that I'm middle-aged, only six in ten Americans stand with Jesus. If trends continue and I die an old man, less than five in ten of my fellow citizens will claim to follow Christ. Perhaps you've seen that reality among your siblings, friends, kids, or grandchildren. Why would that be?

While there are many answers to that crucial question, near the top of the list has to be Jesus himself. The unedited, unfiltered Jesus was, without a doubt, offensive and divisive. Despite his ability to heal the sick and raise the dead, the vast majority of his original audience didn't like him due to his extreme claims of divinity (I'm God) and authority (I always get the last word).

How about you? When Jesus' words are hard to embrace personally and even harder to endorse publicly, will you remain with Jesus? John's gospel, which retells the story of some of Jesus' most offensive moments, gives us a compelling reason to follow Jesus: **"But these are written that you may believe that Jesus is the Messiah, the Son of God, and that by believing you may have life in his name"** (John 20:31).

Yes, Jesus is divisive. Yes, Jesus is offensive. But the name of Jesus is the only way to be fully forgiven, completely pure, and absolutely good enough to live with God. So no matter how many of your friends stay or go, I pray that you stick with Jesus and find eternal life in his name.

DEVOTIONS FOR SPECIAL DAYS

They don't know
Matt Ewart

"Father, forgive them, for they do not know what they are doing" (Luke 23:34).

Jesus spoke those words over the Roman soldiers who were crucifying him. The ironic thing is that they knew exactly what they were doing.

The act of crucifixion had already been around for centuries when it was introduced into the Roman Empire in the 3rd century B.C. The Romans then perfected the art of crucifixion to increase the level and duration of suffering. One of their tactics included nailing their victims to a cross rather than binding them with rope.

The soldiers knew exactly what they were doing. But they were unaware of the consequences.

So it is with us.

If you examine your heart, you will find ways that you have "perfected" the art of sin. You know how to hide it, disguise it, and excuse it. You keep believing that it will satisfy, but it never does. It leaves you ever emptier—an emptiness that can only be filled with death.

The good news of today is that this emptiness has already been filled with the death of another.

Jesus asked his Father to administer forgiveness while he himself was paying its price. Grace was "perfected" on that cross—even for people who have been caught up by sin's deceitfulness.

What sin has been deceiving you, keeping you locked up in chains? Today, Jesus fulfills and speaks these words to you: "Father, forgive them."

Victory!

Nathan Nass

This past fall our local high school football team set a state record by winning its 50th consecutive game. To celebrate, they blasted the song "All I do Is Win" by DJ Khaled over the loudspeakers after every touchdown in their home stadium. What a thrill to keep winning!

Except I don't. I often don't feel like a winner at all. In fact, it often seems like all I do is lose no matter what. I don't do what I know I should do, and I feel guilty about it. I think and do things that I know I should never think and do, and I feel guilty about it. Win? Not me.

Until today. Do you realize what happened today? It's Easter—the day of Jesus' victory. Jesus defeated sin when he died for our sins on a cross. He defeated death when he rose from the dead. Listen to what Jesus does with his victory: **"Thanks be to God! He gives us the victory through our Lord Jesus Christ"** (1 Corinthians 15:57).

Did you catch it? God gives us Jesus' victory! Our sin? Forgiven at the cross! Death? We will rise to live in heaven. I know it looks like the game of life is still in progress, but there's no doubt about the outcome: Jesus won. Victory! Because of Easter, all we do is win through our Lord Jesus Christ!

Mothers

Katrina Harrmann

When my daughter was three, she started every morning by catapulting into my bed and diving under the blankets. She informed me, "I sleep good, Mama."

She loved me with such intensity. "I'll eat you up, I love you so!" we would giggle, quoting her favorite book (*Where the Wild Things Are* by Maurice Sendak). Later in the morning, she always wanted coffee in her tiny pink teacup, "Just like you!"

Isn't parenthood incredible? It never stops astonishing me how these little people change and grow and how we are blessed to watch them do it. I've always loved each version of my kids as they've grown up into young adults.

My daughter is 15 now. And it is still a marvelous thing to be her mama. Motherhood, with all its trials and strains, is a joy, especially in the little, everyday moments.

Today, as we remember and thank the women who had a hand in raising us up as children . . . those who nurtured and protected us . . . cooked for us and wiped away our tears . . . may we use those warm memories to guide us forward as we find others who may need us to nurture, lead, and protect them.

"Only be careful, and watch yourselves closely so that you do not forget the things your eyes have seen or let them fade from your heart as long as you live. Teach them to your children and to their children after them" (Deuteronomy 4:9).

Dads deserve more
Liz Schroeder

We do dads a disservice when we distill them down to their hobbies. Today is a day to honor all that a father represents: a legacy of faith, integrity, sacrifice, and provision—and we give him a new golf club, sports apparel featuring his favorite team, or a gift card to a store for outdoorsmen. Like most American holidays, Father's Day has been hijacked by clever marketing to dupe buyers into yet more conspicuous consumption.

Sons, daughters, wives—we can do better. Gifts are certainly nice, but we also have other love languages in our toolboxes.

We can use our words to offer appreciation. This can be a phone call to tell your dad what his role in your life has meant to you. It doesn't have to sound like a greeting card; the truth is that most of those cards paint a simplistic and too-rosy picture of what is often a complicated and nuanced relationship.

We can volunteer to help, which can look like doing yardwork as a token of thanks for all the hard work he has done for you. Do whatever communicates this to your dad: "I see the sacrifices you make for me, and I want to honor you for it."

Finally, thank your heavenly Father for making you the beneficiary of blessings that were sown in faithfulness long before you were born. **"Know therefore that the LORD your God is God; he is the faithful God, keeping his covenant of love to a thousand generations of those who love him and keep his commandments"** (Deuteronomy 7:9).

The joy of not owning
Daron Lindemann

When you're staying at a hotel, do you bring pictures along and nail them up on the walls? Do you leave the water running all day? Do you rip up the towels and use them as rags to clean your car? No. Because you don't own the hotel room.

The Bible says that **"the earth is the Lord's, and everything in it"** (Psalm 24:1). We aren't owners of our stuff. We are stewards.

Steward is a word that means "caretaker." God owns all your stuff and asks you to take care of it in a way that honors him, thanks him, and shows him that you can handle bigger and better things.

Do you appreciate the great joy in this? Think back to the hotel. Do you have to make the bed, wash the towels, or fix the air conditioner? No! The owner is obligated to take care of that.

"And God is able to bless you abundantly, so that in all things at all times, having all that you need, you will abound in every good work" (2 Corinthians 9:8).

Instead of your stuff owning you, God owns your stuff and owns you. By his gracious choice, he's obligated.

More than that, he is able.

Dear God, your gifts and grace to me are too generous. And my appreciation is less than I'd like. Teach me true joy in your ownership, joy that frees me from owning what already belongs to you. Amen.

About the Writers

Pastor Mike Novotny pours his Jesus-based joy into his ministry as a pastor at The CORE (Appleton, Wisconsin) and as the lead speaker for Time of Grace, a global media ministry that connects people to God through television, print, and digital resources. Unafraid to bring grace and truth to the toughest topics of our time, he has written numerous books, including *3 Words That Will Change Your Life*; *What's Big Starts Small*; *You Know God Loves You, Right?*; and *When Life Hurts*. Mike lives with his wife, Kim, and their two daughters, Brooklyn and Maya; runs long distances; and plays soccer with other middle-aged men whose best days are long behind them. To find more books by Pastor Mike, go to timeofgrace.store.

Linda Buxa is a freelance communications professional as well as a regular blogger and contributing writer for Time of Grace Ministry. Linda is the author of *Dig In! Family Devotions to Feed Your Faith*, *Parenting by Prayer*, *Made for Friendship*, and *Visible Faith: Living a Fruitful Life in Christ*. She and her husband, Greg, have lived in Alaska, Washington D.C., and California. After retiring from the military, they moved to Wisconsin, where they settled on 11.7 acres and now keep track of chickens, multiple cats, and 1 black Lab. Their 3 children insist on getting older and following their dreams, so Greg and Linda have entered the empty-nest stage. The sign in her kitchen sums up their lives: "You call it chaos; we call it family."

Andrea Delwiche lives in Wisconsin with her husband, three kids, dog, cat, and a goldfish pond full of fish. She enjoys reading, knitting, and road-tripping with her family. Although a lifelong believer, she began to come into a deeper understanding of what it means to follow Christ far into adulthood (always a beginner on that journey!). Andrea has facilitated a Christian discussion group for women for many years and recently published a book of poetry—*The Book of Burning Questions*.

Pastor Jon Enter served as a pastor in West Palm Beach, Florida, for ten years. He is now a campus pastor and instructor at St. Croix Lutheran Academy in St. Paul, Minnesota. Jon also serves as a regular speaker on Grace Talks video devotions and a contributing writer to the ministry. He once led a tour at his college, and the Lord had him meet his future wife, Debbi. They are now drowning in pink and glitter with their four daughters: Violet, Lydia, Eden, and Maggie.

Pastor Matt Ewart and his wife, Amy, have been blessed with three children who keep life interesting. Matt is currently a pastor in Lakeville, Minnesota, and has previously served as a pastor in Colorado and Arizona.

Jan Gompper spent most of her career teaching theatre at Wisconsin Lutheran College in Milwaukee. She also served six years as a cohost for *Time of Grace* during its start-up years. She has collaborated on two faith-based musicals, numerous Christian songs, and has written and codirected scripts for a Christian video series. She and her husband now reside in the Tampa area, where she continues to practice her acting craft and coach aspiring acting students as opportunities arise. She also assists with Sunday school and other church-related activities.

Katrina Harrmann lives in southwest Michigan with her photographer husband, Nathan, and their three kids. A lifelong Christian, she attended journalism school at the University of Missouri, Columbia, and worked at the *Green Bay Press-Gazette* and the *Sheboygan Press* before taking on the full-time job of motherhood. Currently, she writes and lives along the shores of Lake Michigan and enjoys gardening, hiking, camping, doing puzzles, and playing with her chihuahua in her free time.

Ann Jahns and her husband live in Wisconsin as recent empty nesters, having had the joy of raising three boys to adulthood. She is a marketing coordinator for a Christian church body and a freelance proofreader and copy editor. Ann has been privileged to teach Sunday school and lead Bible studies for women of all ages. One of her passions is supporting women in the "sandwich generation" as they experience the unique joys and challenges of raising children while supporting aging parents.

Pastor Daron Lindemann loves the journey—exploring God's paths in life, riding open highways on his Harley with his wife, or discovering even more about Jesus and the Bible. He serves as a pastor in Pflugerville, Texas, with a passion for life-changing faith and for smoking brisket.

Pastor Nathan Nass serves at Christ the King Lutheran Church in Tulsa, Oklahoma. Prior to moving to Oklahoma, he served at churches in Wisconsin, Minnesota, Texas, and Georgia. He and his wife, Emily, have four children. You can find more sermons and devotions on his blog: upsidedownsavior.home.blog.

Jason Nelson had a career as a teacher, counselor, and leader. He has a bachelor's degree in education, did graduate work in theology, and has a master's degree in counseling psychology. After his career ended in disabling back pain, he wrote the book *Miserable Joy: Chronic Pain in My Christian Life*. He has written and spoken extensively on a variety of topics related to the Christian life. Jason has been a contributing writer for Time of Grace since 2010. He has authored many Grace Moments devotions and several books. Jason lives with his wife, Nancy, in Wisconsin.

Pastor David Scharf served as a pastor in Greenville, Wisconsin, and now serves as a professor of theology at Martin Luther College in Minnesota. He has presented at numerous leadership, outreach, and missionary conferences across the country. He is a contributing writer for Time of Grace and a speaker for Grace Talks video devotions. Dave and his wife have six children.

Liz Schroeder is a Resilient Recovery coach, a ministry that allows her to go into sober living homes and share the love and hope of Jesus with men and women recently out of rehab or prison. It has been a dream of hers to write Grace Moments, a resource she has used for years in homeschooling her five children. After going on a mission trip to Malawi through an organization called Kingdom Workers, she now serves on its U.S. board of directors. She and her husband, John, are privileged to live in Phoenix and call CrossWalk their church home.

Pastor Clark Schultz loves Jesus; his wife, Kristin, and their three boys; the Green Bay Packers; Milwaukee Brewers; Wisconsin Badgers; and—of course—Batman. His ministry stops are all in Wisconsin and include a vicar year in Green Bay, tutoring and recruiting for Christian ministry at a high school in Watertown, teacher/coach at a Christian high school in Lake Mills, and a pastor in Cedar Grove. He currently serves as a pastor in West Bend and is the author of the book *5-Minute Bible Studies: For Teens*. Pastor Clark's favorite quote is, "Find something you love to do and you will never work a day in your life."

Karen Spiegelberg lives in Wisconsin with her husband, Jim. She has three married daughters, five grandchildren, and has been a foster mom to many. She is a member of her city's common council as an alderman and loves sharing her faith through that role. Besides reading, cycling, and traveling, she enjoys spending a lot of time growing in grace with her growing family!

About Time of Grace

Time of Grace is for people who are experiencing the highest of highs or have hit rock bottom or are anywhere in between. That's because through Time of Grace, you will be reminded that the One who can help you in your life, the God of forgiveness and grace and mercy, is not far away. He is right here with you. GOD is here! He will help you on your spiritual journey. Walk with us at timeofgrace.org.

.

**To discover more, please visit
timeofgrace.org or call 800.661.3311.**

Help share God's message of grace!

Every gift you give helps Time of Grace reach people around the world with the good news of Jesus. Your generosity and prayer support take the gospel of grace to others through our ministry outreach and help them experience a satisfied life as they see God all around them.

**Give today at timeofgrace.org/give
or by calling 800.661.3311.**

Thank you!